DISNEY | SQUARESOFT

KINGDOM HEARTS

2

Adapted by
Shiro Amano

TOKYOPOP®

HAMBURG // LONDON // LOS ANGELES // TOKYO

Kingdom Hearts Vol. 2
Adapted by
Shiro Amano

Associate Editor - Peter Ahlstrom
Copy Editor - Eric Althoff
Retouch and Lettering - Jose Macasocol, Jr.
Production Artist - Jose Macasocol, Jr. and Ana Lopez
Cover Layout - Gary Shum

Editor - Bryce P. Coleman
Digital Imaging Manager - Chris Buford
Production Managers - Jennifer Miller and Mutsumi Miyazaki
Managing Editor - Lindsey Johnston
VP of Production - Ron Klamert
Publisher and E.I.C. - Mike Kiley
President and C.O.O. - John Parker
C.E.O. - Stuart Levy

A TOKYOPOP® Manga

TOKYOPOP Inc.
5900 Wilshire Blvd. Suite 2000
Los Angeles, CA 90036

E-mail: info@TOKYOPOP.com
Come visit us online at www.TOKYOPOP.com

ISBN: 1-59816-218-7

First TOKYOPOP printing: January 2006
10 9 8 7 6 5 4 3
Printed in the USA

KINGDOM HEARTS

Our Story So Far...

After being swept away from his island home and his friends Kairi and Riku, Sora finds himself lost in a mysterious new land. Soon, he meets Court Wizard Donald and Captain Goofy, who are desperately trying to find their missing King. Now the trio must band together to stop the Heartless—nasty creatures who feed on the darkness in people's hearts—before they destroy all the worlds! Armed with the magical Keyblade, Sora and his companions will travel from one world to the next, searching for their friends and the secret text that will stop the Heartless...

KINGDOM HEARTS: VOLUME 2
TABLE OF CONTENTS

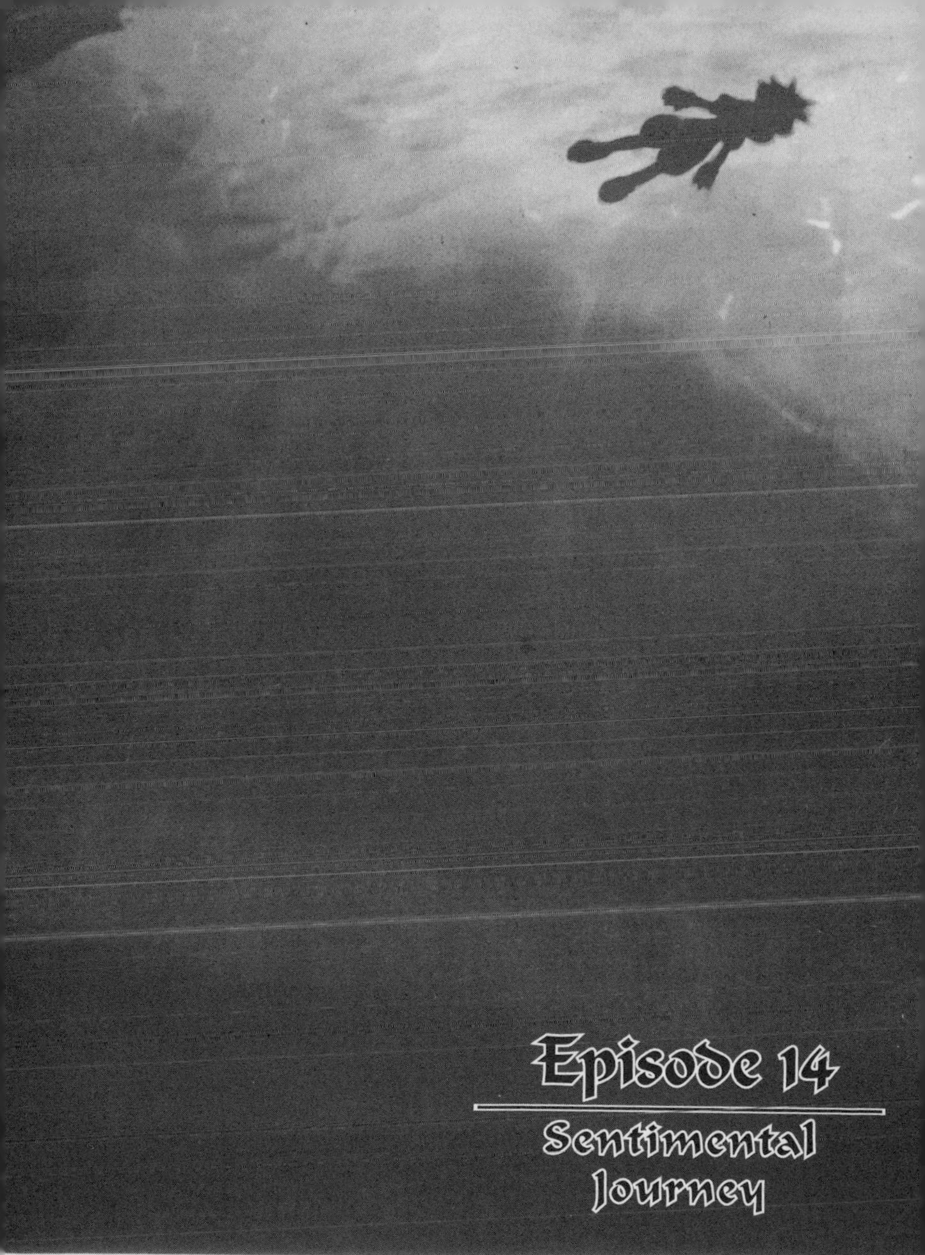

Episode 14

Sentimental Journey

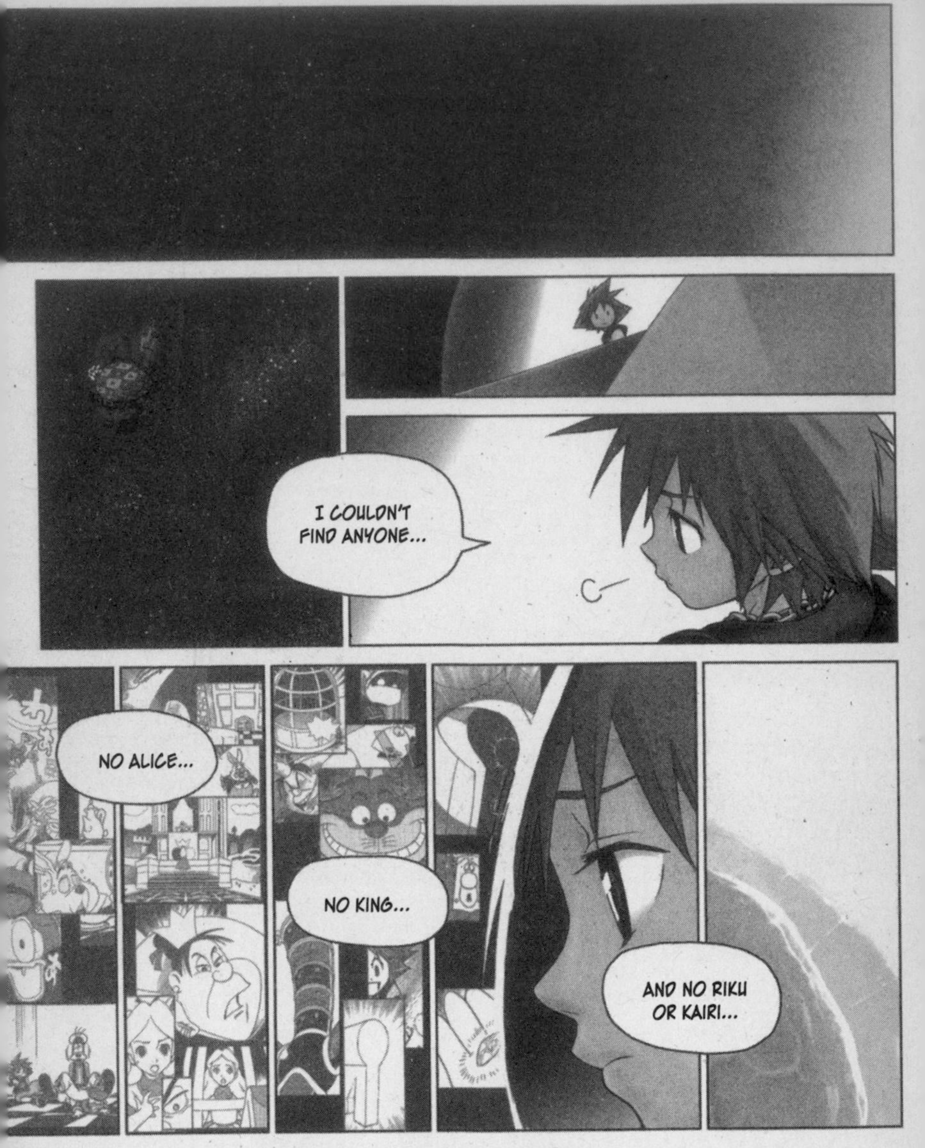
I COULDN'T FIND ANYONE...
NO ALICE...
NO KING...
AND NO RIKU OR KAIRI...

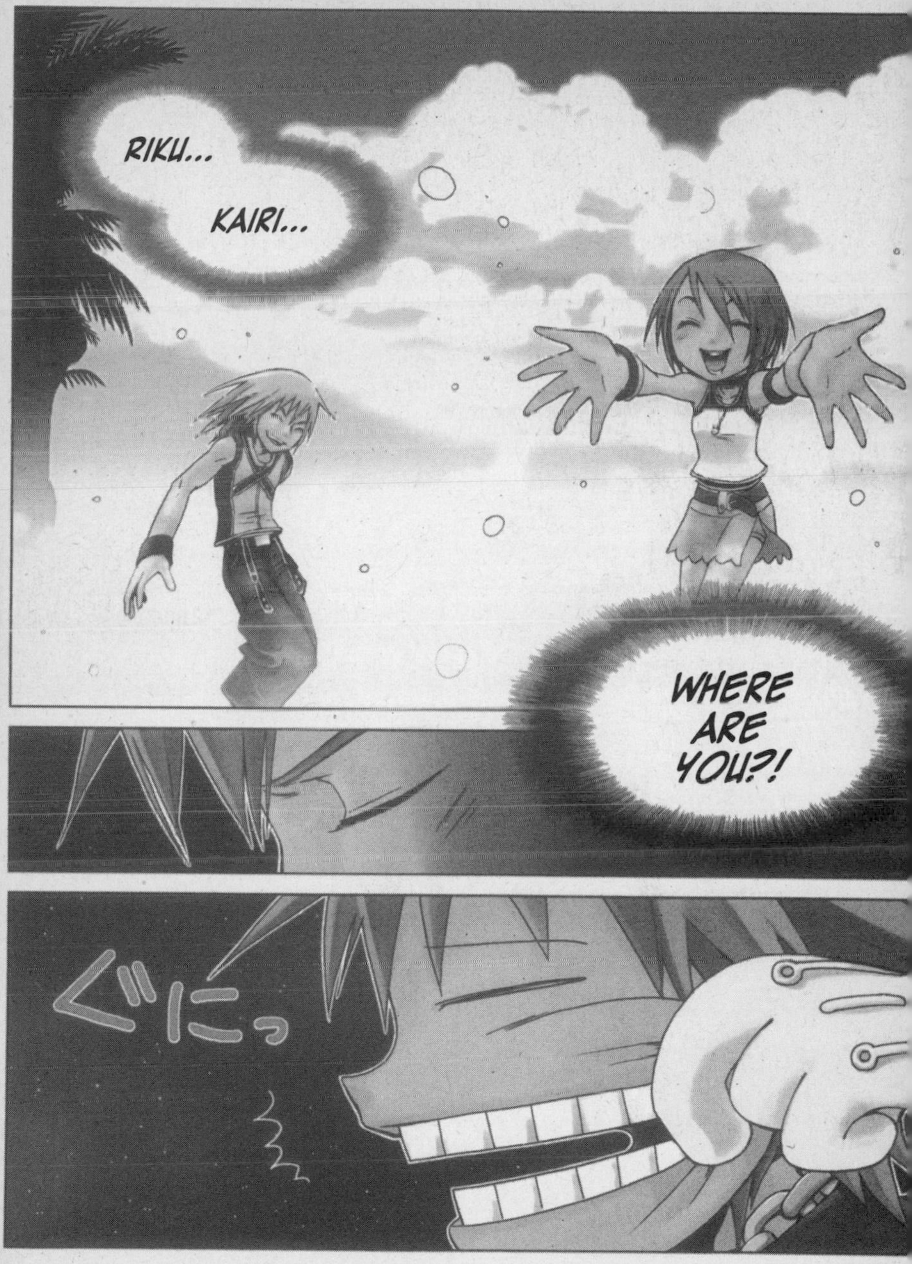
RIKU...
KAIRI...
WHERE ARE YOU?!
ぐにっ

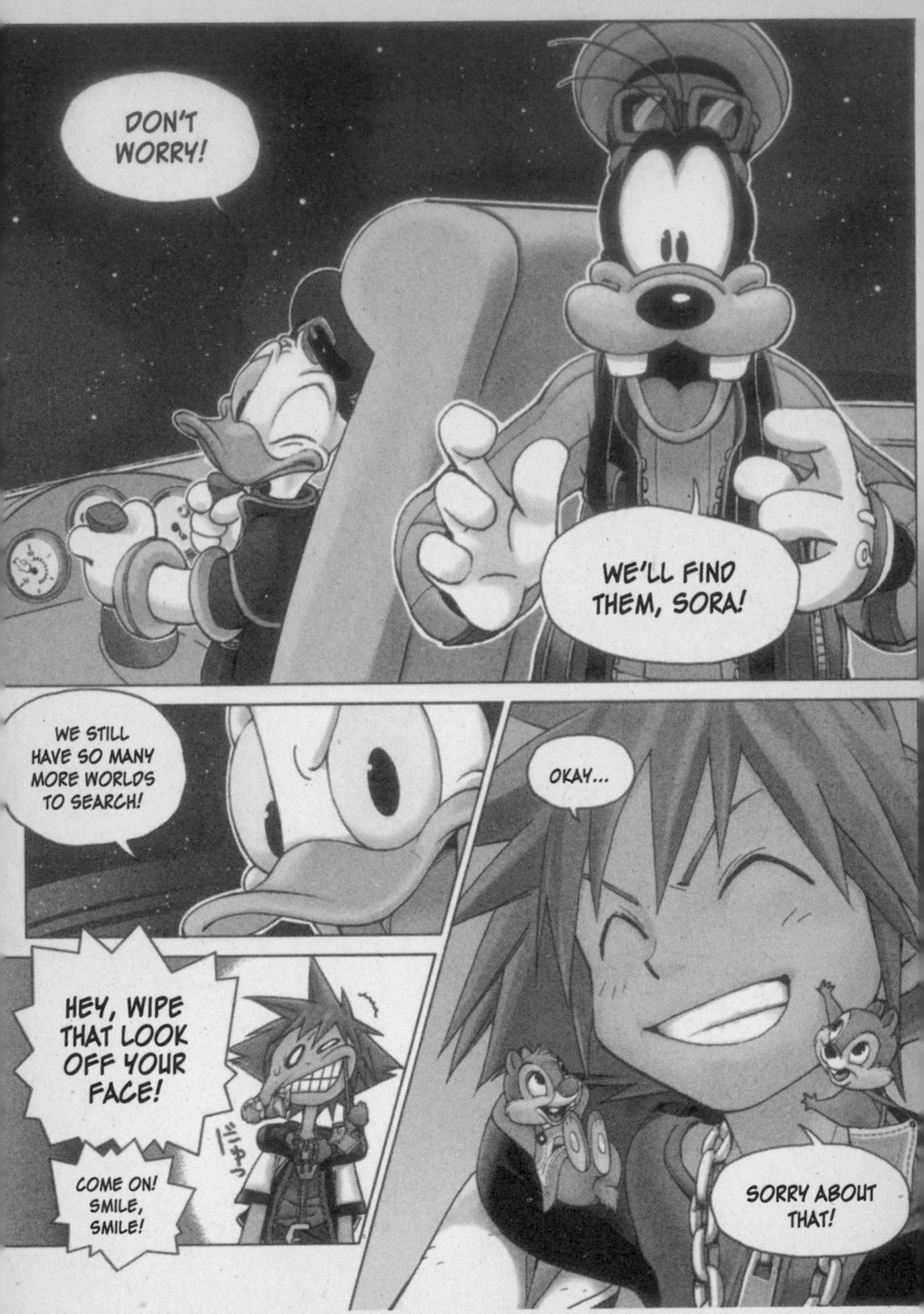
DON'T WORRY!
WE'LL FIND THEM, SORA!
WE STILL HAVE SO MANY MORE WORLDS TO SEARCH!
HEY, WIPE THAT LOOK OFF YOUR FACE!
COME ON! SMILE, SMILE!
OKAY...
SORRY ABOUT THAT!

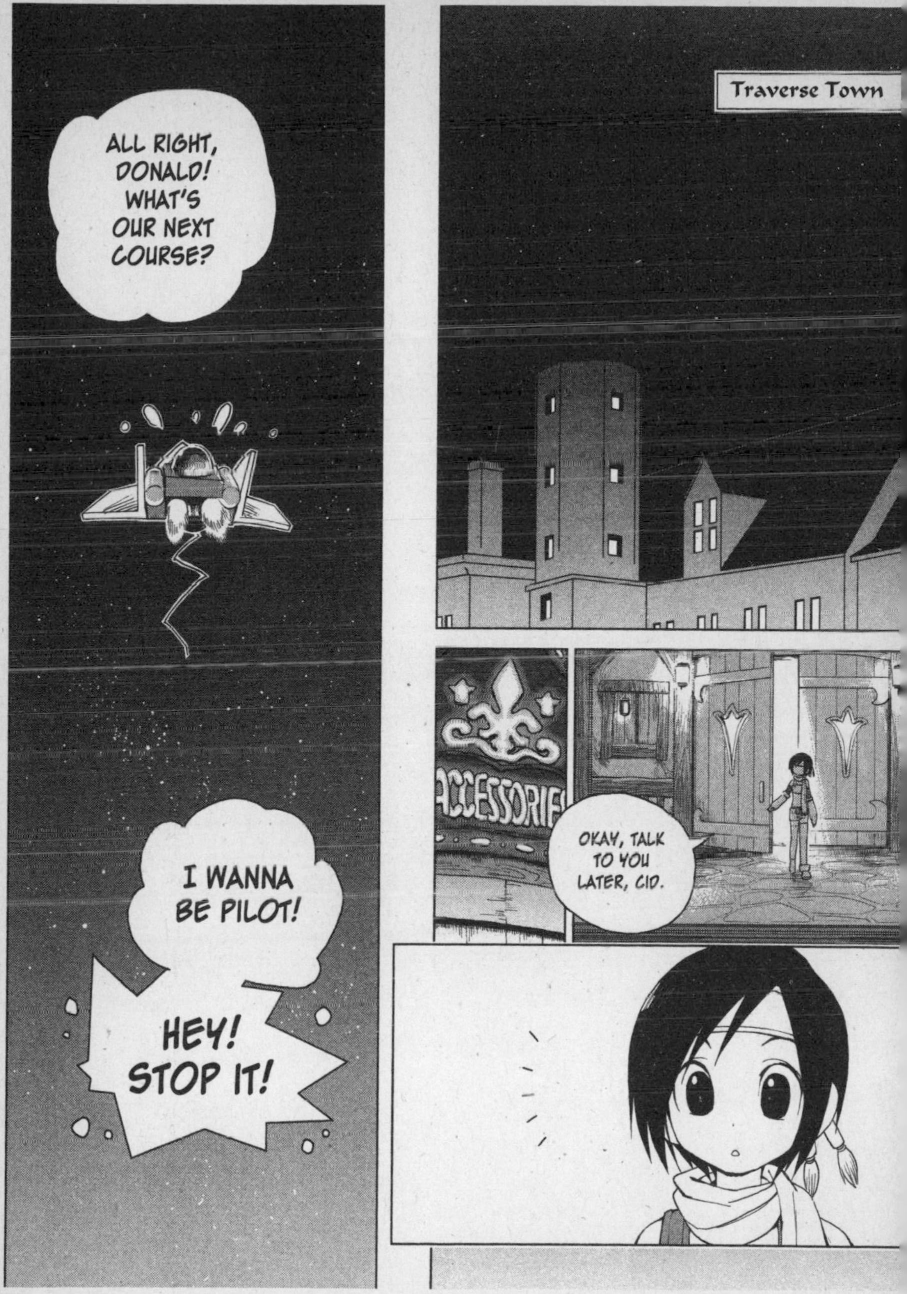

ALL RIGHT, DONALD! WHAT'S OUR NEXT COURSE?
I WANNA BE PILOT!
HEY! STOP IT!
Traverse Town
OKAY, TALK TO YOU LATER, CID.

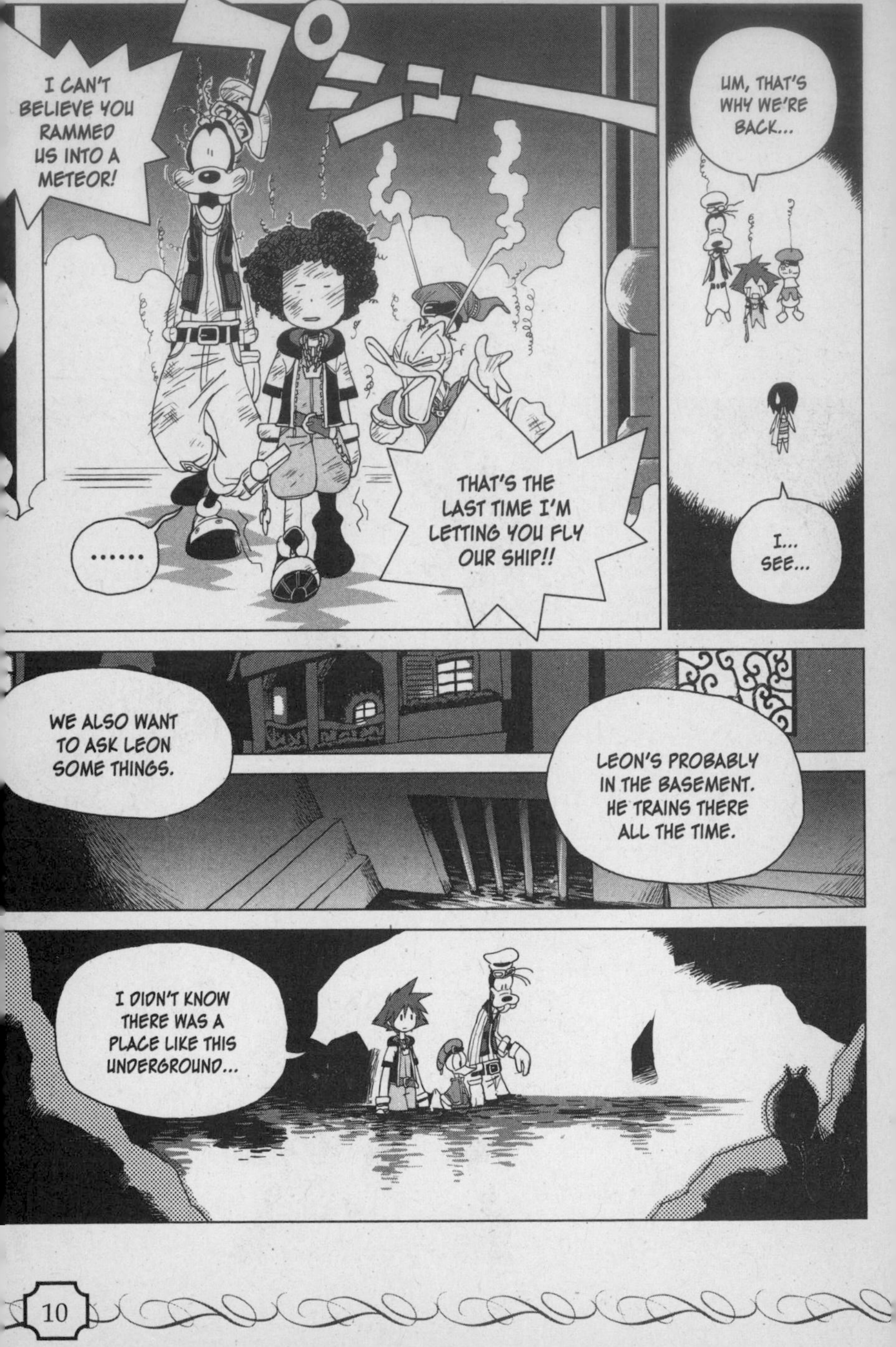

プシュー
I CAN'T BELIEVE YOU RAMMED US INTO A METEOR!
......
THAT'S THE LAST TIME I'M LETTING YOU FLY OUR SHIP!!
UM, THAT'S WHY WE'RE BACK...
I... SEE...
WE ALSO WANT TO ASK LEON SOME THINGS.
LEON'S PROBABLY IN THE BASEMENT. HE TRAINS THERE ALL THE TIME.
I DIDN'T KNOW THERE WAS A PLACE LIKE THIS UNDERGROUND...

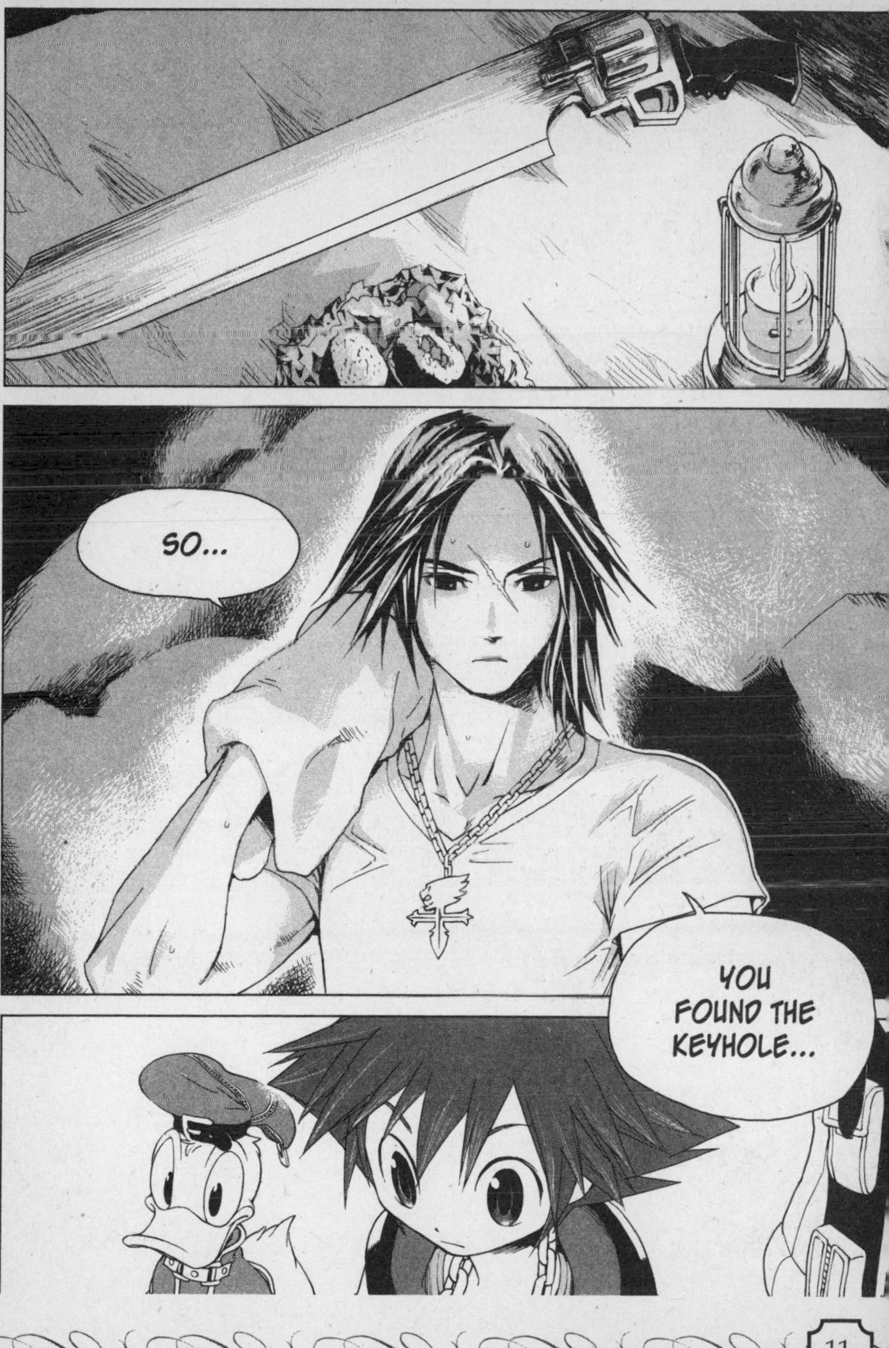
SO...
YOU FOUND THE KEYHOLE...

Episode 15

The Chosen One

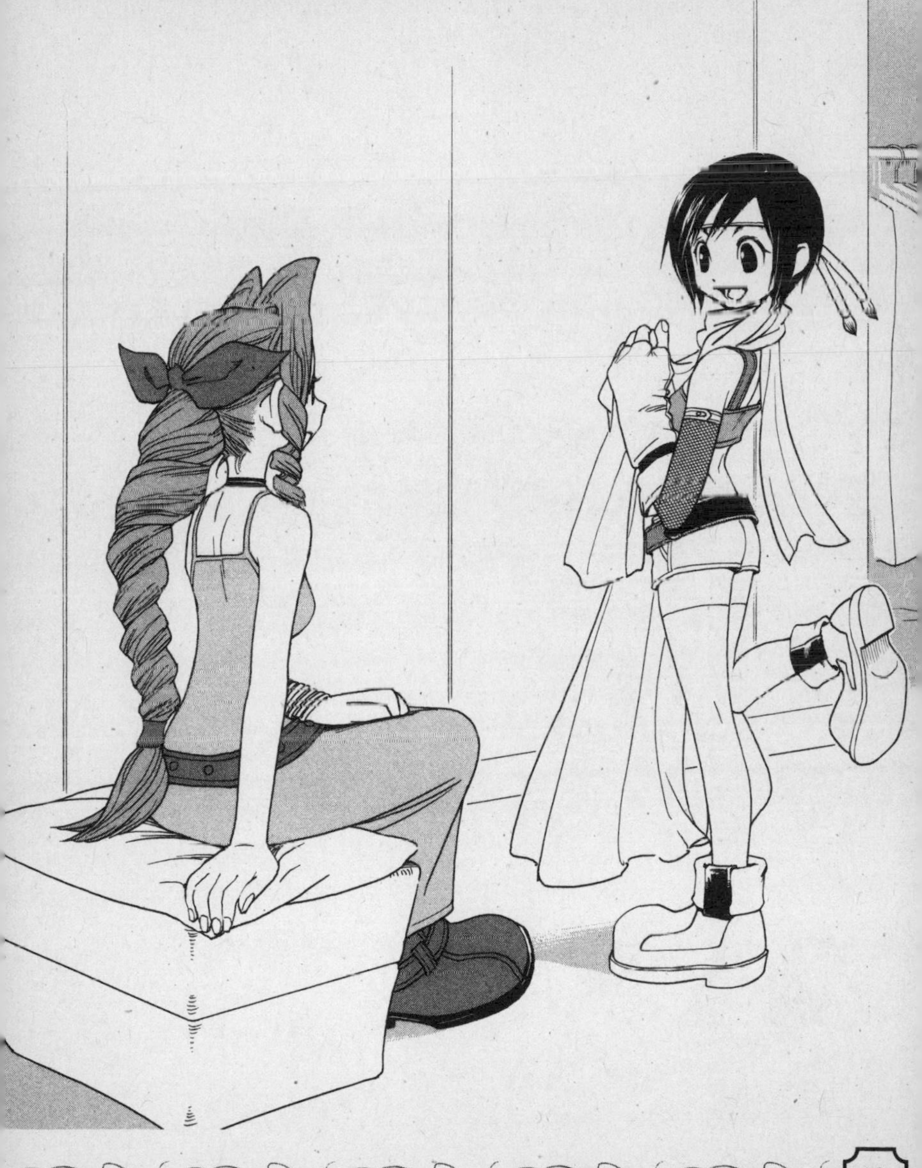

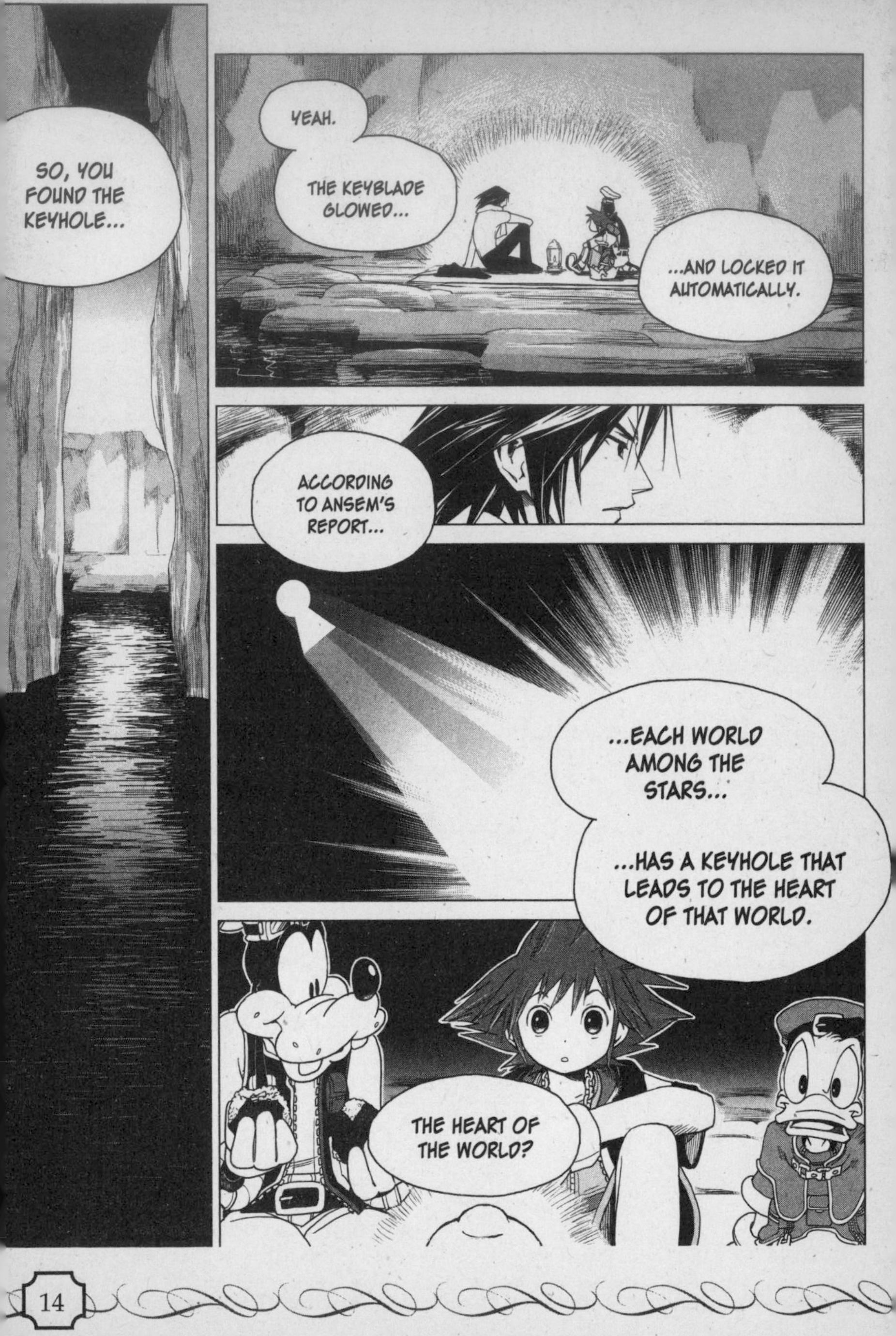
SO, YOU FOUND THE KEYHOLE...
YEAH.
THE KEYBLADE GLOWED...
...AND LOCKED IT AUTOMATICALLY.
ACCORDING TO ANSEM'S REPORT...
...EACH WORLD AMONG THE STARS...
...HAS A KEYHOLE THAT LEADS TO THE HEART OF THAT WORLD.
THE HEART OF THE WORLD?

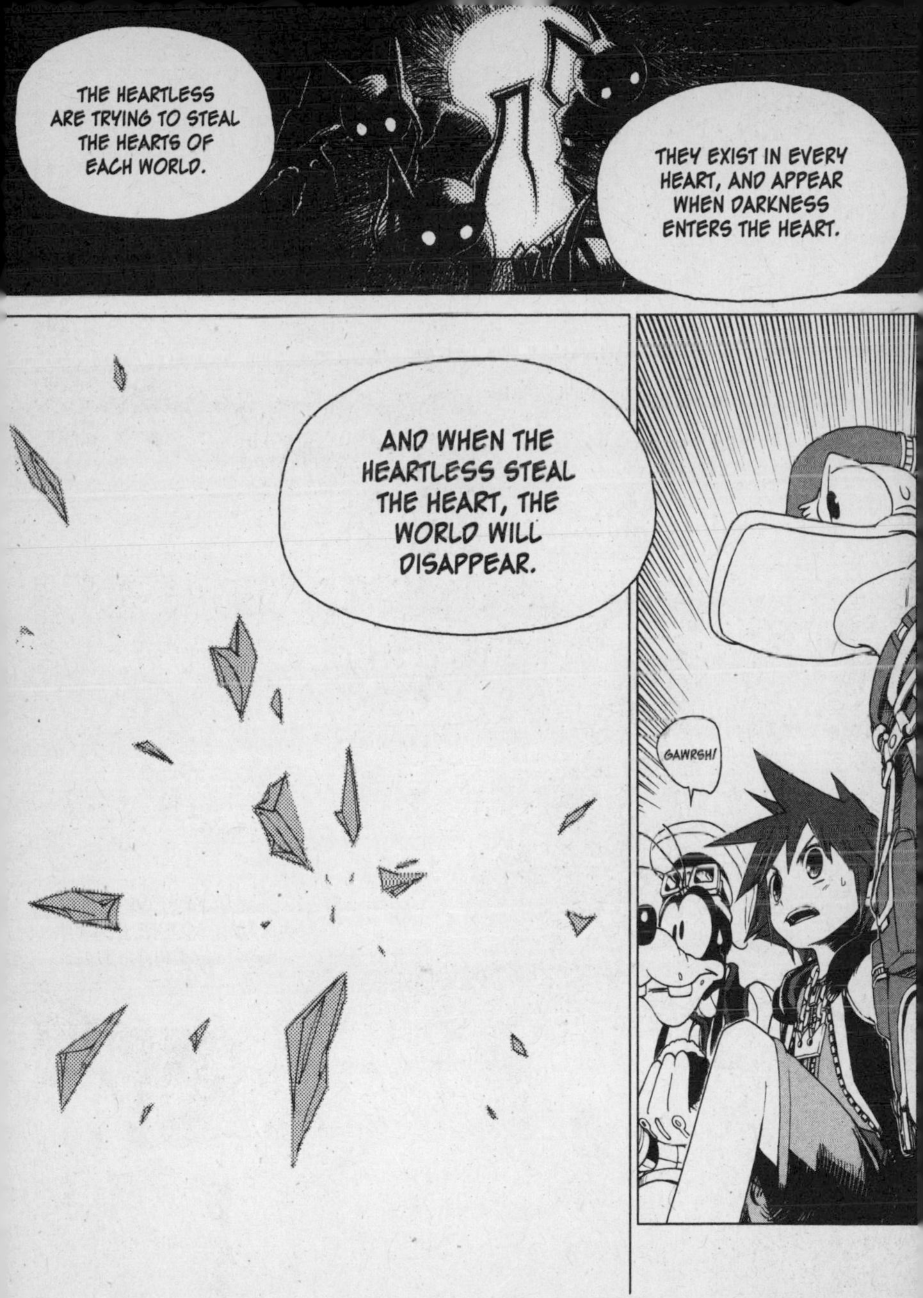
THE HEARTLESS ARE TRYING TO STEAL THE HEARTS OF EACH WORLD.
THEY EXIST IN EVERY HEART, AND APPEAR WHEN DARKNESS ENTERS THE HEART.
AND WHEN THE HEARTLESS STEAL THE HEART, THE WORLD WILL DISAPPEAR.
GAWRSH!

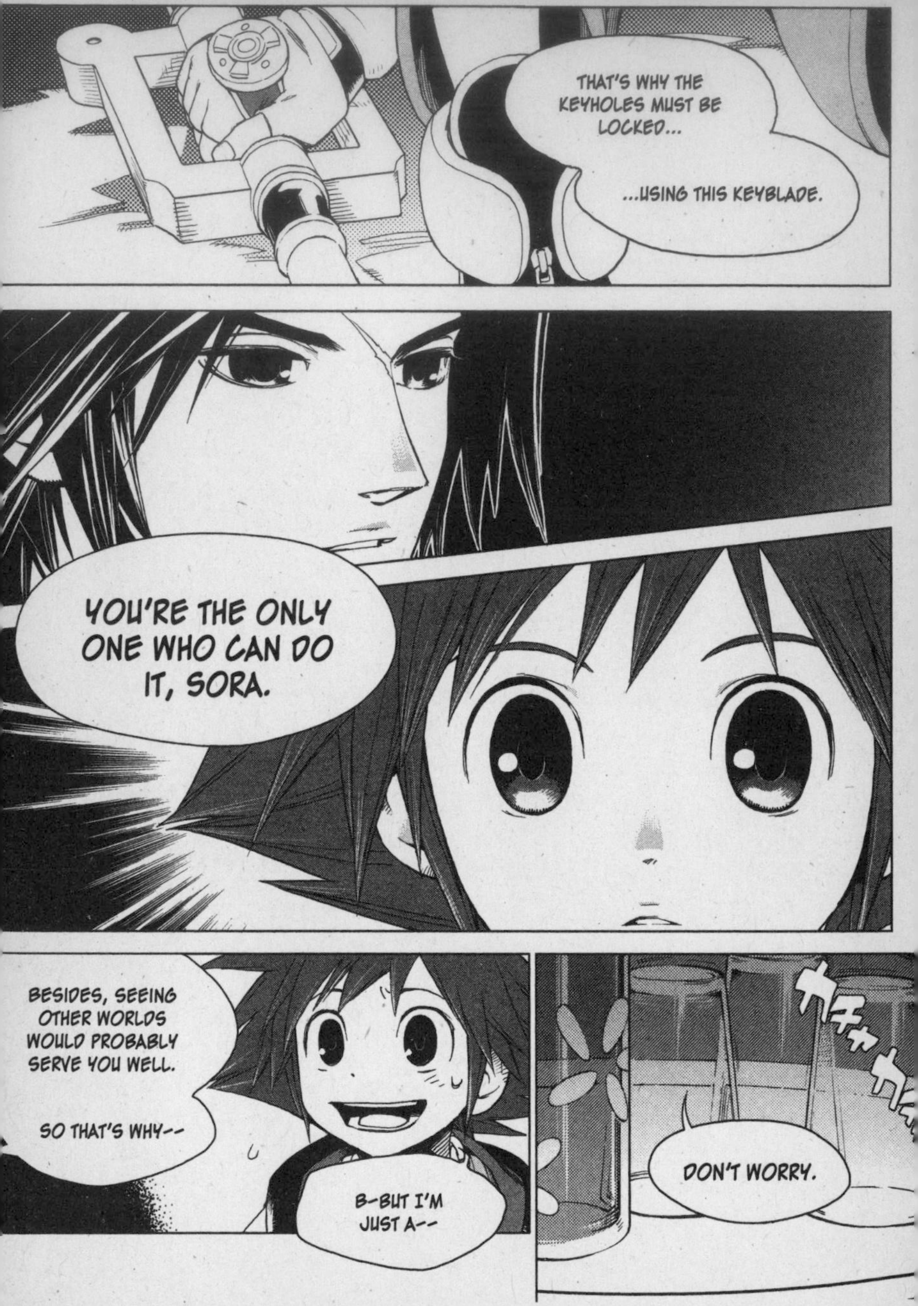
THAT'S WHY THE KEYHOLES MUST BE LOCKED...
...USING THIS KEYBLADE.
YOU'RE THE ONLY ONE WHO CAN DO IT, SORA.
BESIDES, SEEING OTHER WORLDS WOULD PROBABLY SERVE YOU WELL.
SO THAT'S WHY--
B-BUT I'M JUST A--
DON'T WORRY.

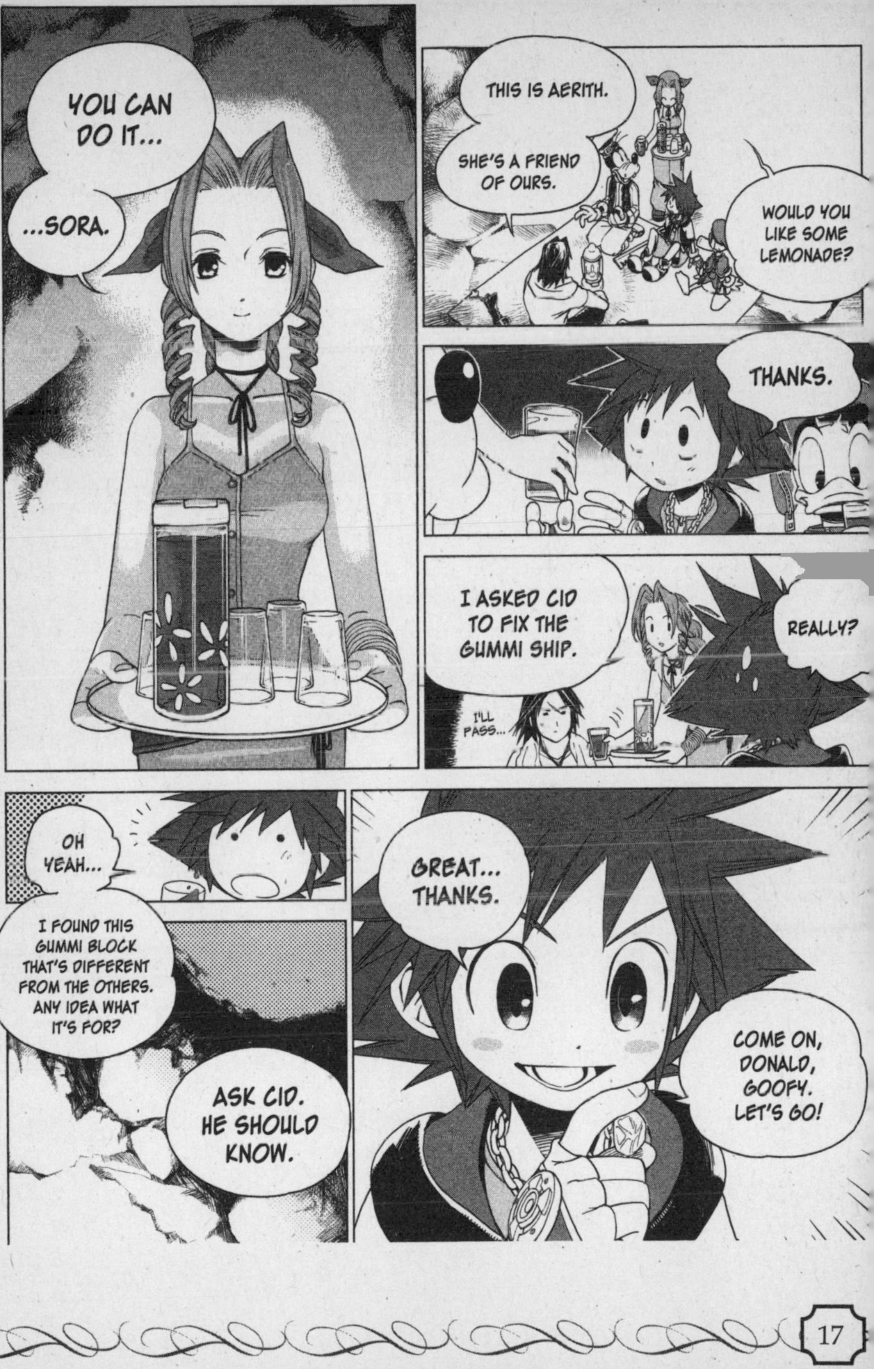

YOU CAN DO IT...
...SORA.
THIS IS AERITH.
SHE'S A FRIEND OF OURS.
WOULD YOU LIKE SOME LEMONADE?
THANKS.
I ASKED CID TO FIX THE GUMMI SHIP.
REALLY?
I'LL PASS...
OH YEAH...
I FOUND THIS GUMMI BLOCK THAT'S DIFFERENT FROM THE OTHERS. ANY IDEA WHAT IT'S FOR?
ASK CID. HE SHOULD KNOW.
GREAT... THANKS.
COME ON, DONALD, GOOFY. LET'S GO!

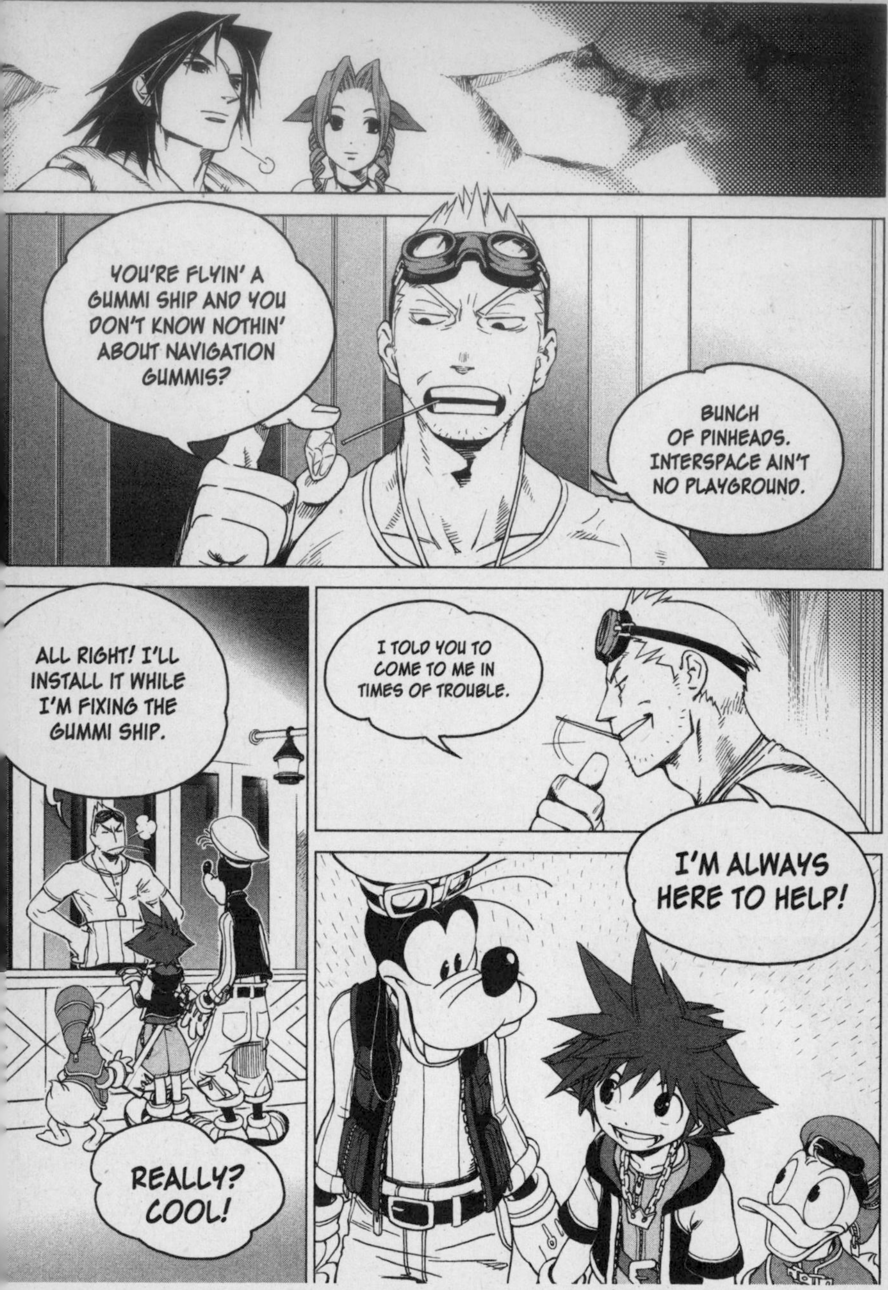
YOU'RE FLYIN' A GUMMI SHIP AND YOU DON'T KNOW NOTHIN' ABOUT NAVIGATION GUMMIS?
BUNCH OF PINHEADS. INTERSPACE AIN'T NO PLAYGROUND.
ALL RIGHT! I'LL INSTALL IT WHILE I'M FIXING THE GUMMI SHIP.
REALLY? COOL!
I TOLD YOU TO COME TO ME IN TIMES OF TROUBLE.
I'M ALWAYS HERE TO HELP!

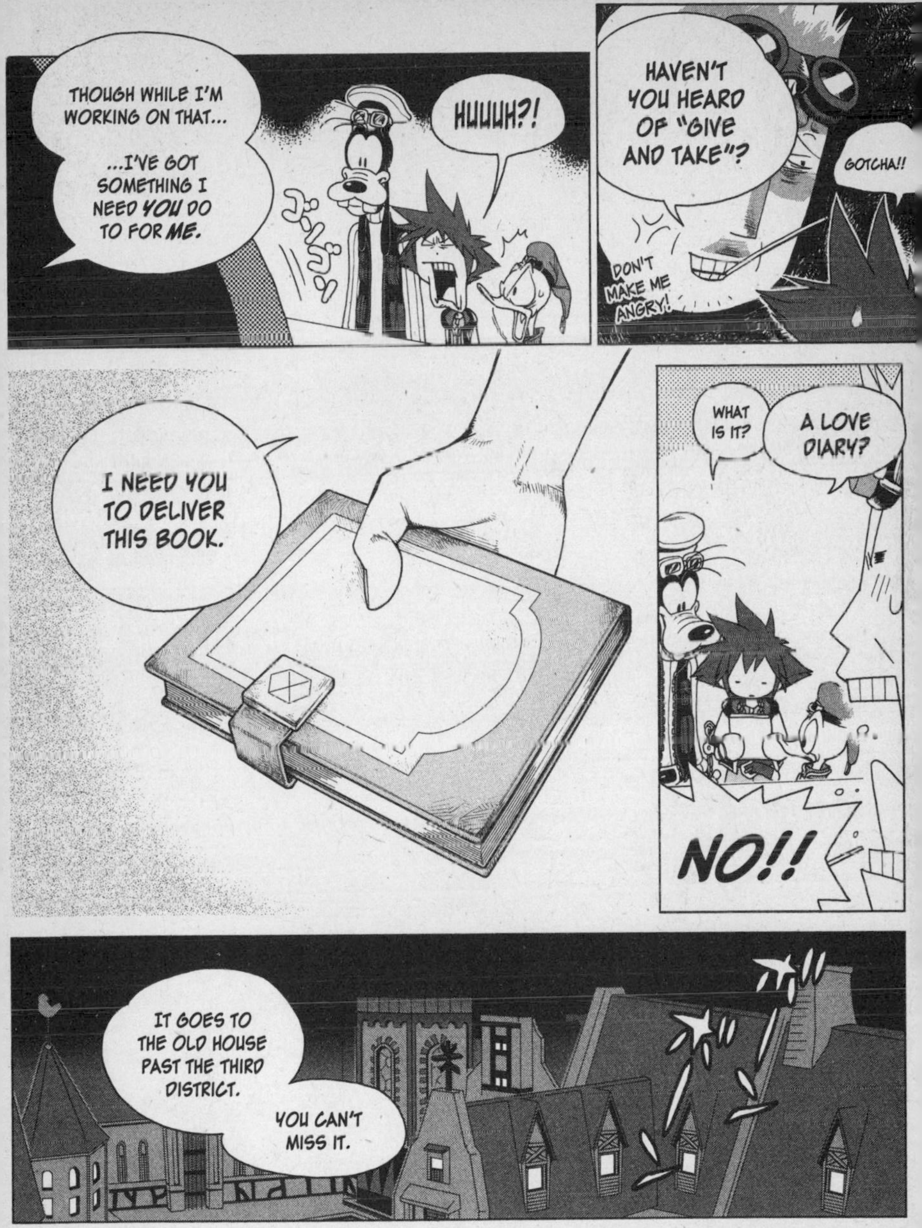
THOUGH WHILE I'M WORKING ON THAT...
...I'VE GOT SOMETHING I NEED YOU DO TO FOR ME.
HUUUH?!
HAVEN'T YOU HEARD OF "GIVE AND TAKE"?
GOTCHA!!
DON'T MAKE ME ANGRY!
I NEED YOU TO DELIVER THIS BOOK.
WHAT IS IT?
A LOVE DIARY?
NO!!
IT GOES TO THE OLD HOUSE PAST THE THIRD DISTRICT.
YOU CAN'T MISS IT.

Episode 16

Wizard's House

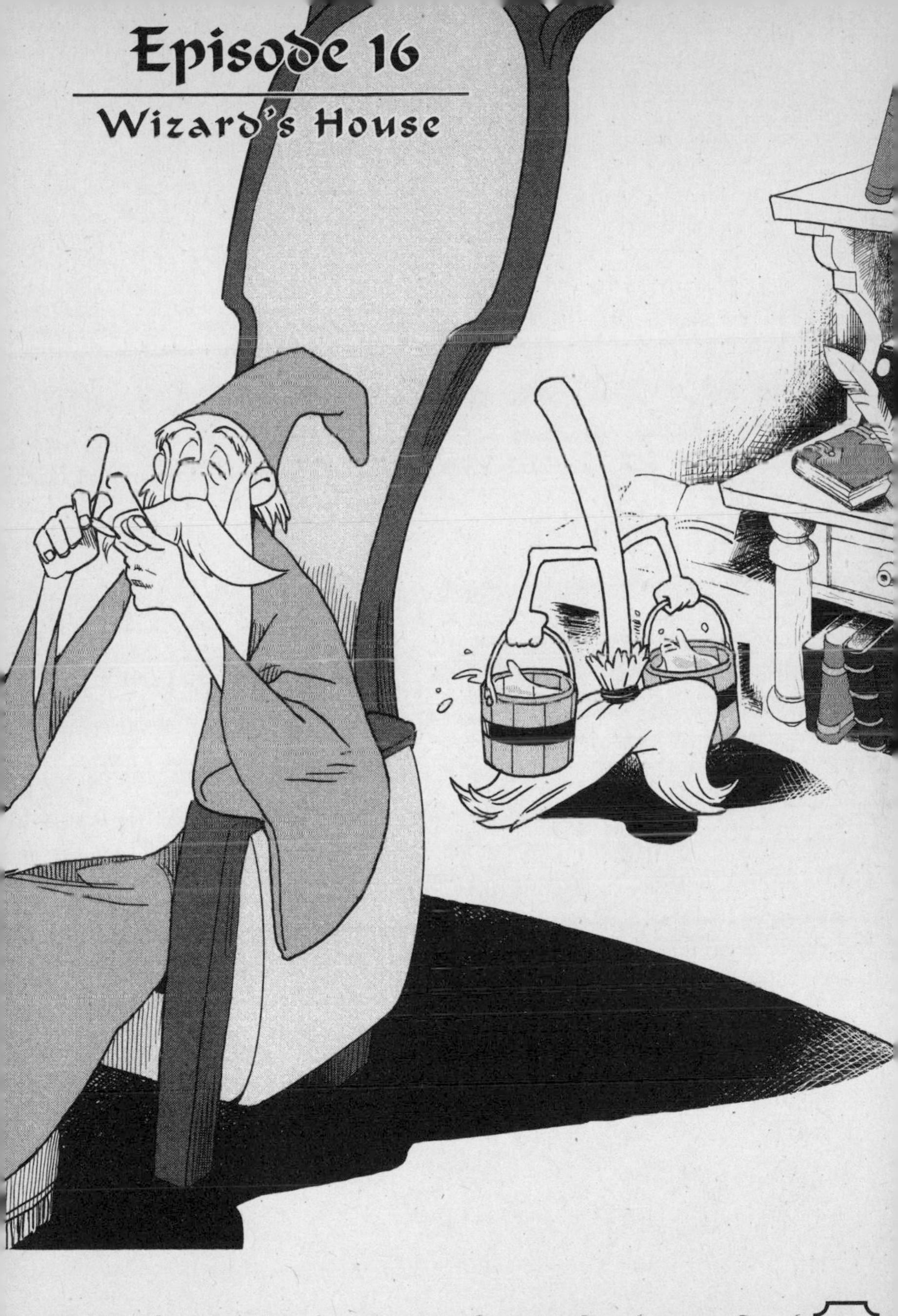

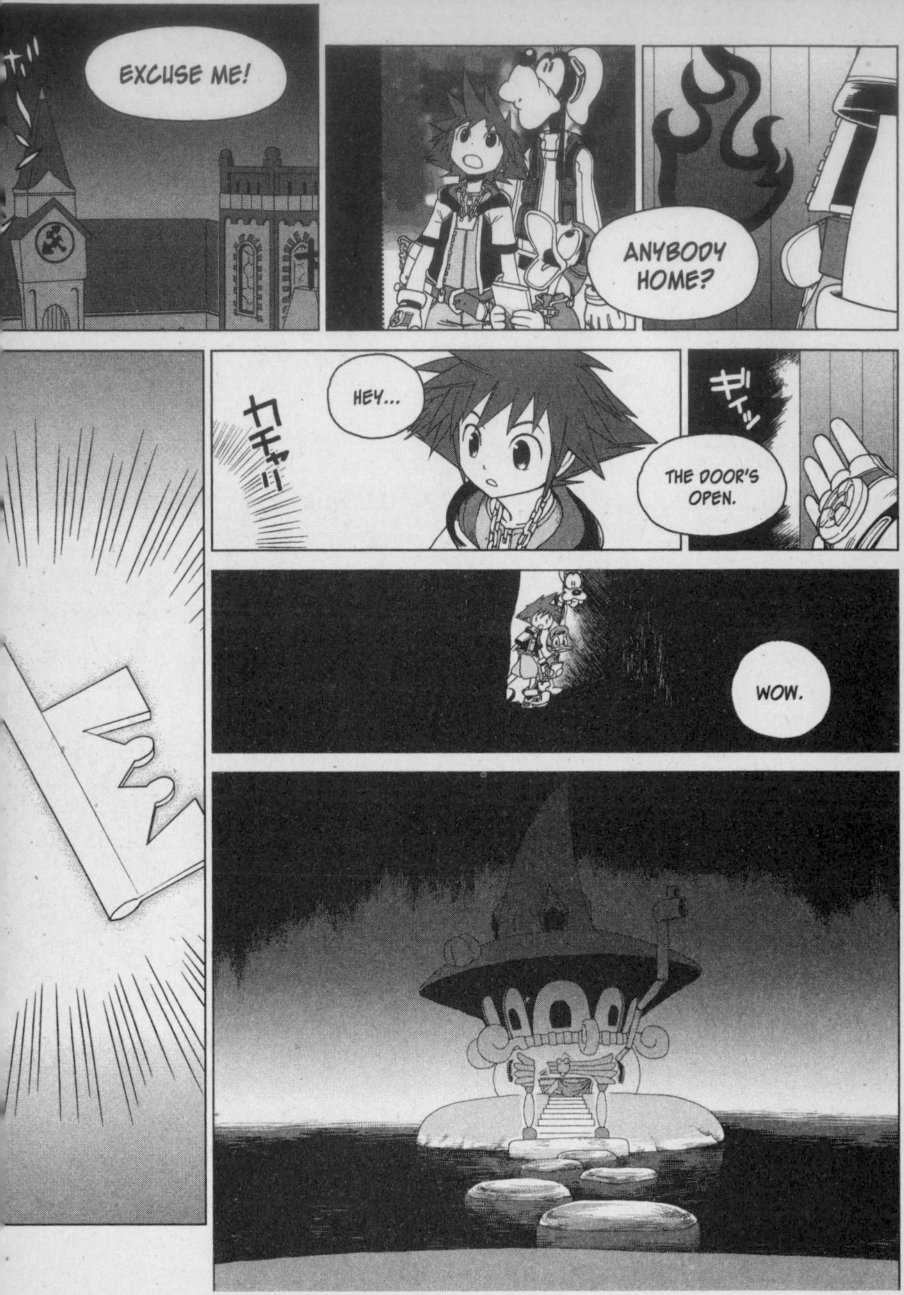
EXCUSE ME!
ANYBODY HOME?
HEY...
カチャリ
ギイッ
THE DOOR'S OPEN.
WOW.

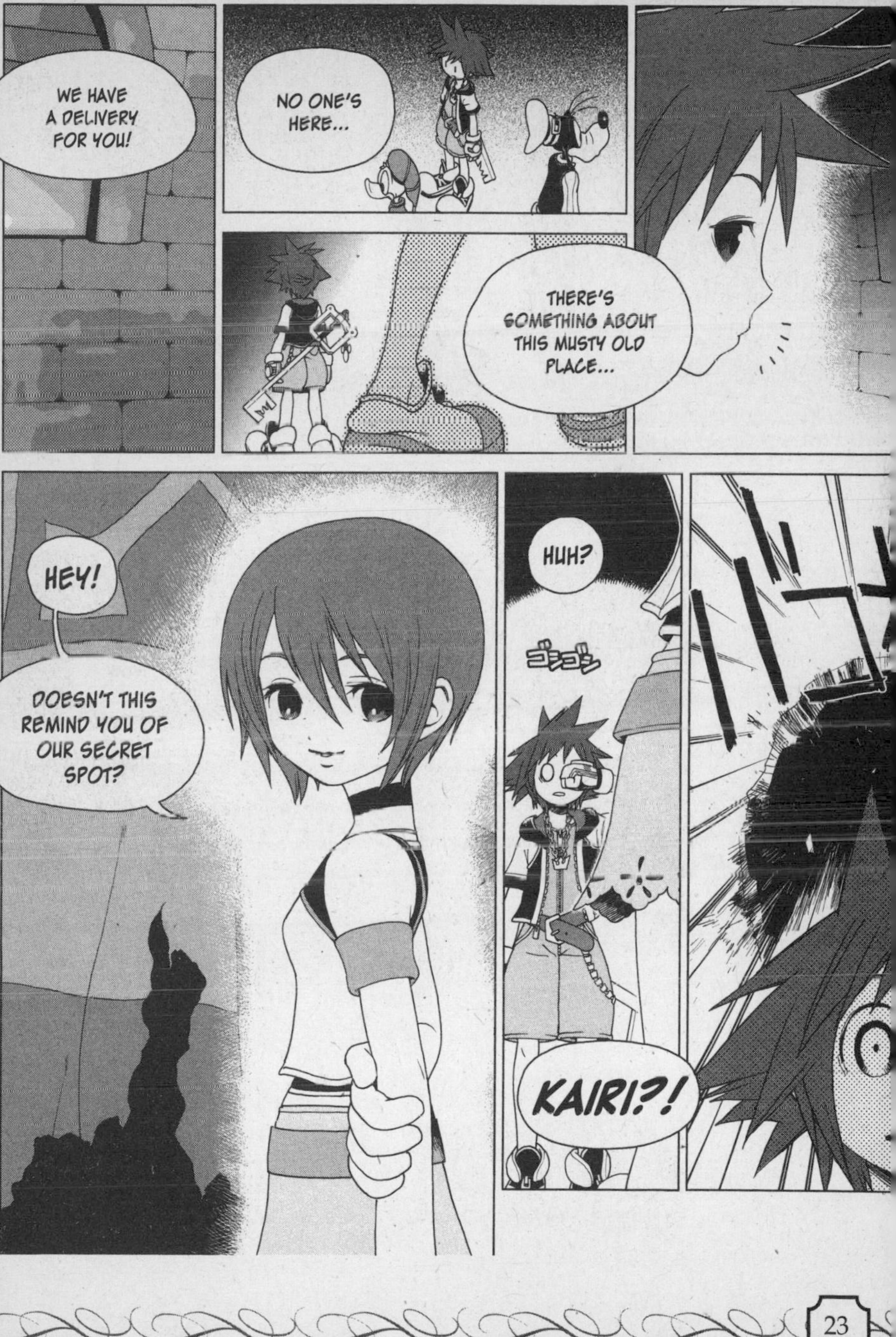
WE HAVE A DELIVERY FOR YOU!
NO ONE'S HERE...
THERE'S SOMETHING ABOUT THIS MUSTY OLD PLACE...
HEY!
DOESN'T THIS REMIND YOU OF OUR SECRET SPOT?
HUH?
ゴシゴシ
KAIRI?!

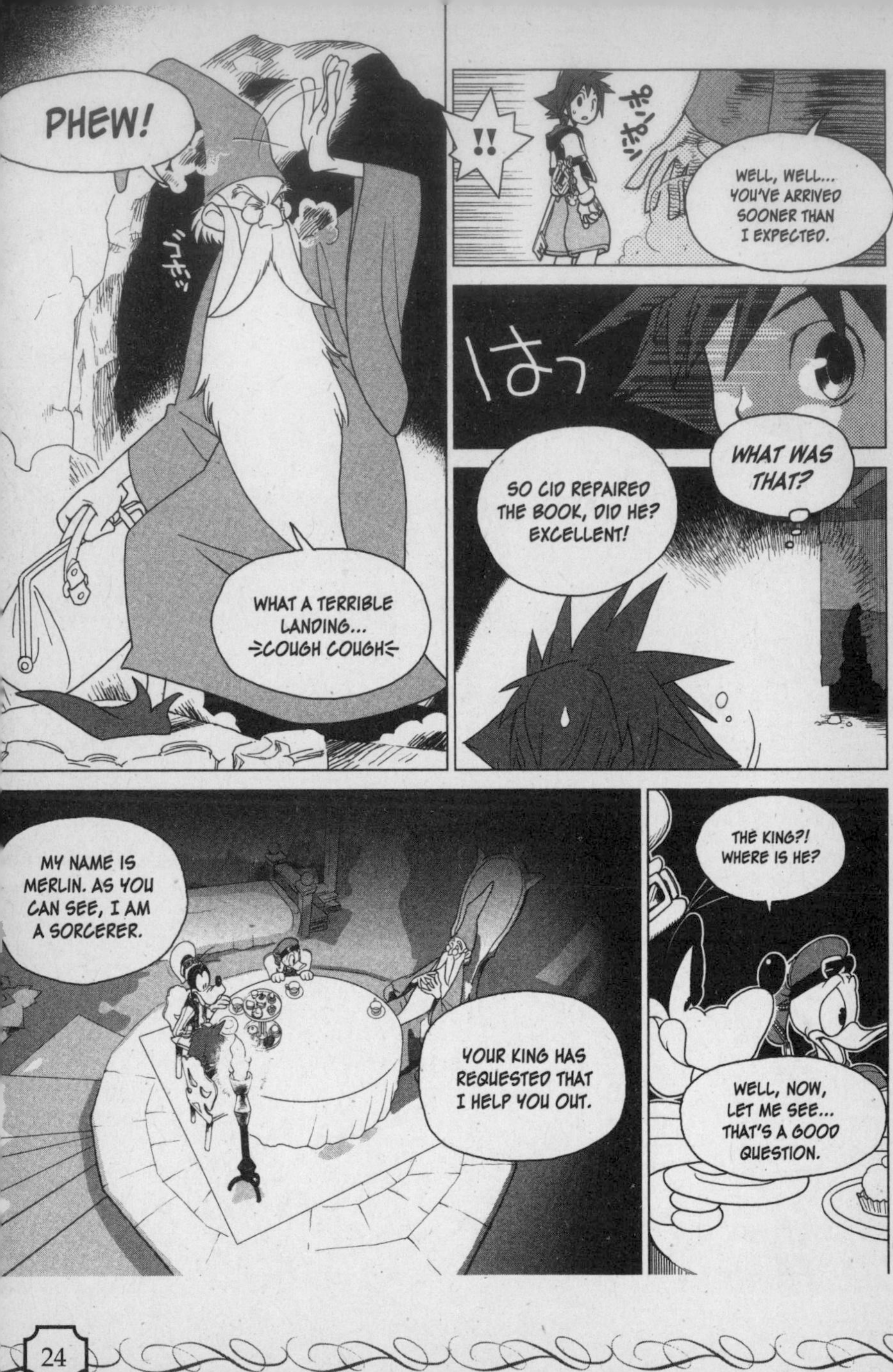
PHEW!
WHAT A TERRIBLE LANDING... =COUGH COUGH=
!!
WELL, WELL... YOU'VE ARRIVED SOONER THAN I EXPECTED.
はっ
WHAT WAS THAT?
SO CID REPAIRED THE BOOK, DID HE? EXCELLENT!
MY NAME IS MERLIN. AS YOU CAN SEE, I AM A SORCERER.
YOUR KING HAS REQUESTED THAT I HELP YOU OUT.
THE KING?! WHERE IS HE?
WELL, NOW, LET ME SEE... THAT'S A GOOD QUESTION.

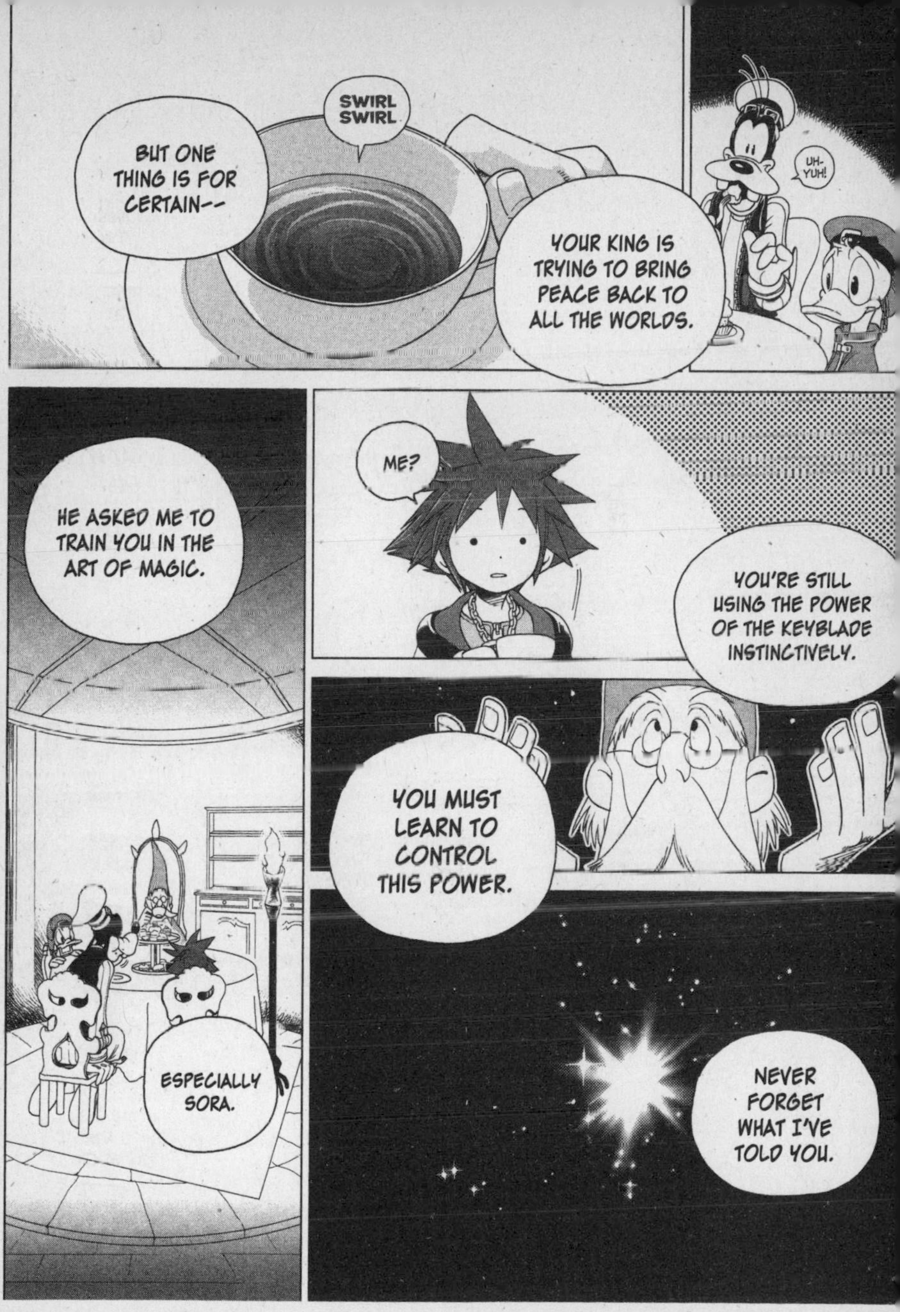
SWIRL SWIRL
BUT ONE THING IS FOR CERTAIN--
YOUR KING IS TRYING TO BRING PEACE BACK TO ALL THE WORLDS.
UH-YUH!
HE ASKED ME TO TRAIN YOU IN THE ART OF MAGIC.
ESPECIALLY SORA.
ME?
YOU'RE STILL USING THE POWER OF THE KEYBLADE INSTINCTIVELY.
YOU MUST LEARN TO CONTROL THIS POWER.
NEVER FORGET WHAT I'VE TOLD YOU.

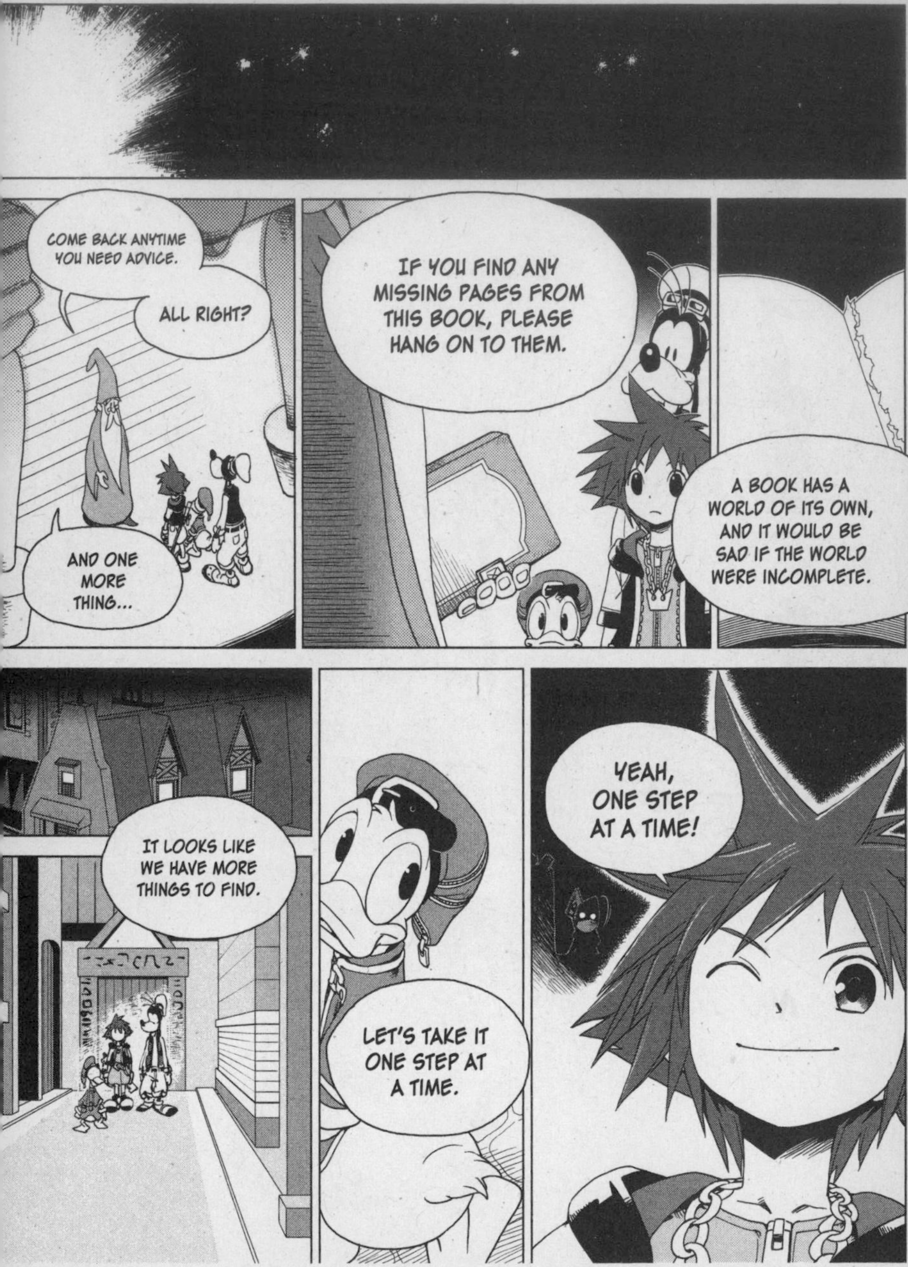
COME BACK ANYTIME YOU NEED ADVICE.
ALL RIGHT?
AND ONE MORE THING...
IF YOU FIND ANY MISSING PAGES FROM THIS BOOK, PLEASE HANG ON TO THEM.
A BOOK HAS A WORLD OF ITS OWN, AND IT WOULD BE SAD IF THE WORLD WERE INCOMPLETE.
IT LOOKS LIKE WE HAVE MORE THINGS TO FIND.
LET'S TAKE IT ONE STEP AT A TIME.
YEAH, ONE STEP AT A TIME!

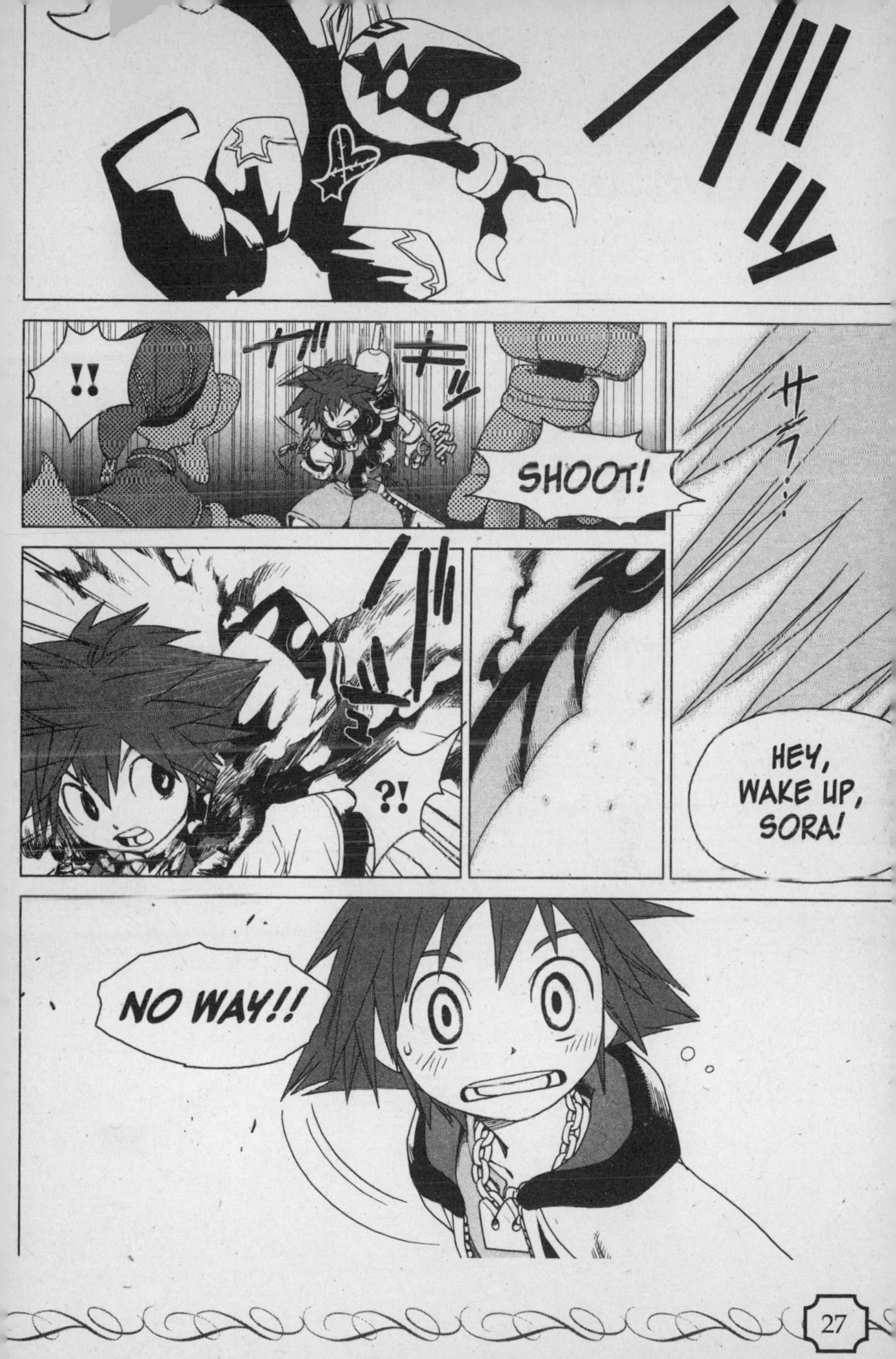
!!
SHOOT!
?!
HEY, WAKE UP, SORA!
NO WAY!!

Episode 17

Reunion

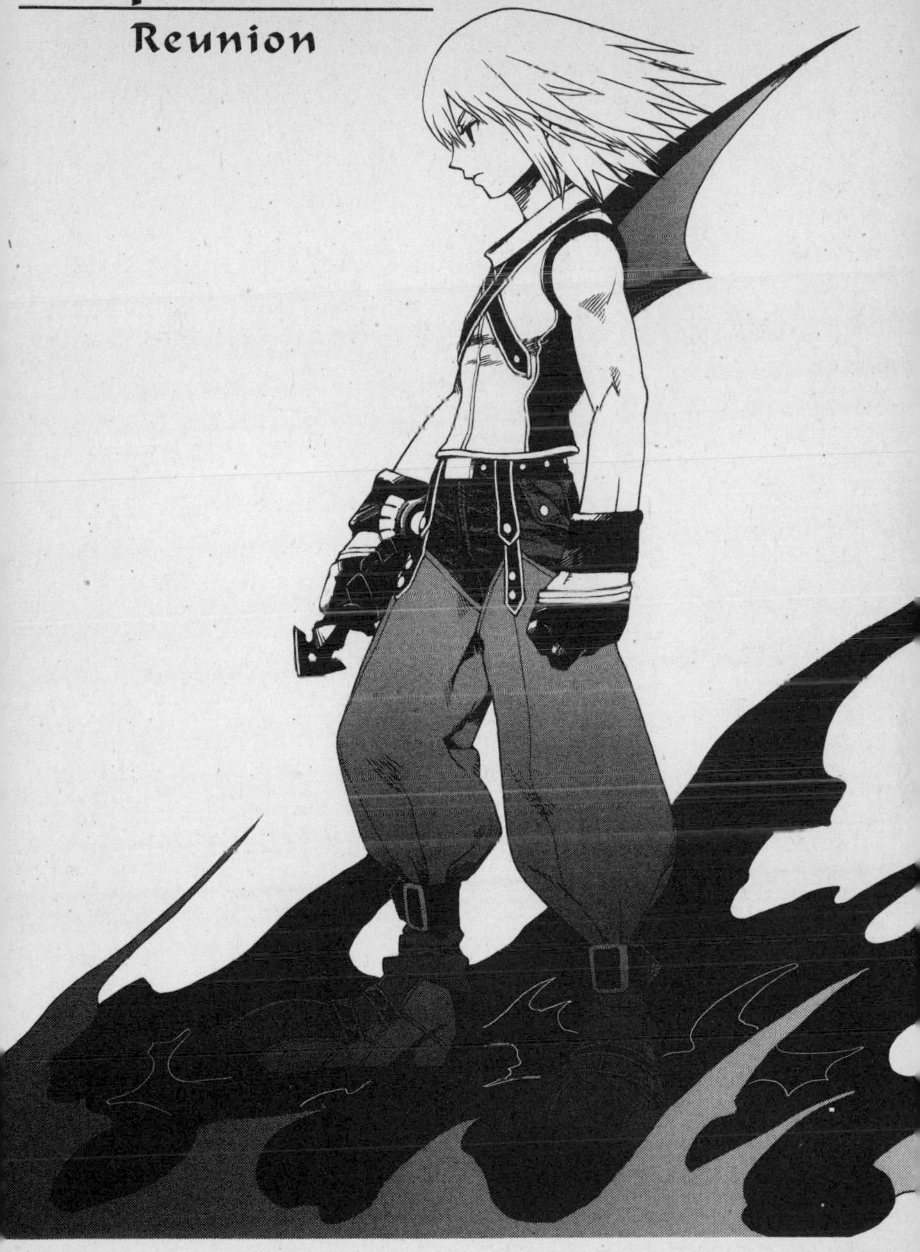

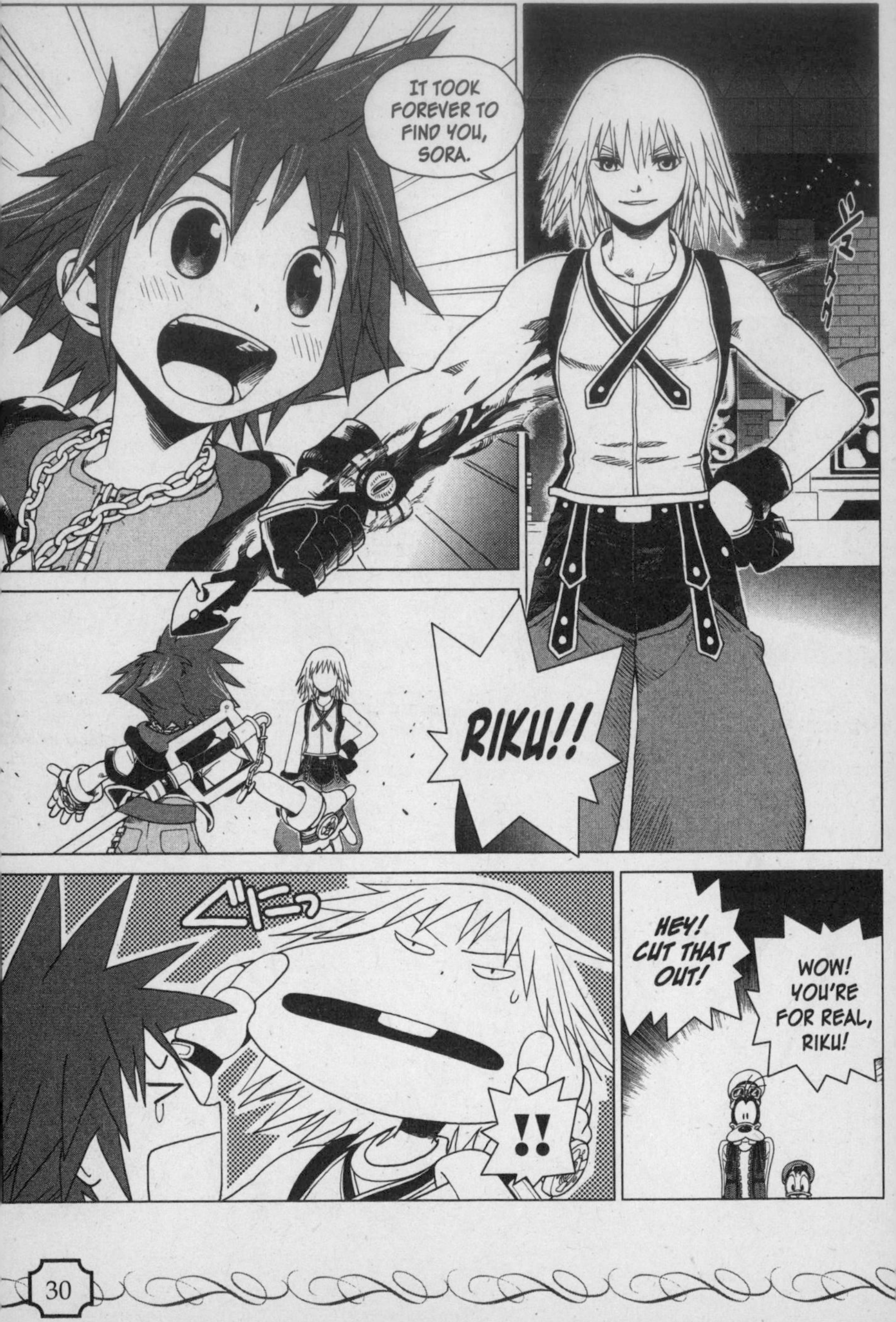
IT TOOK FOREVER TO FIND YOU, SORA.
RIKU!!
!!
HEY! CUT THAT OUT!
WOW! YOU'RE FOR REAL, RIKU!

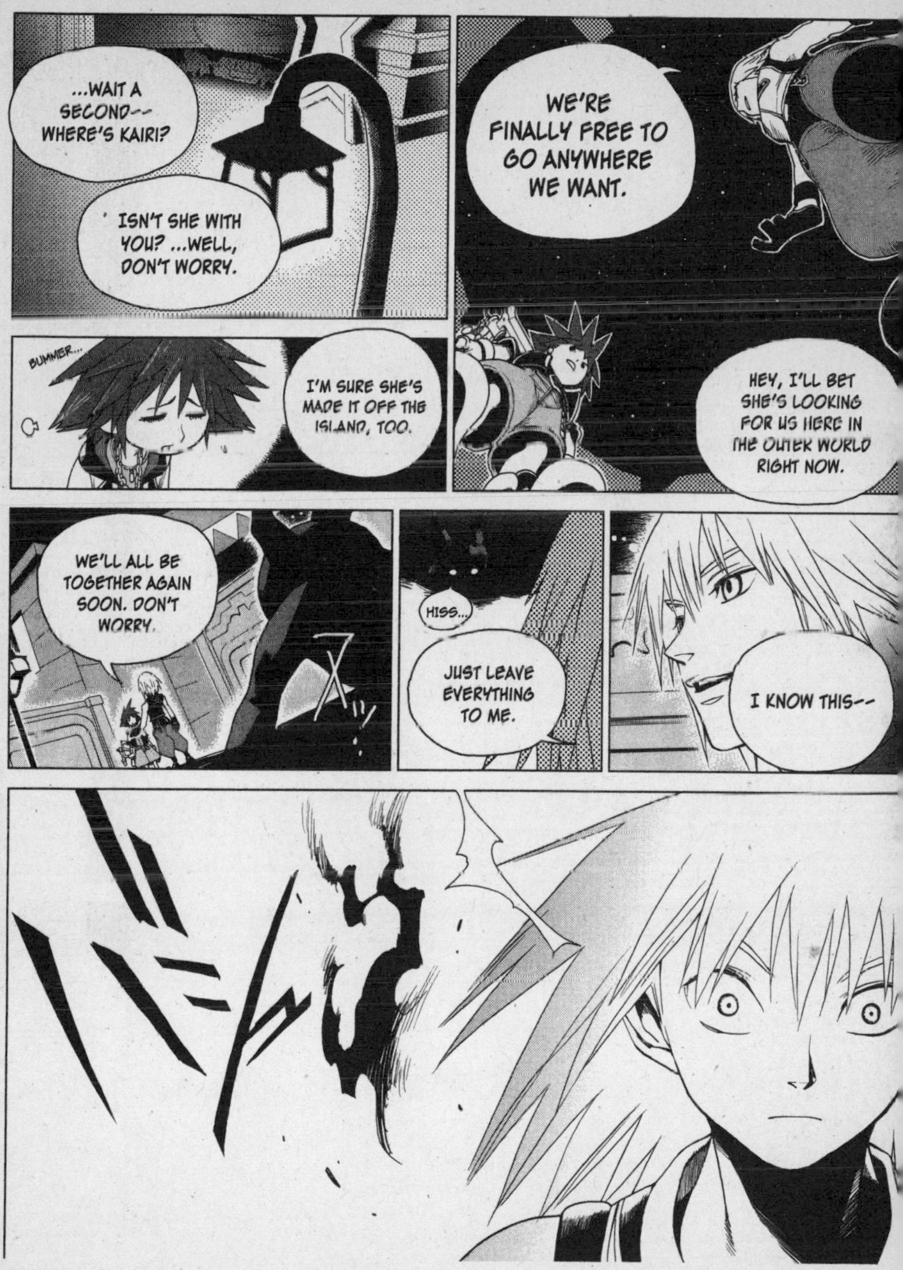
...WAIT A SECOND-- WHERE'S KAIRI?
ISN'T SHE WITH YOU? ...WELL, DON'T WORRY.
WE'RE FINALLY FREE TO GO ANYWHERE WE WANT.
BUMMER...
I'M SURE SHE'S MADE IT OFF THE ISLAND, TOO.
HEY, I'LL BET SHE'S LOOKING FOR US HERE IN THE OUTER WORLD RIGHT NOW.
WE'LL ALL BE TOGETHER AGAIN SOON. DON'T WORRY.
HISS...
JUST LEAVE EVERYTHING TO ME.
I KNOW THIS--

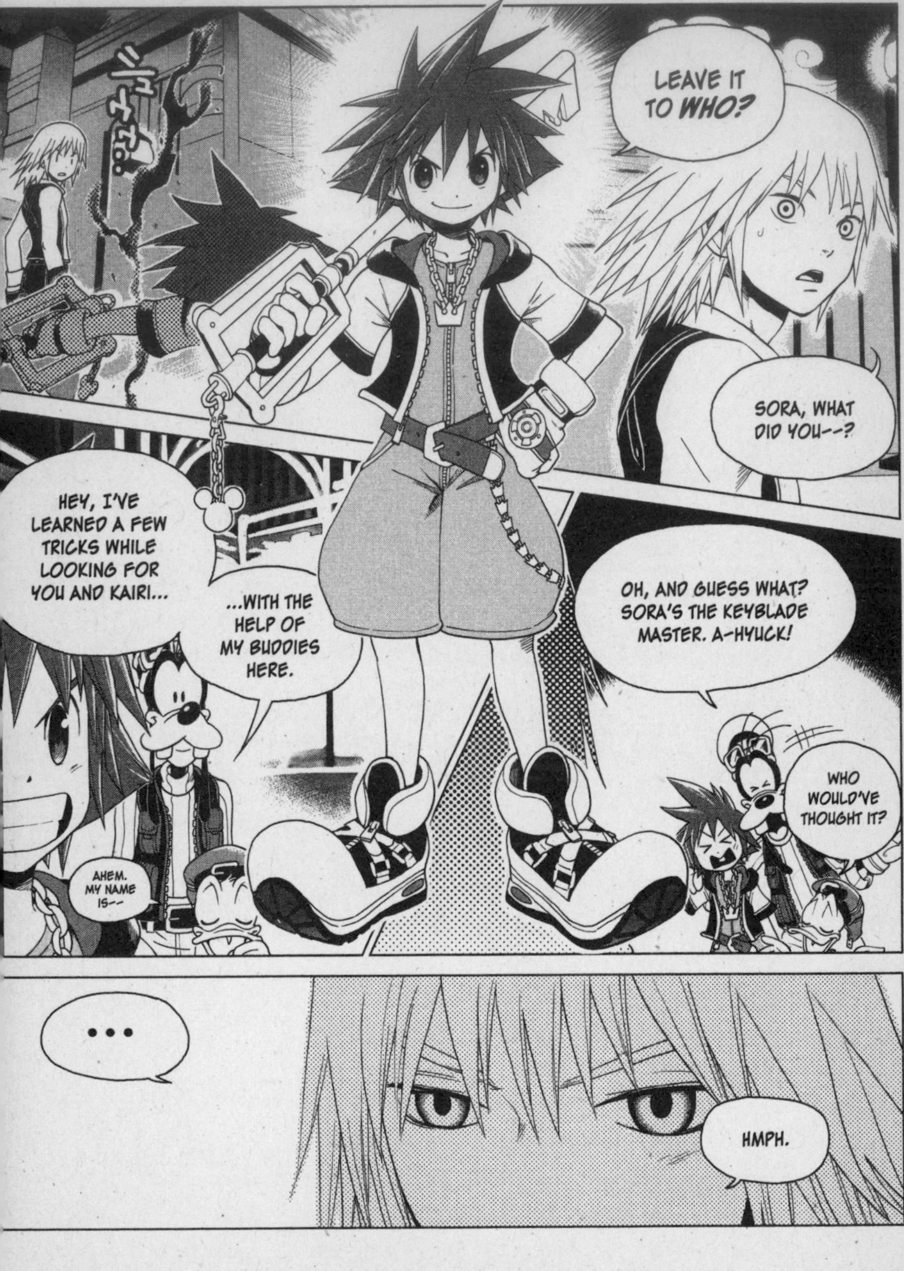

シュウゥ..
LEAVE IT TO *WHO?*
SORA, WHAT DID YOU--?
HEY, I'VE LEARNED A FEW TRICKS WHILE LOOKING FOR YOU AND KAIRI...
...WITH THE HELP OF MY BUDDIES HERE.
AHEM. MY NAME IS--
OH, AND GUESS WHAT? SORA'S THE KEYBLADE MASTER. A-HYUCK!
WHO WOULD'VE THOUGHT IT?
...
HMPH.

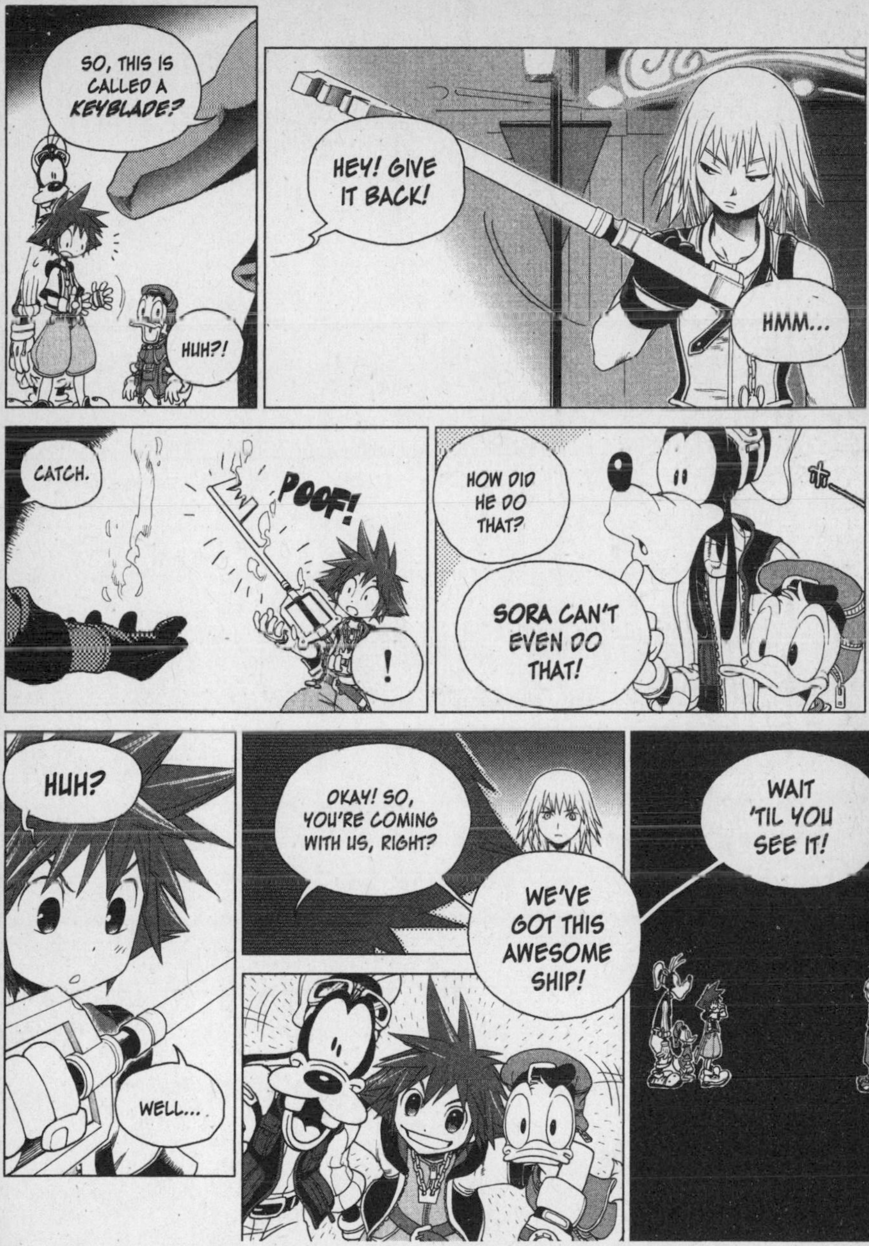
SO, THIS IS CALLED A KEYBLADE?
HUH?!
HEY! GIVE IT BACK!
HMM...
CATCH.
POOF!
!
HOW DID HE DO THAT?
SORA CAN'T EVEN DO THAT!
HUH?
WELL...
OKAY! SO, YOU'RE COMING WITH US, RIGHT?
WE'VE GOT THIS AWESOME SHIP!
WAIT 'TIL YOU SEE IT!

SORA! YOU CAN'T JUST DECIDE THINGS ON YOUR OWN!

OH, COME ON! HE'S MY FRIEND!

I'M SURE RIKU WANTS TO JOIN US.

RIGHT, RIKU?

HEY...

RIKU!

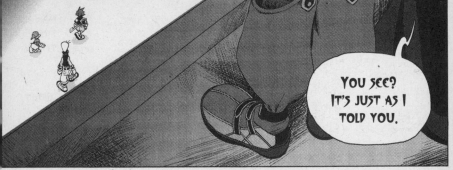

YOU SEE? IT'S JUST AS I TOLD YOU.

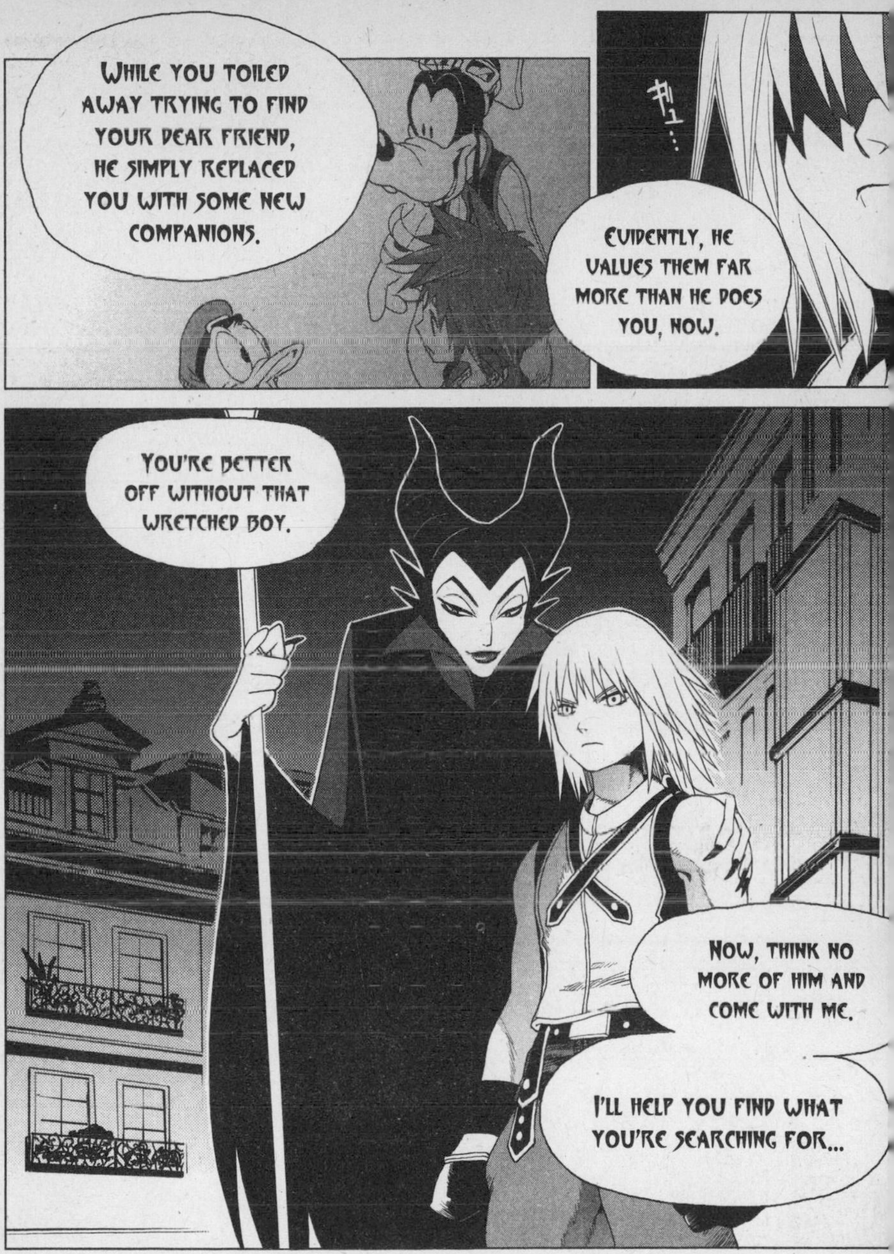
WHILE YOU TOILED AWAY TRYING TO FIND YOUR DEAR FRIEND, HE SIMPLY REPLACED YOU WITH SOME NEW COMPANIONS.
EVIDENTLY, HE VALUES THEM FAR MORE THAN HE DOES YOU, NOW.
YOU'RE BETTER OFF WITHOUT THAT WRETCHED BOY.
NOW, THINK NO MORE OF HIM AND COME WITH ME.
I'LL HELP YOU FIND WHAT YOU'RE SEARCHING FOR...

Episode 18

Maleficent

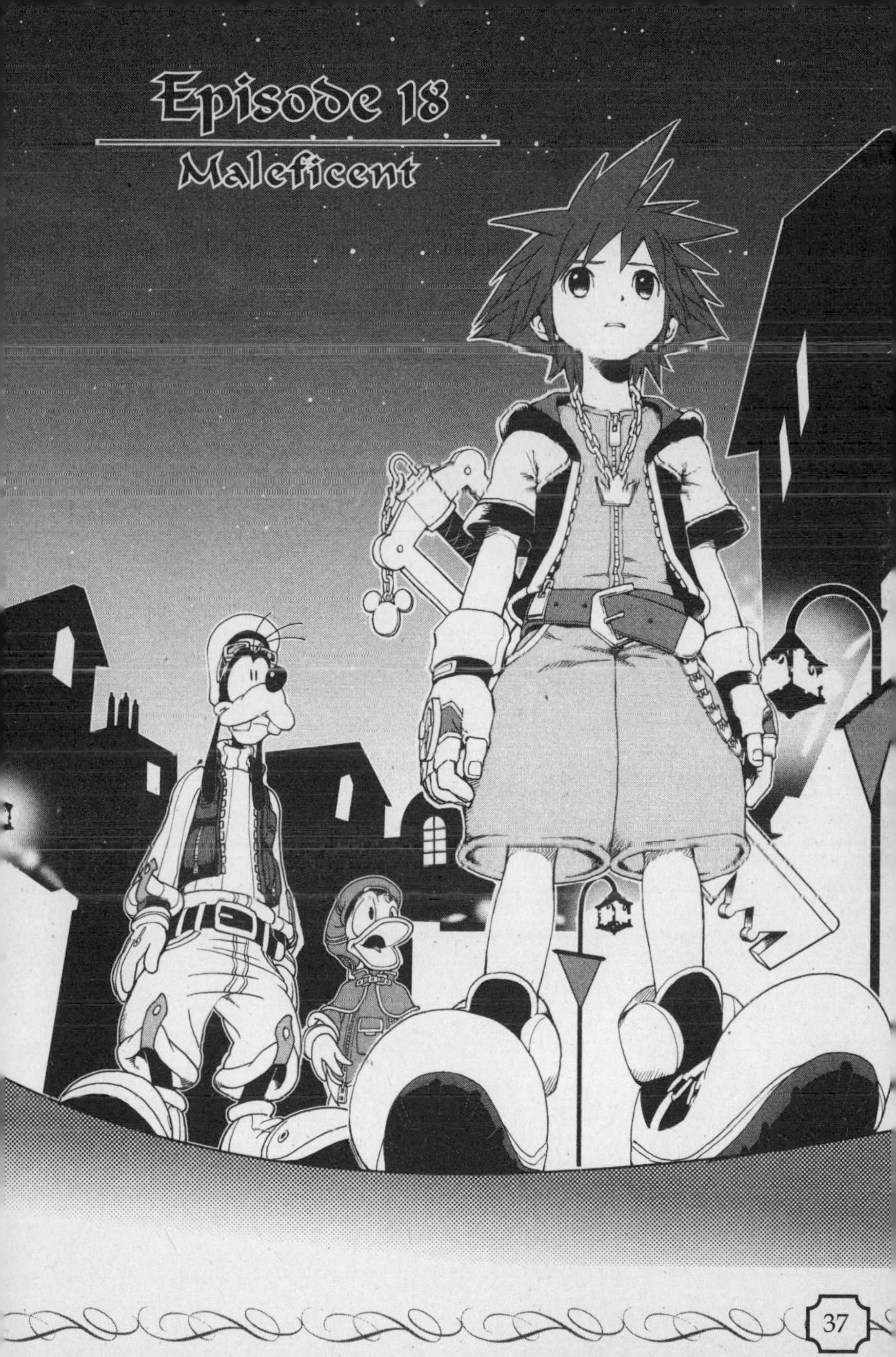

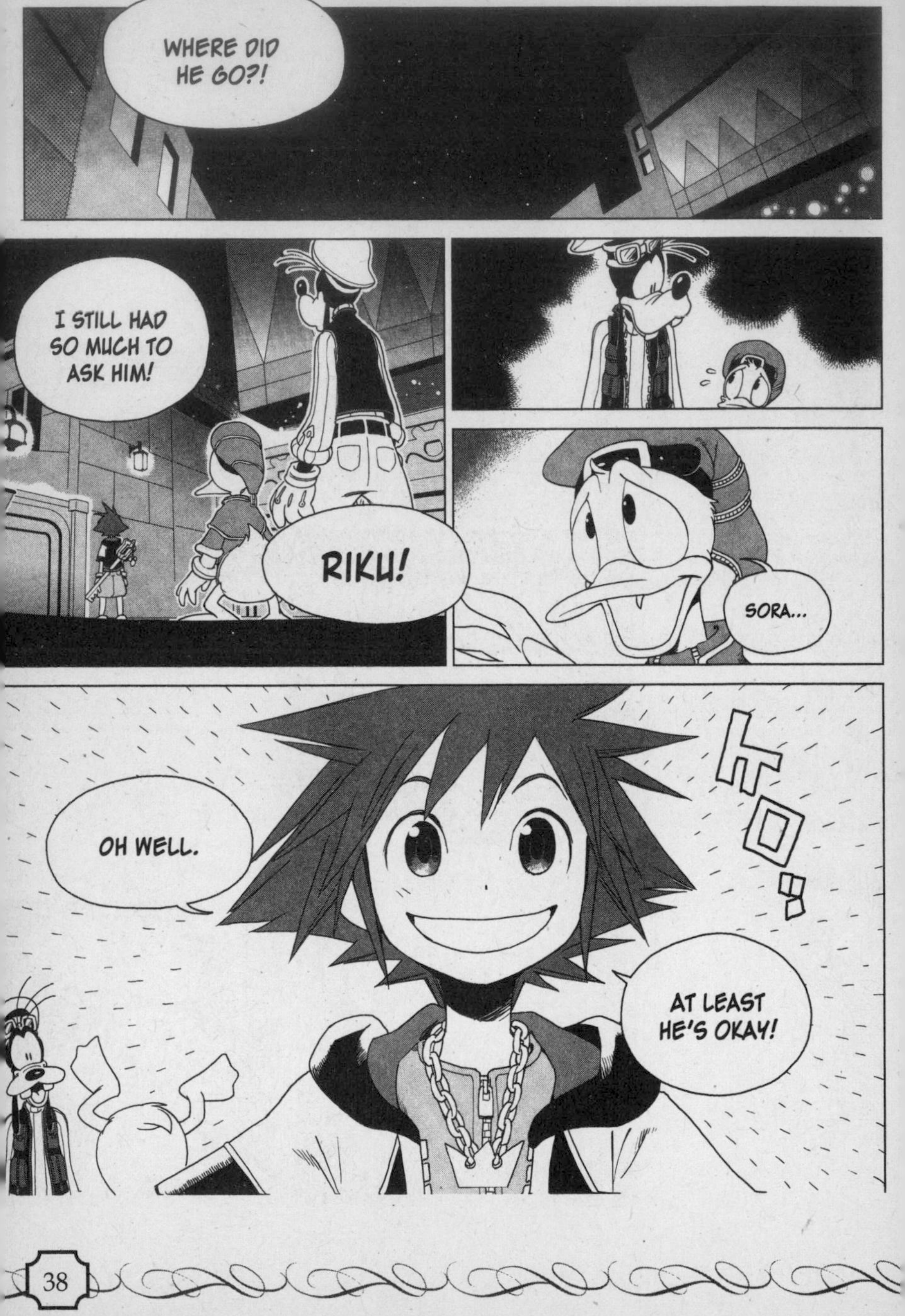

WHERE DID HE GO?!
I STILL HAD SO MUCH TO ASK HIM!
RIKU!
SORA...
OH WELL.
AT LEAST HE'S OKAY!

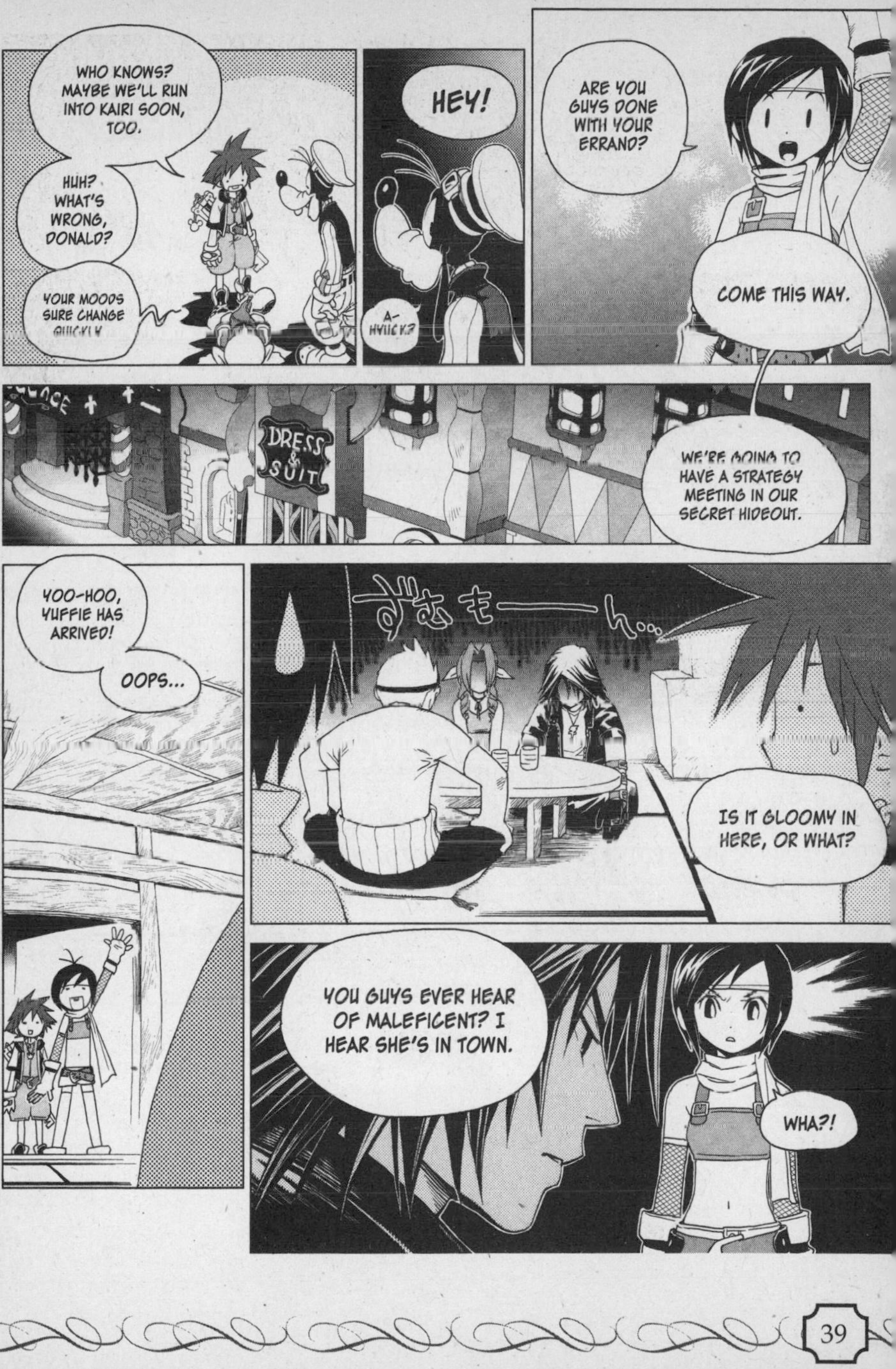
WHO KNOWS? MAYBE WE'LL RUN INTO KAIRI SOON, TOO.
HUH? WHAT'S WRONG, DONALD?
YOUR MOODS SURE CHANGE QUICKLY
HEY!
A-HYUCK?
ARE YOU GUYS DONE WITH YOUR ERRAND?
COME THIS WAY.
DRESS & SUIT
WE'RE GOING TO HAVE A STRATEGY MEETING IN OUR SECRET HIDEOUT.
YOO-HOO, YUFFIE HAS ARRIVED!
OOPS...
ずむもーーん...
IS IT GLOOMY IN HERE, OR WHAT?
YOU GUYS EVER HEAR OF MALEFICENT? I HEAR SHE'S IN TOWN.
WHA?!

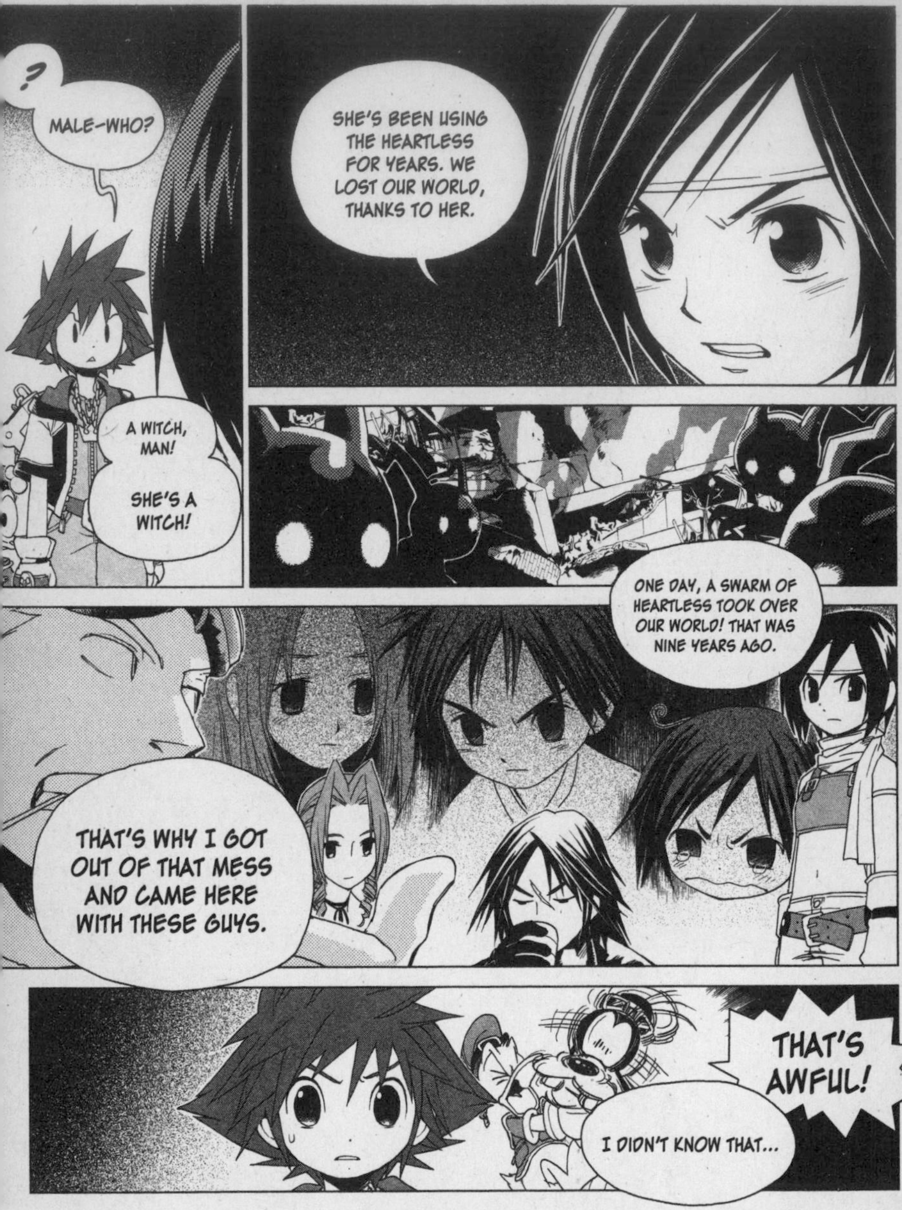
?
MALE-WHO?
A WITCH, MAN!
SHE'S A WITCH!
SHE'S BEEN USING THE HEARTLESS FOR YEARS. WE LOST OUR WORLD, THANKS TO HER.
ONE DAY, A SWARM OF HEARTLESS TOOK OVER OUR WORLD! THAT WAS NINE YEARS AGO.
THAT'S WHY I GOT OUT OF THAT MESS AND CAME HERE WITH THESE GUYS.
I DIDN'T KNOW THAT...
THAT'S AWFUL!

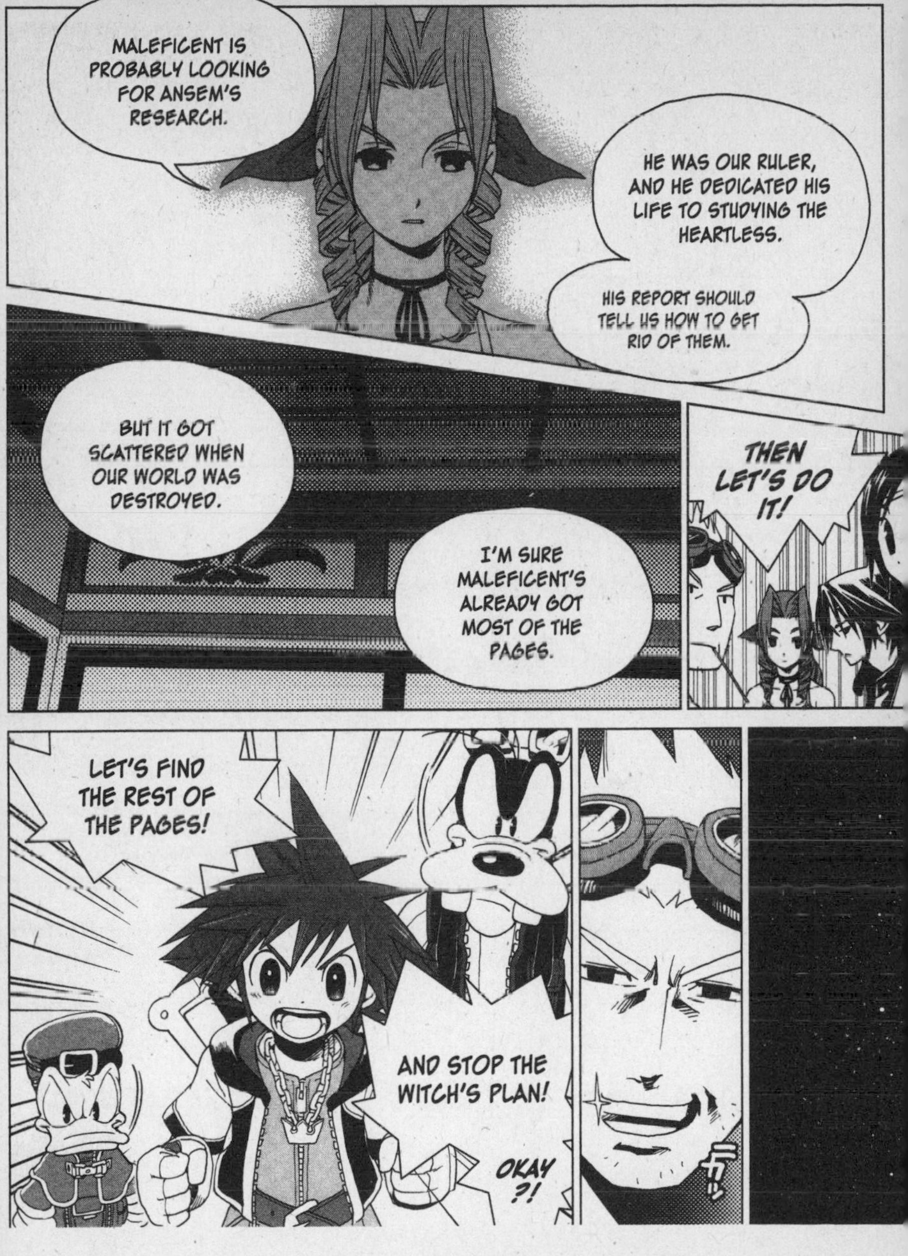
MALEFICENT IS PROBABLY LOOKING FOR ANSEM'S RESEARCH.
HE WAS OUR RULER, AND HE DEDICATED HIS LIFE TO STUDYING THE HEARTLESS.
HIS REPORT SHOULD TELL US HOW TO GET RID OF THEM.
BUT IT GOT SCATTERED WHEN OUR WORLD WAS DESTROYED.
I'M SURE MALEFICENT'S ALREADY GOT MOST OF THE PAGES.
THEN LET'S DO IT!
LET'S FIND THE REST OF THE PAGES!
AND STOP THE WITCH'S PLAN!
OKAY ?!

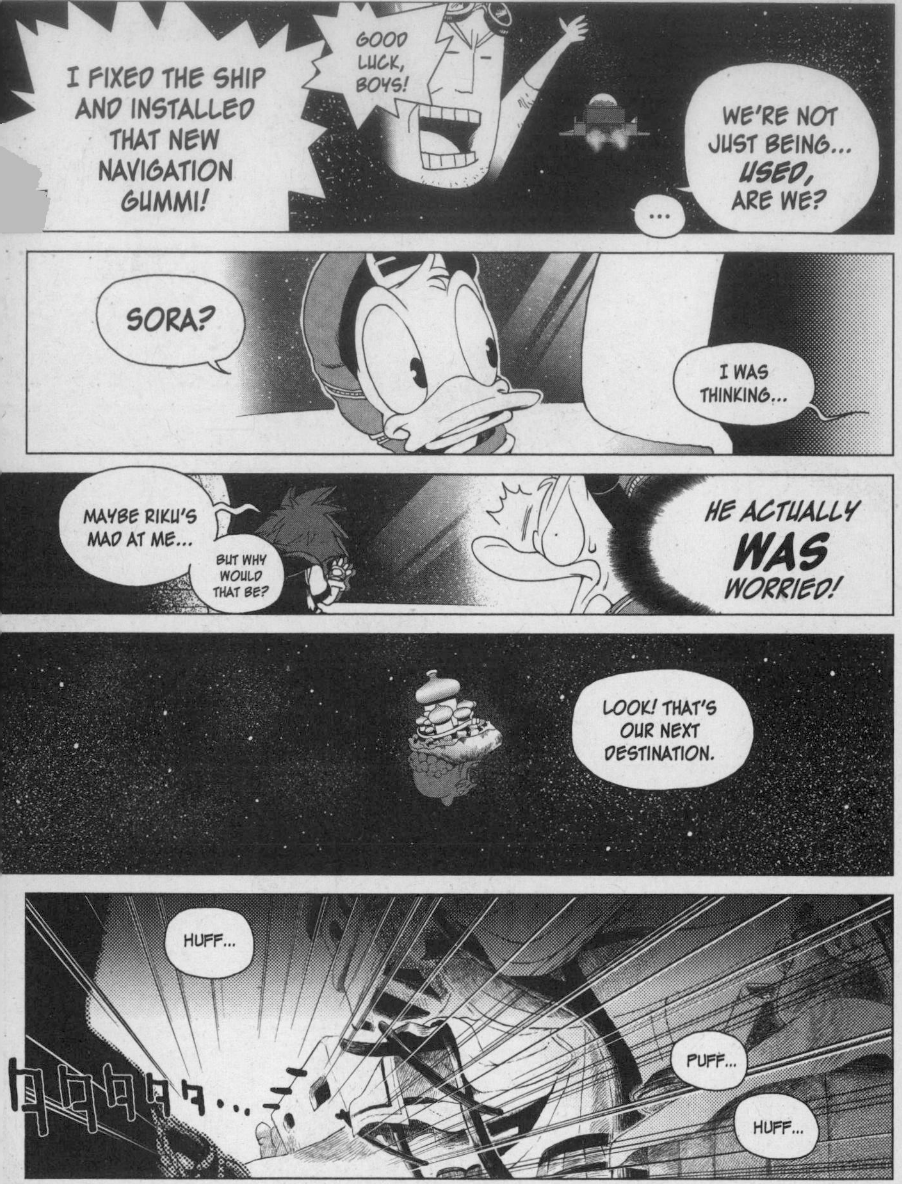
I FIXED THE SHIP AND INSTALLED THAT NEW NAVIGATION GUMMI!
GOOD LUCK, BOYS!
WE'RE NOT JUST BEING... USED, ARE WE?
...
SORA?
I WAS THINKING...
MAYBE RIKU'S MAD AT ME...
BUT WHY WOULD THAT BE?
HE ACTUALLY WAS WORRIED!
LOOK! THAT'S OUR NEXT DESTINATION.
HUFF...
タタタタタ...
PUFF...
HUFF...

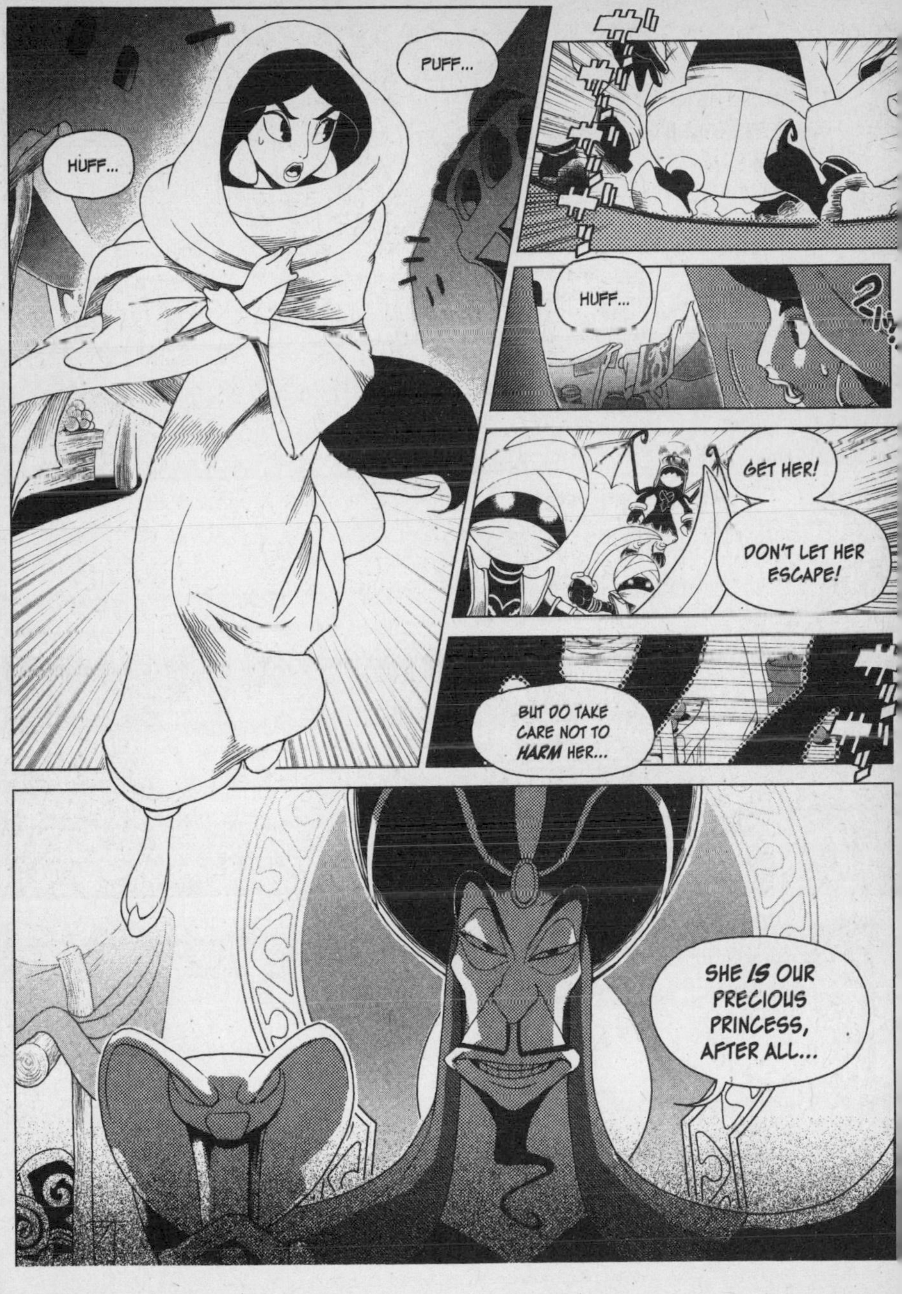
HUFF...
PUFF...
HUFF...
GET HER!
DON'T LET HER ESCAPE!
BUT DO TAKE CARE NOT TO *HARM* HER...
SHE *IS* OUR PRECIOUS PRINCESS, AFTER ALL...

Episode 19

Agrabah

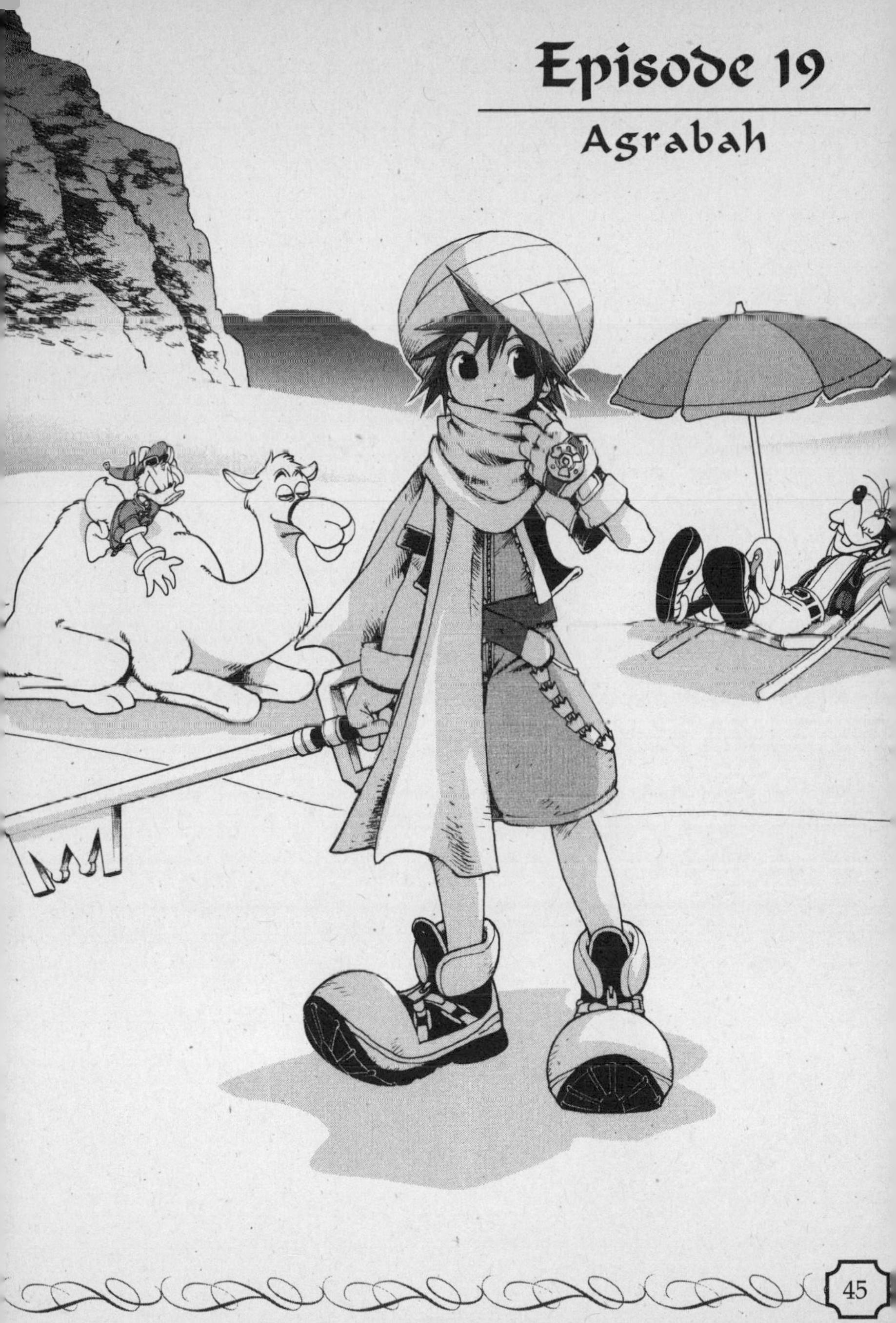

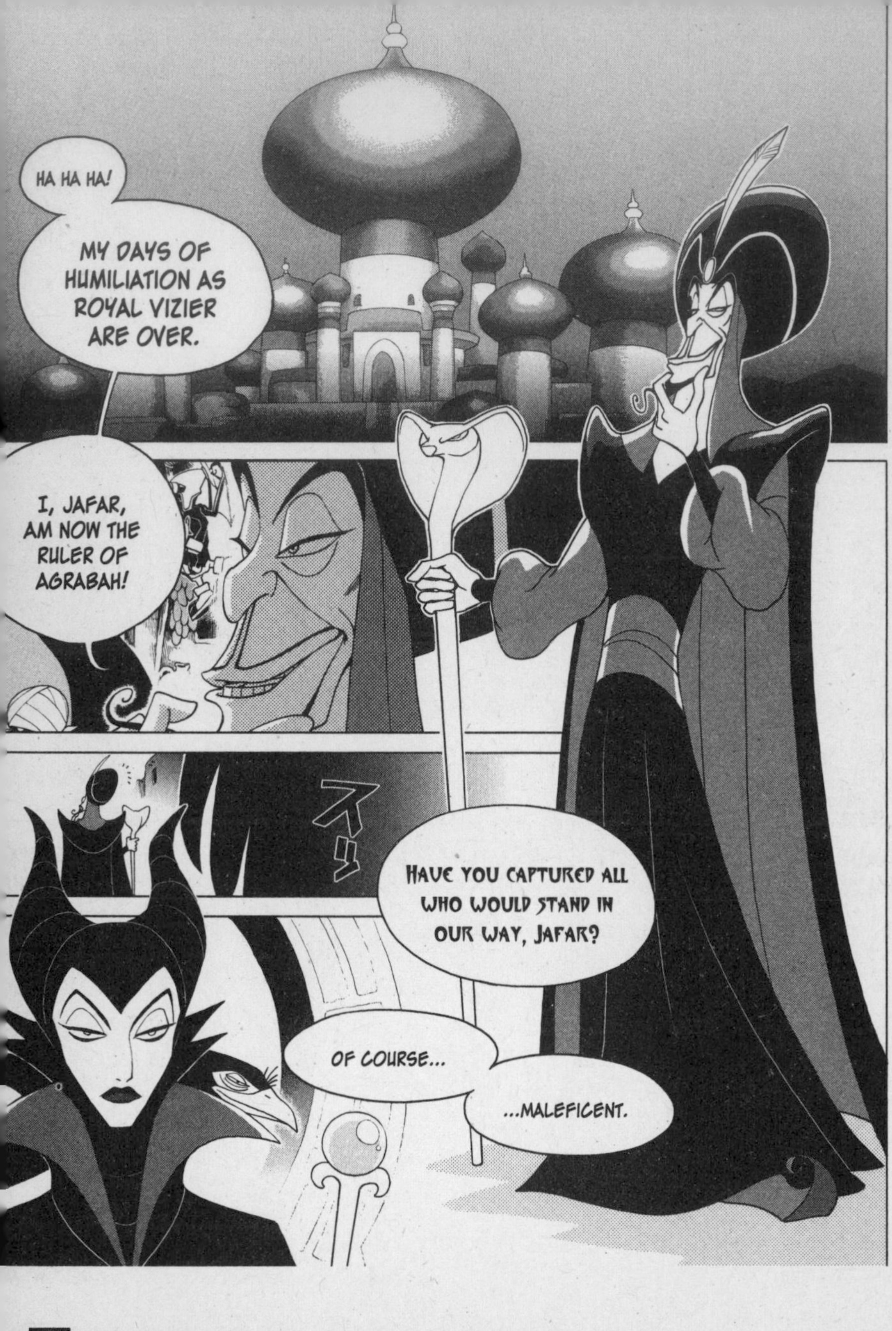
HA HA HA!
MY DAYS OF HUMILIATION AS ROYAL VIZIER ARE OVER.
I, JAFAR, AM NOW THE RULER OF AGRABAH!
スッ
HAVE YOU CAPTURED ALL WHO WOULD STAND IN OUR WAY, JAFAR?
OF COURSE...
...MALEFICENT.

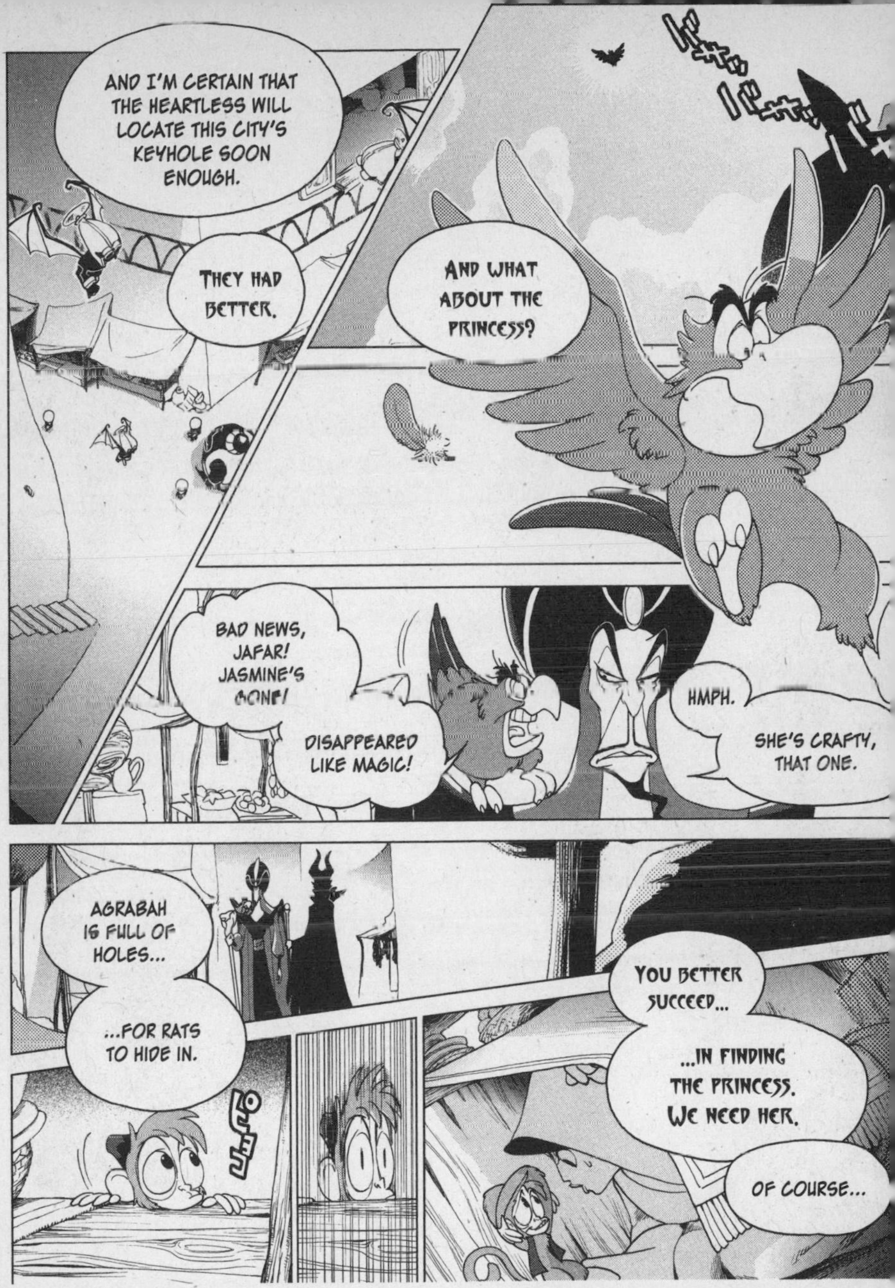
AND I'M CERTAIN THAT THE HEARTLESS WILL LOCATE THIS CITY'S KEYHOLE SOON ENOUGH.
THEY HAD BETTER.
AND WHAT ABOUT THE PRINCESS?
BAD NEWS, JAFAR! JASMINE'S GONE!
DISAPPEARED LIKE MAGIC!
HMPH.
SHE'S CRAFTY, THAT ONE.
AGRABAH IS FULL OF HOLES...
...FOR RATS TO HIDE IN.
YOU BETTER SUCCEED...
...IN FINDING THE PRINCESS. WE NEED HER.
OF COURSE...

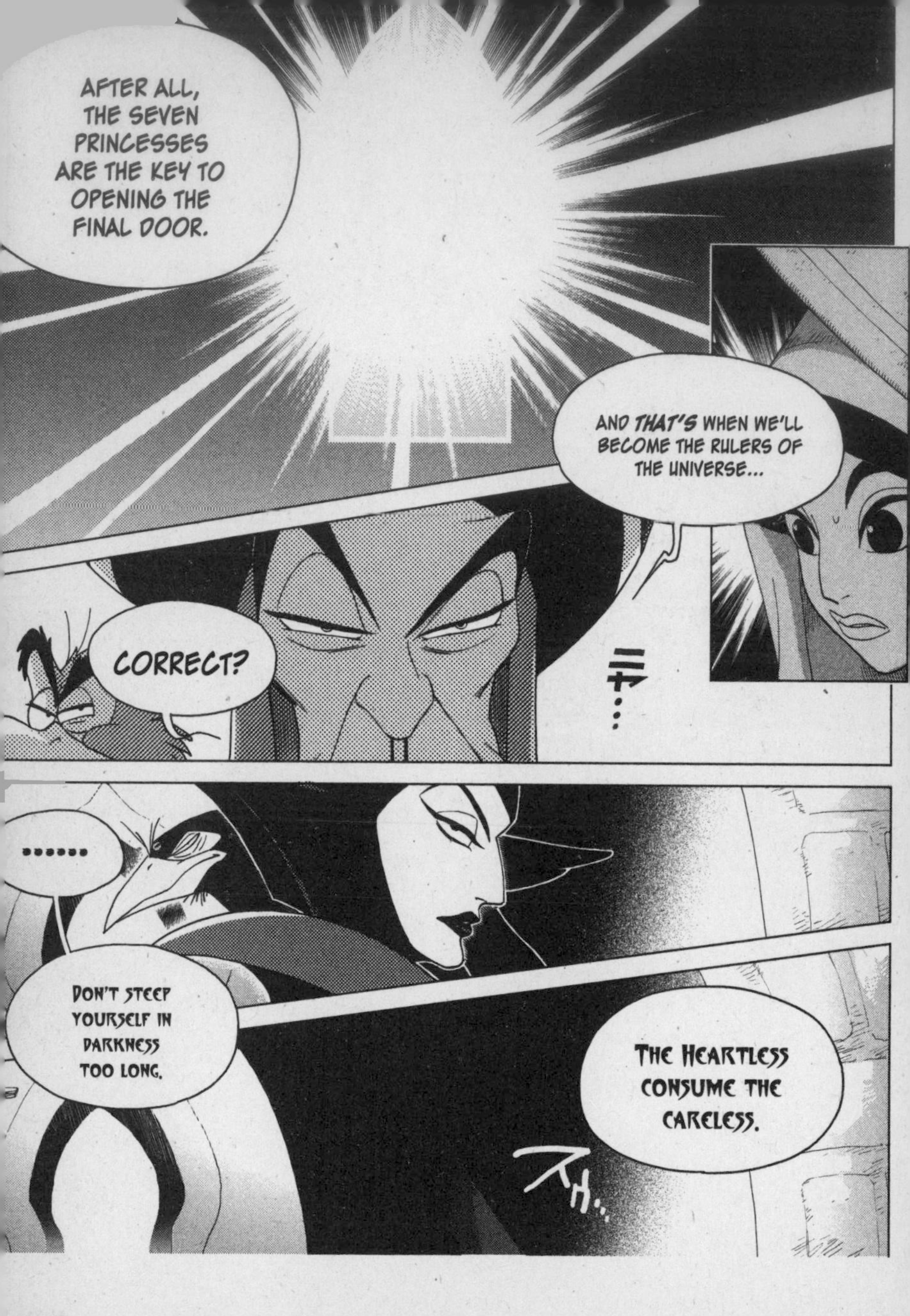
AFTER ALL, THE SEVEN PRINCESSES ARE THE KEY TO OPENING THE FINAL DOOR.
AND *THAT'S* WHEN WE'LL BECOME THE RULERS OF THE UNIVERSE...
CORRECT?
ニヤ...
......
DON'T STEEP YOURSELF IN DARKNESS TOO LONG.
THE HEARTLESS CONSUME THE CARELESS.

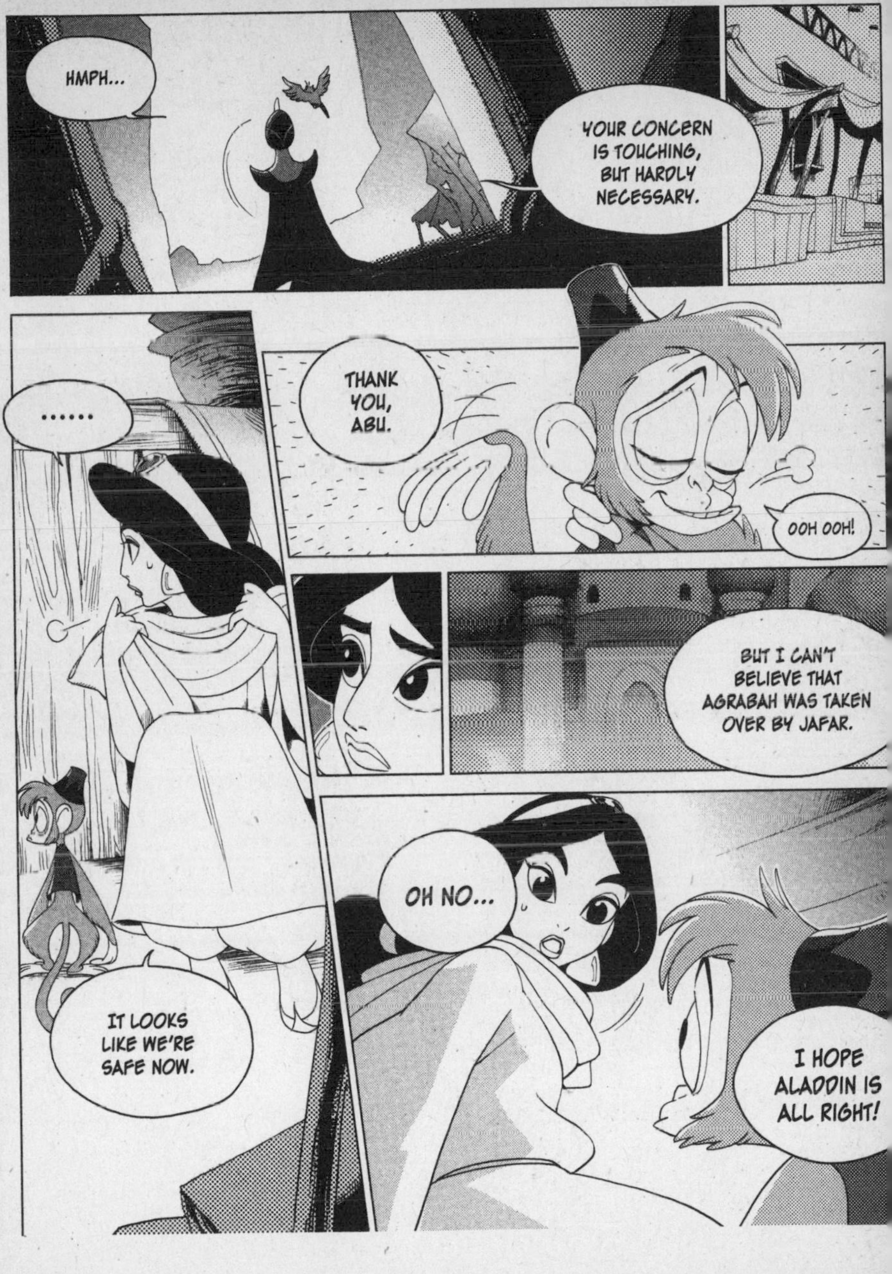
HMPH...
YOUR CONCERN IS TOUCHING, BUT HARDLY NECESSARY.
......
THANK YOU, ABU.
OOH OOH!
BUT I CAN'T BELIEVE THAT AGRABAH WAS TAKEN OVER BY JAFAR.
IT LOOKS LIKE WE'RE SAFE NOW.
OH NO...
I HOPE ALADDIN IS ALL RIGHT!

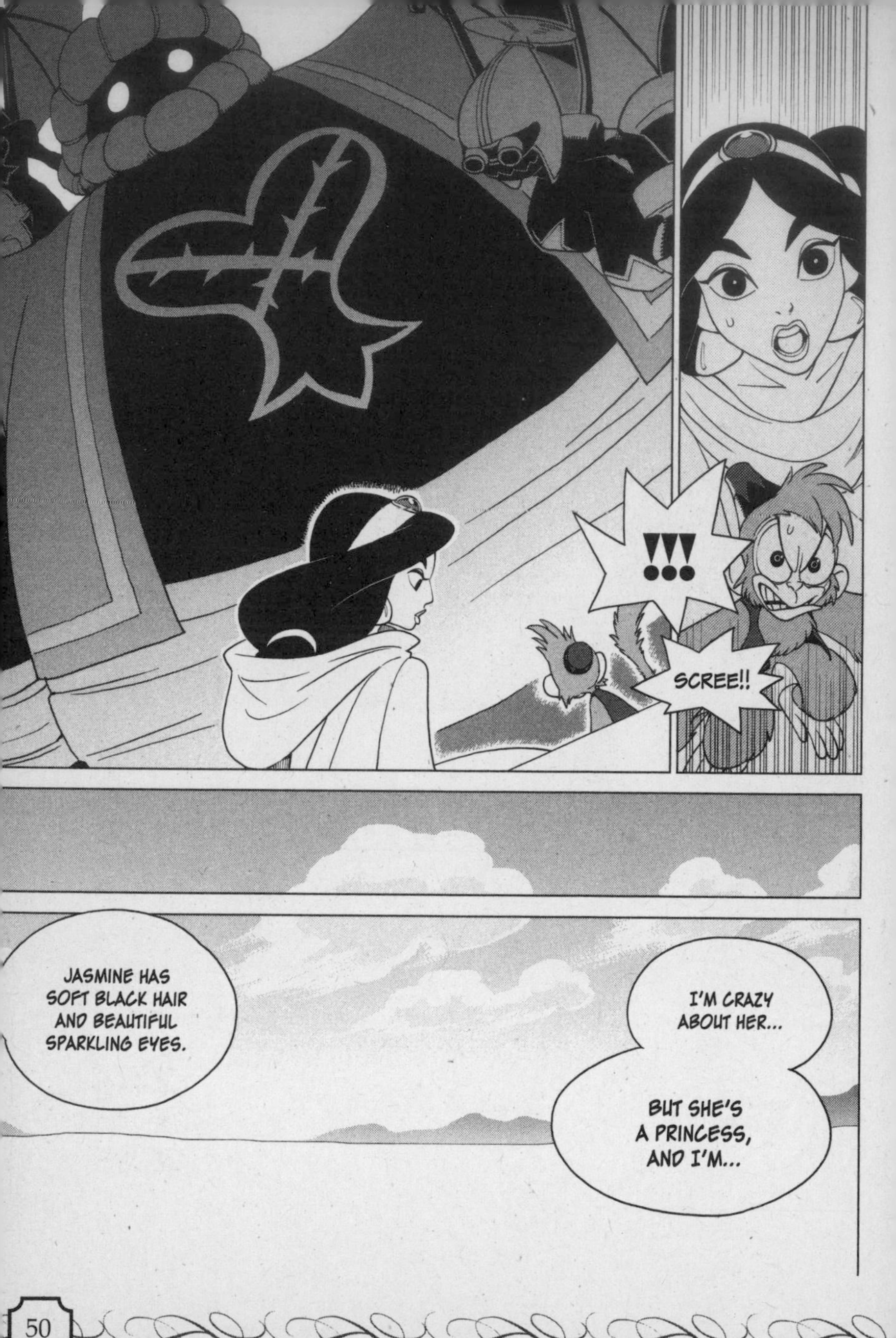
!!!
SCREE!!
JASMINE HAS SOFT BLACK HAIR AND BEAUTIFUL SPARKLING EYES.
I'M CRAZY ABOUT HER...
BUT SHE'S A PRINCESS, AND I'M...

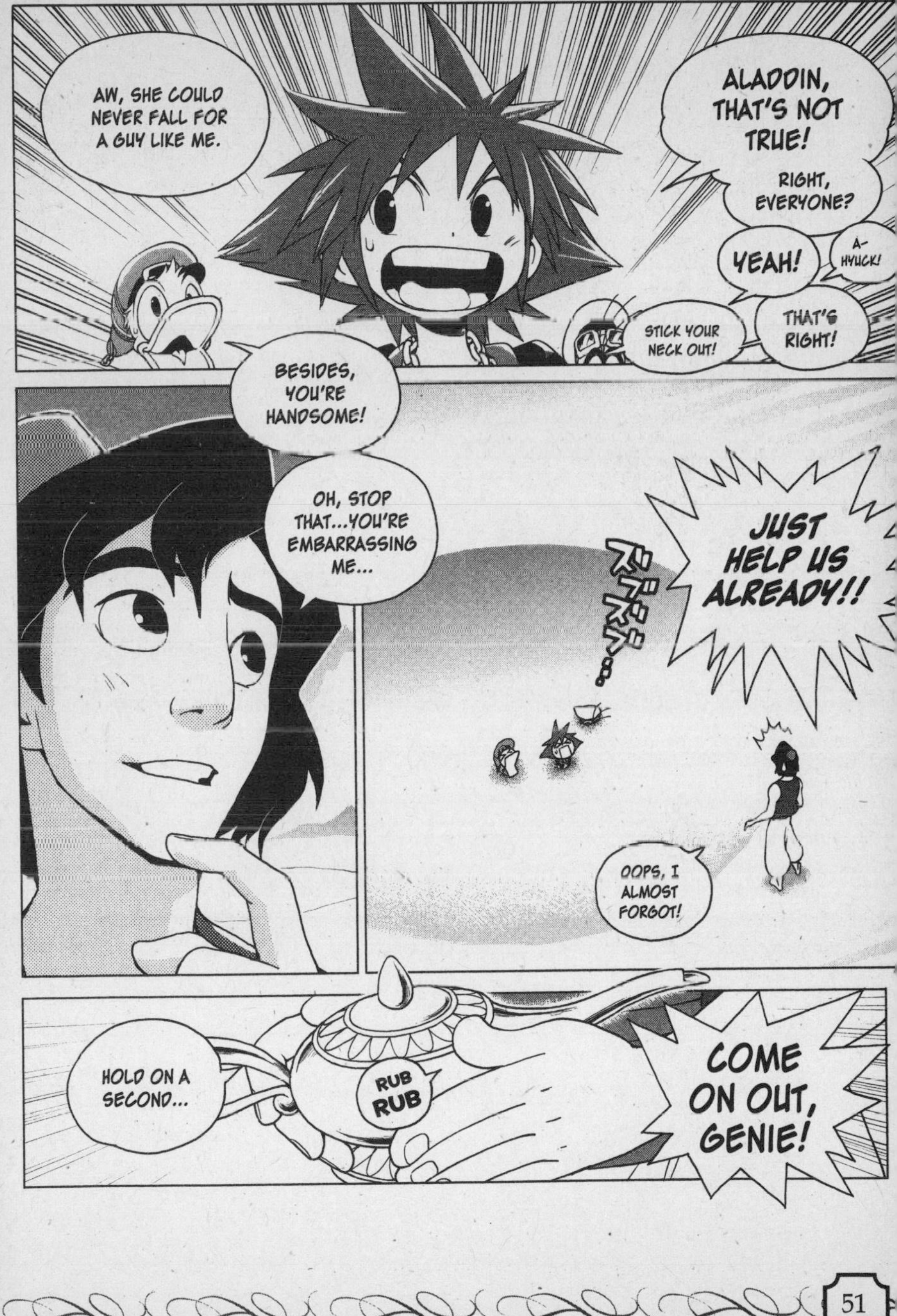

AW, SHE COULD NEVER FALL FOR A GUY LIKE ME.
ALADDIN, THAT'S NOT TRUE!
RIGHT, EVERYONE?
YEAH!
A-HYUCK!
STICK YOUR NECK OUT!
THAT'S RIGHT!
BESIDES, YOU'RE HANDSOME!
OH, STOP THAT...YOU'RE EMBARRASSING ME...
JUST HELP US ALREADY!!
OOPS, I ALMOST FORGOT!
HOLD ON A SECOND...
RUB RUB
COME ON OUT, GENIE!

Episode 20

The Genie of the Lamp

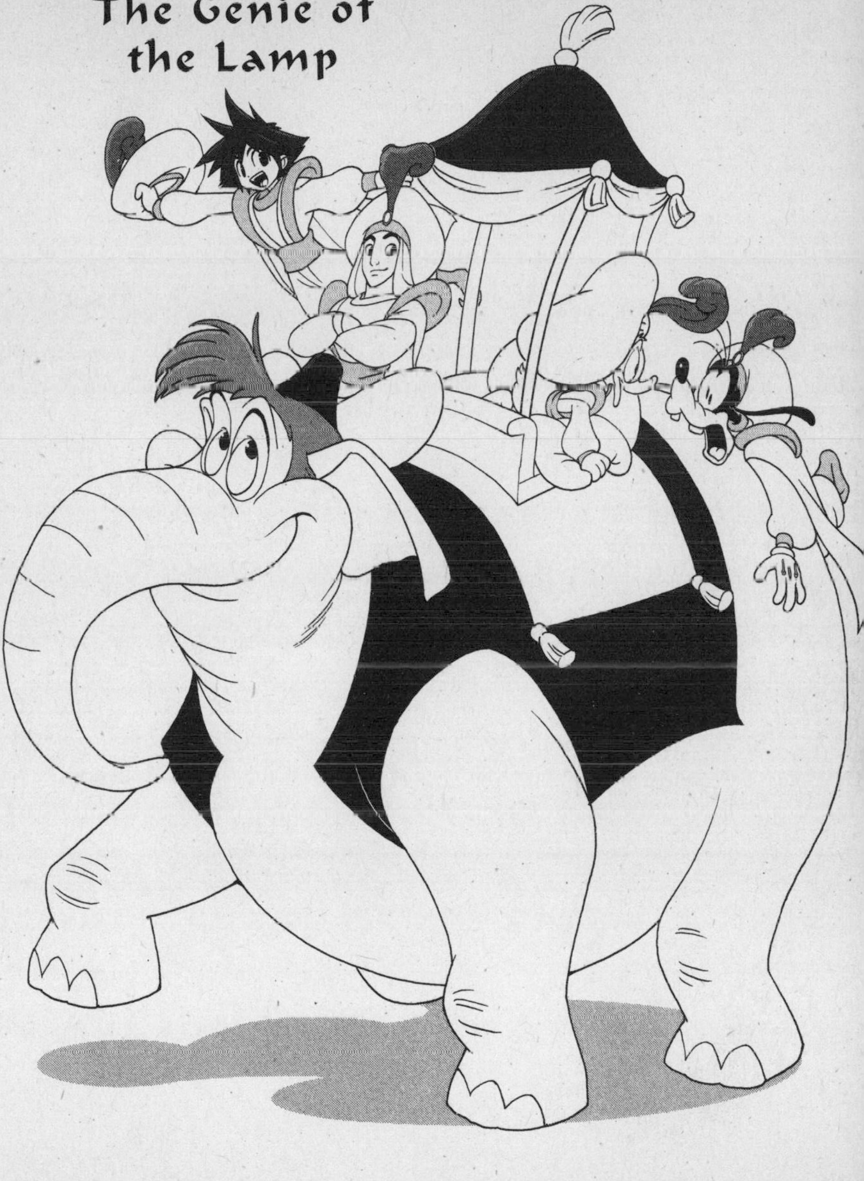

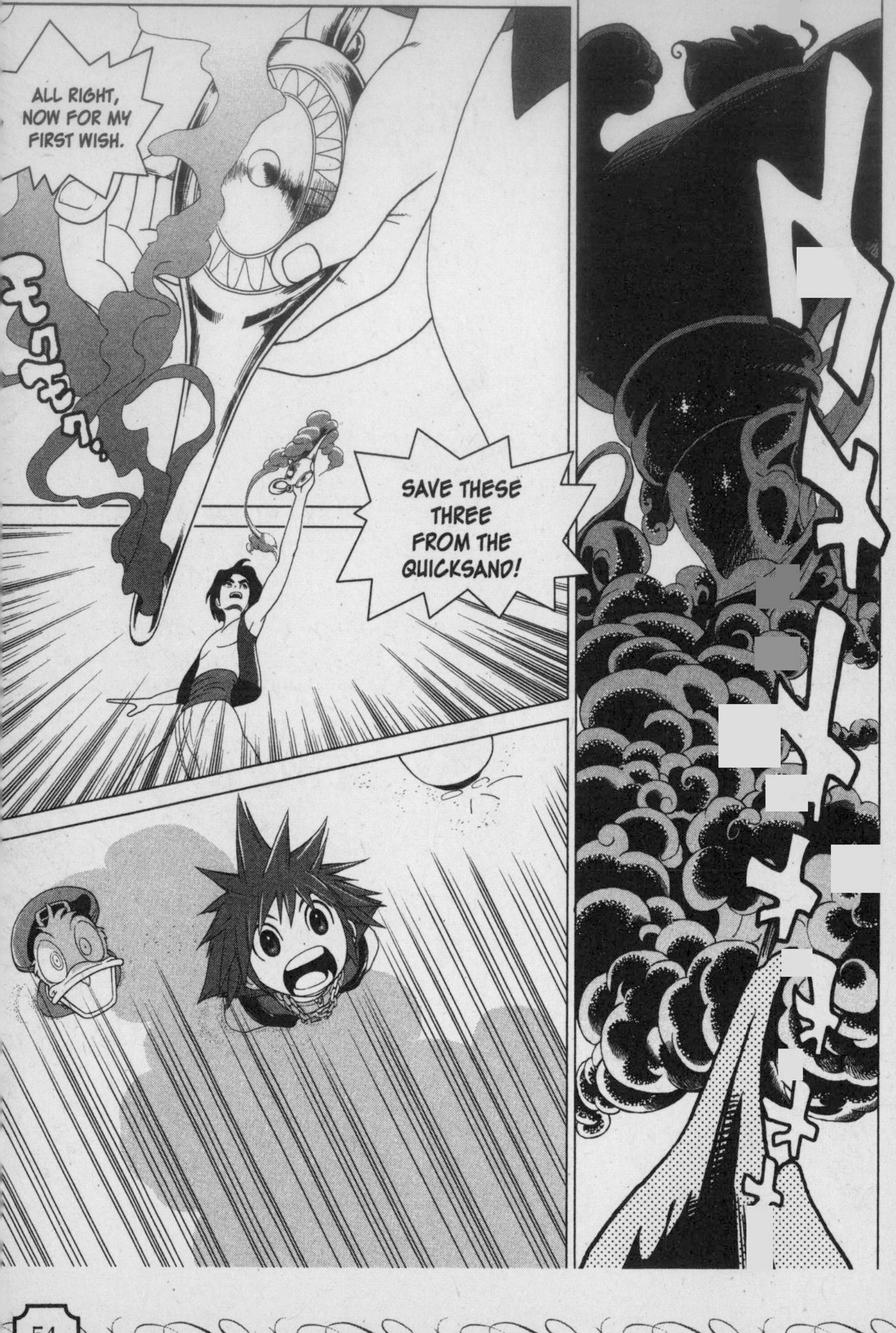
ALL RIGHT, NOW FOR MY FIRST WISH.
SAVE THESE THREE FROM THE QUICKSAND!

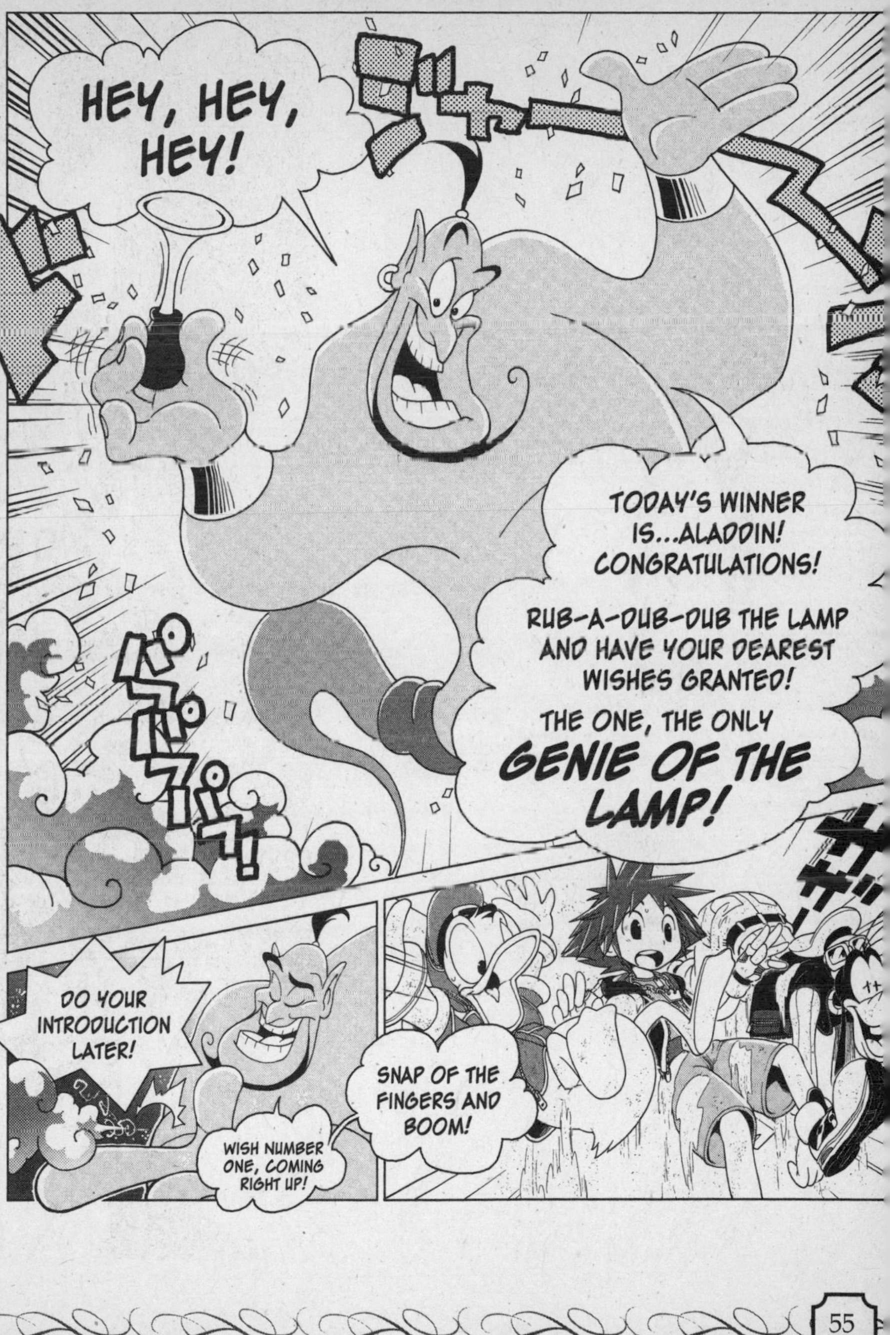
HEY, HEY, HEY!
TODAY'S WINNER IS...ALADDIN! CONGRATULATIONS!
RUB-A-DUB-DUB THE LAMP AND HAVE YOUR DEAREST WISHES GRANTED!
THE ONE, THE ONLY GENIE OF THE LAMP!
DO YOUR INTRODUCTION LATER!
WISH NUMBER ONE, COMING RIGHT UP!
SNAP OF THE FINGERS AND BOOM!

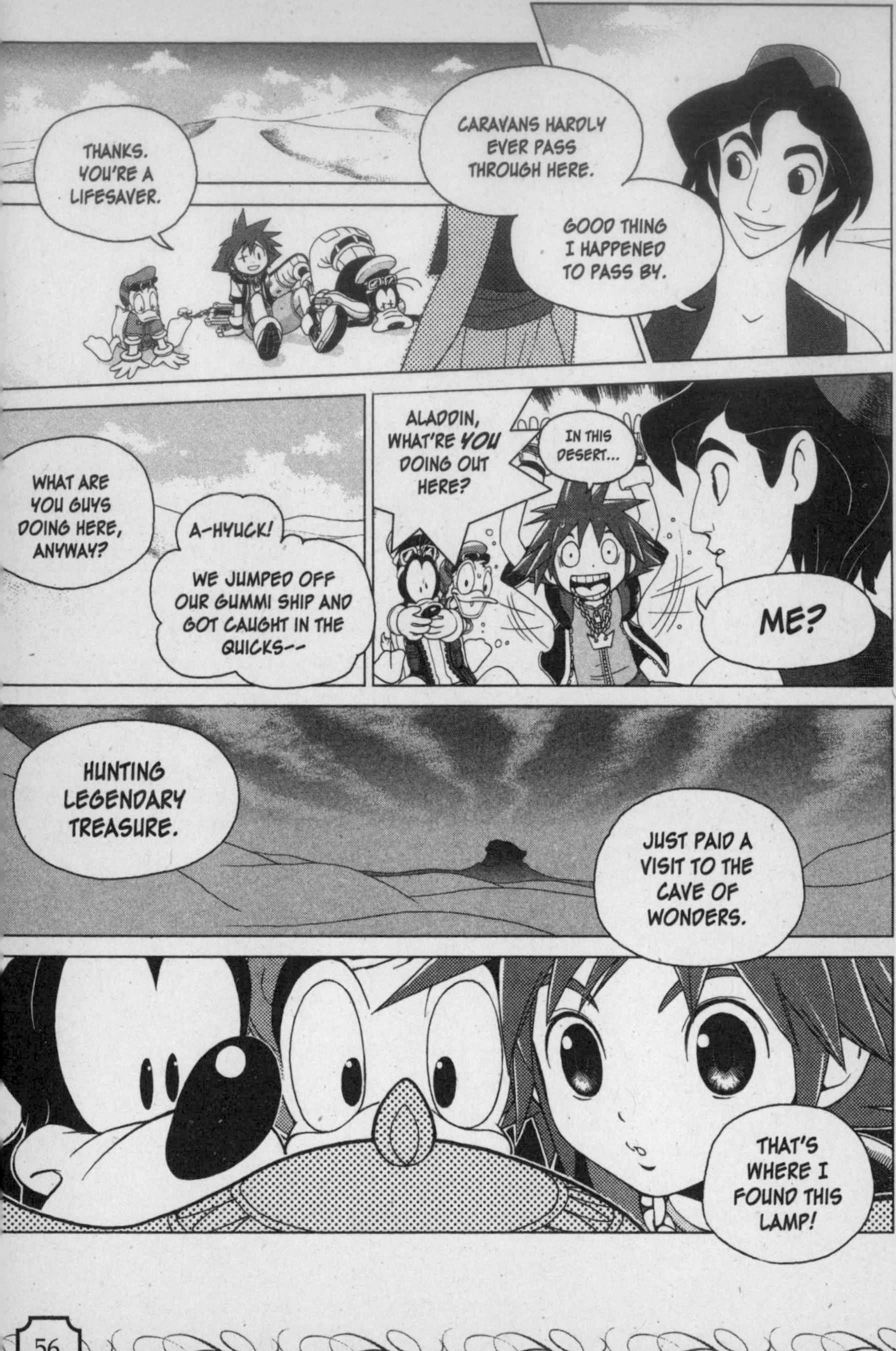
THANKS. YOU'RE A LIFESAVER.
CARAVANS HARDLY EVER PASS THROUGH HERE.
GOOD THING I HAPPENED TO PASS BY.
WHAT ARE YOU GUYS DOING HERE, ANYWAY?
A-HYUCK!
WE JUMPED OFF OUR GUMMI SHIP AND GOT CAUGHT IN THE QUICKS--
ALADDIN, WHAT'RE *YOU* DOING OUT HERE?
IN THIS DESERT...
ME?
HUNTING LEGENDARY TREASURE.
JUST PAID A VISIT TO THE CAVE OF WONDERS.
THAT'S WHERE I FOUND THIS LAMP!

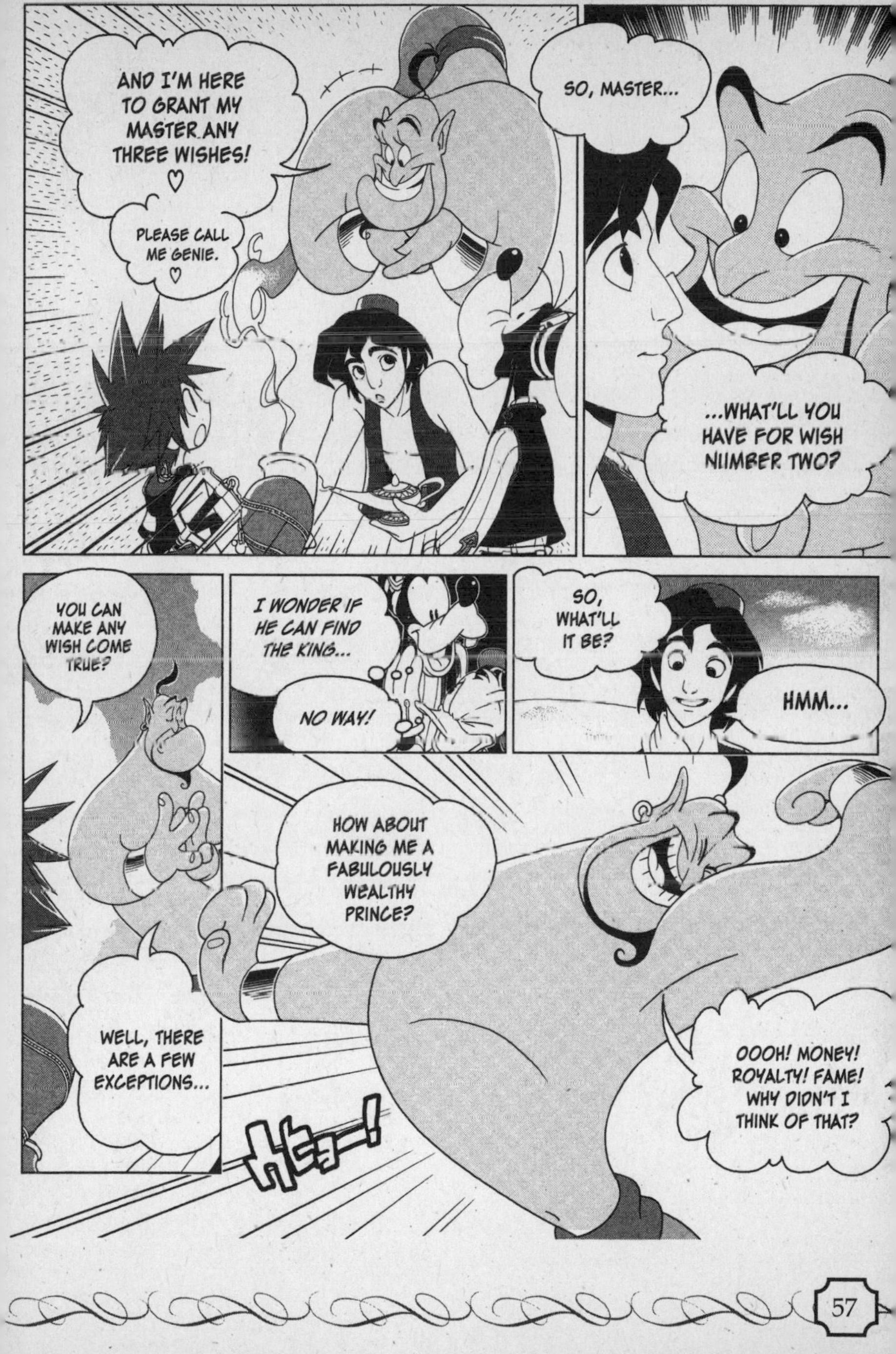
AND I'M HERE TO GRANT MY MASTER ANY THREE WISHES! ♡
PLEASE CALL ME GENIE. ♡
SO, MASTER...
...WHAT'LL YOU HAVE FOR WISH NUMBER TWO?
YOU CAN MAKE ANY WISH COME TRUE?
WELL, THERE ARE A FEW EXCEPTIONS...
I WONDER IF HE CAN FIND THE KING...
NO WAY!
SO, WHAT'LL IT BE?
HMM...
HOW ABOUT MAKING ME A FABULOUSLY WEALTHY PRINCE?
OOOH! MONEY! ROYALTY! FAME! WHY DIDN'T I THINK OF THAT?

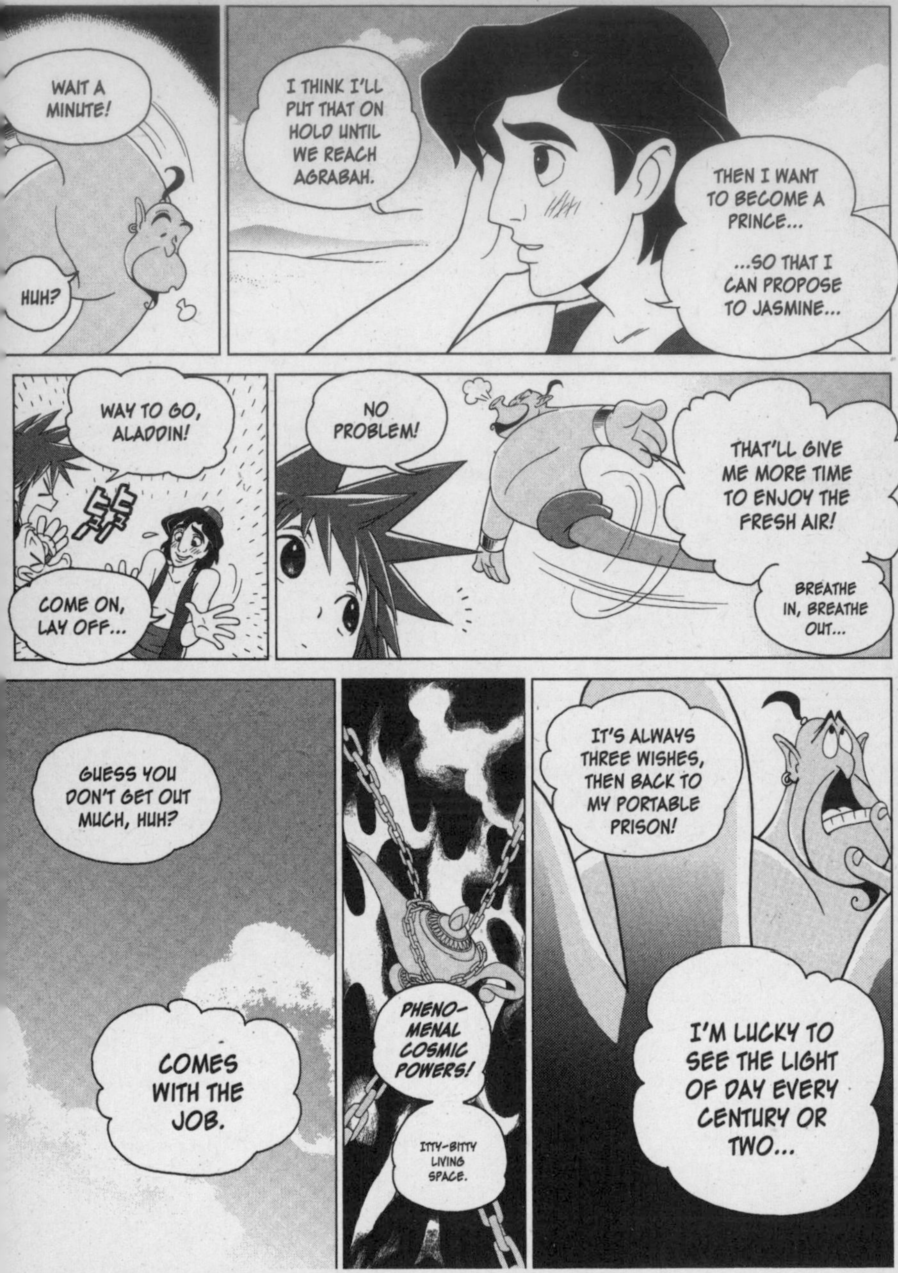
WAIT A MINUTE!
HUH?
I THINK I'LL PUT THAT ON HOLD UNTIL WE REACH AGRABAH.
THEN I WANT TO BECOME A PRINCE...
...SO THAT I CAN PROPOSE TO JASMINE...
WAY TO GO, ALADDIN!
COME ON, LAY OFF...
NO PROBLEM!
THAT'LL GIVE ME MORE TIME TO ENJOY THE FRESH AIR!
BREATHE IN, BREATHE OUT...
GUESS YOU DON'T GET OUT MUCH, HUH?
COMES WITH THE JOB.
PHENO-MENAL COSMIC POWERS!
ITTY-BITTY LIVING SPACE.
IT'S ALWAYS THREE WISHES, THEN BACK TO MY PORTABLE PRISON!
I'M LUCKY TO SEE THE LIGHT OF DAY EVERY CENTURY OR TWO...

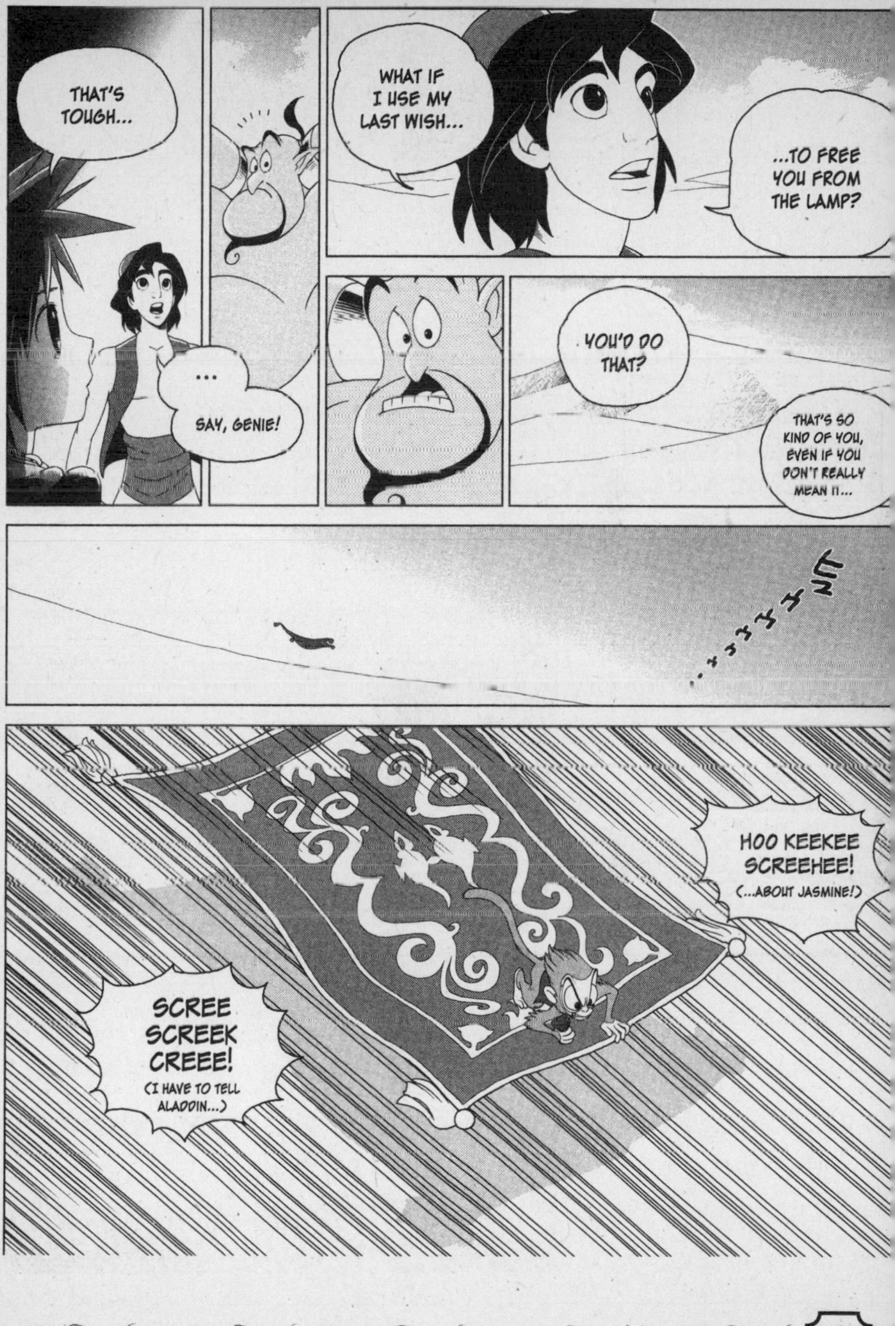
THAT'S TOUGH...
... SAY, GENIE!
WHAT IF I USE MY LAST WISH...
...TO FREE YOU FROM THE LAMP?
YOU'D DO THAT?
THAT'S SO KIND OF YOU, EVEN IF YOU DON'T REALLY MEAN IT...
SCREE SCREEK CREEE! (I HAVE TO TELL ALADDIN...)
HOO KEEKEE SCREEHEE! (...ABOUT JASMINE!)

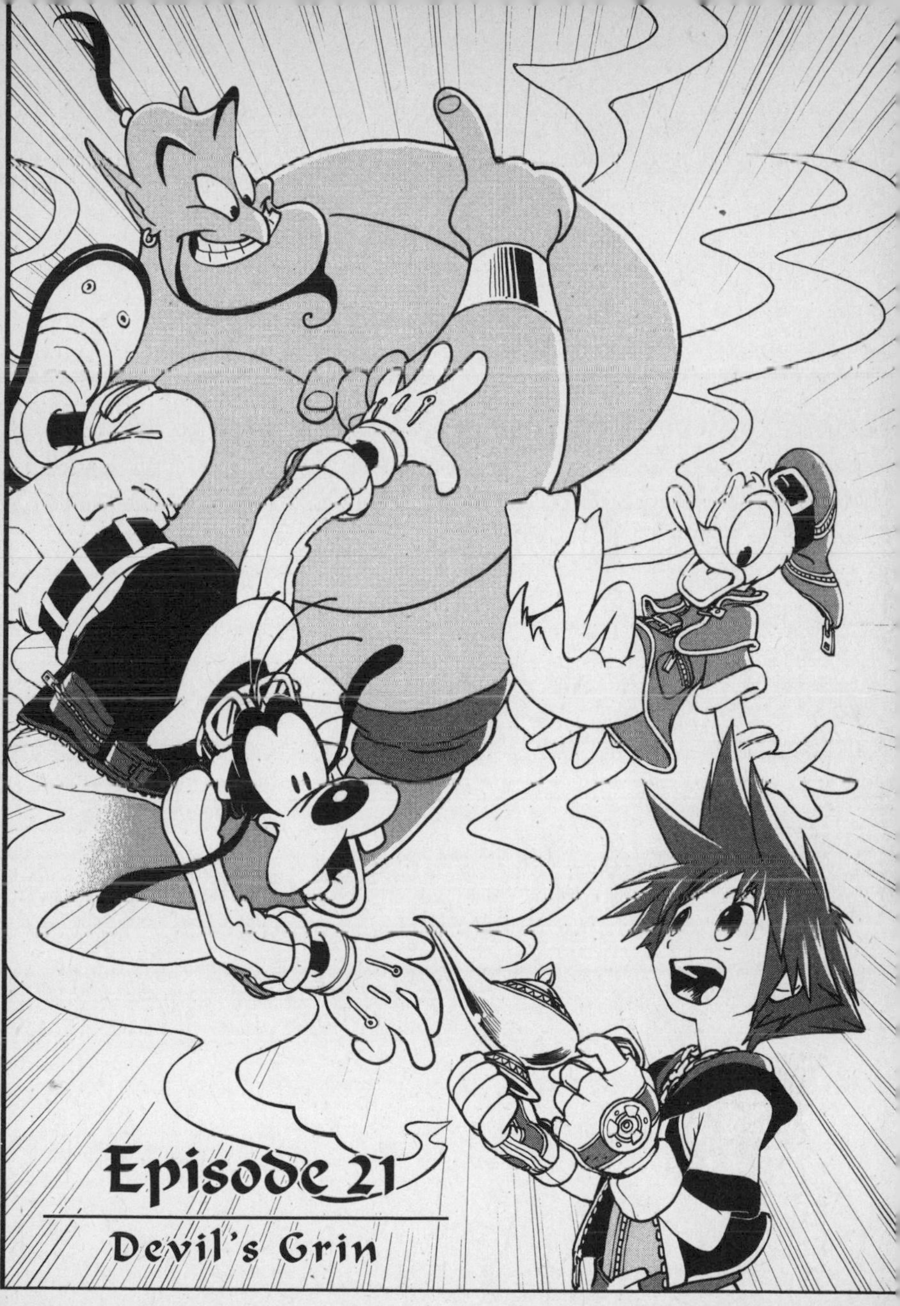
Episode 21
Devil's Grin

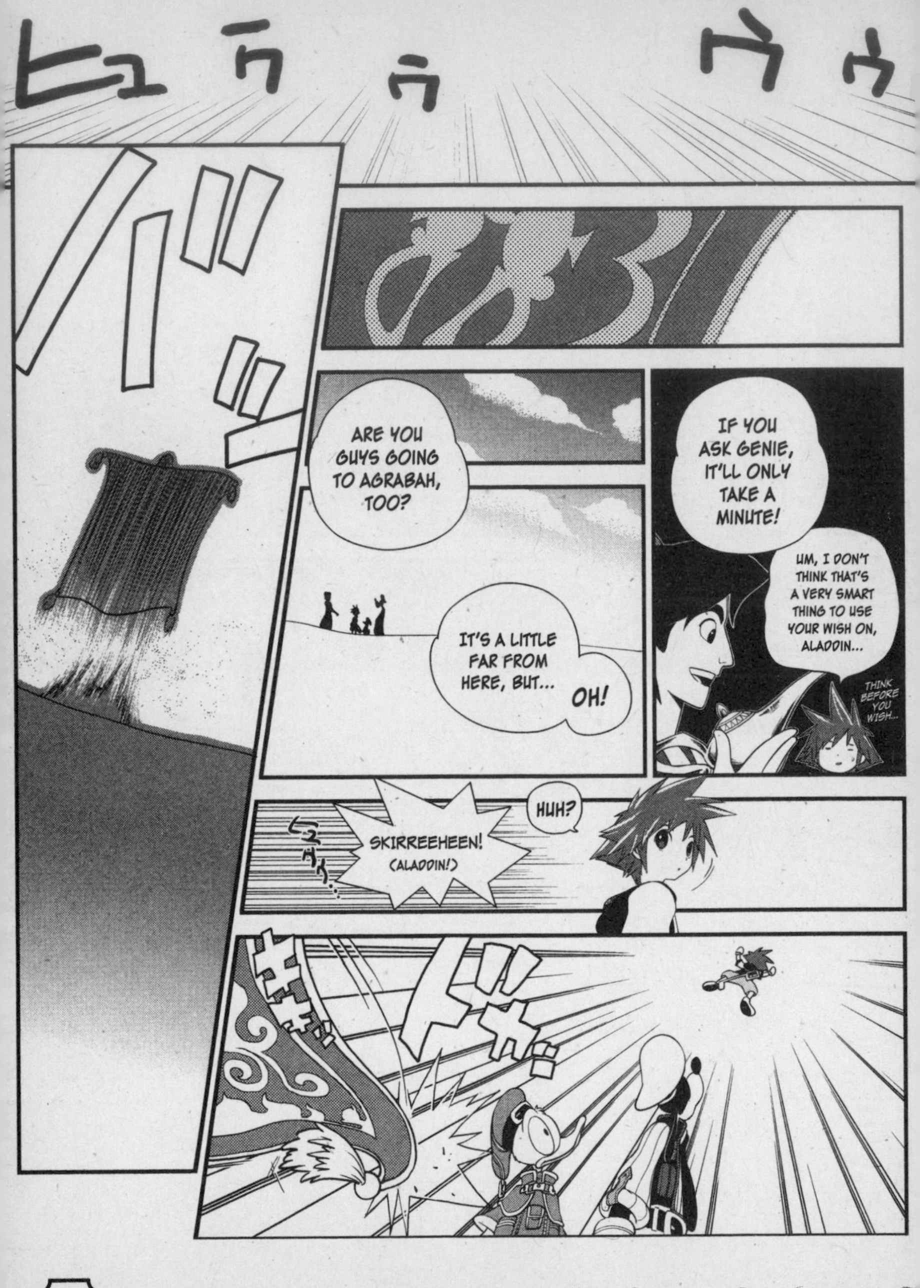
ARE YOU GUYS GOING TO AGRABAH, TOO?
IT'S A LITTLE FAR FROM HERE, BUT...
OH!
IF YOU ASK GENIE, IT'LL ONLY TAKE A MINUTE!
UM, I DON'T THINK THAT'S A VERY SMART THING TO USE YOUR WISH ON, ALADDIN...
THINK BEFORE YOU WISH...
SKIRREEHEEN!
(ALADDIN!)
HUH?

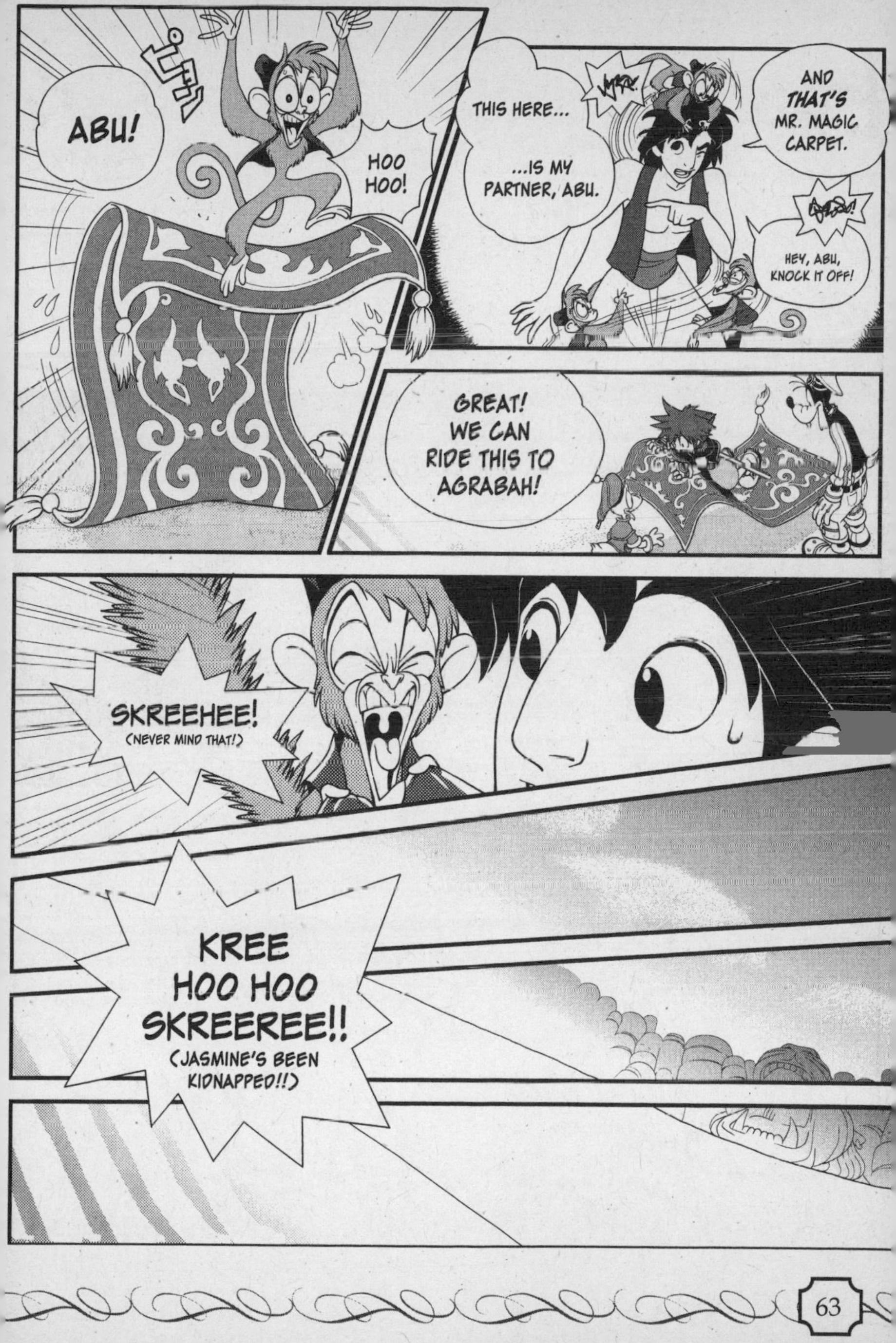
ABU!
HOO HOO!
THIS HERE...
...IS MY PARTNER, ABU.
AND THAT'S MR. MAGIC CARPET.
HEY, ABU, KNOCK IT OFF!
GREAT! WE CAN RIDE THIS TO AGRABAH!
SKREEHEE!
(NEVER MIND THAT!)
KREE HOO HOO SKREEREE!!
(JASMINE'S BEEN KIDNAPPED!!)

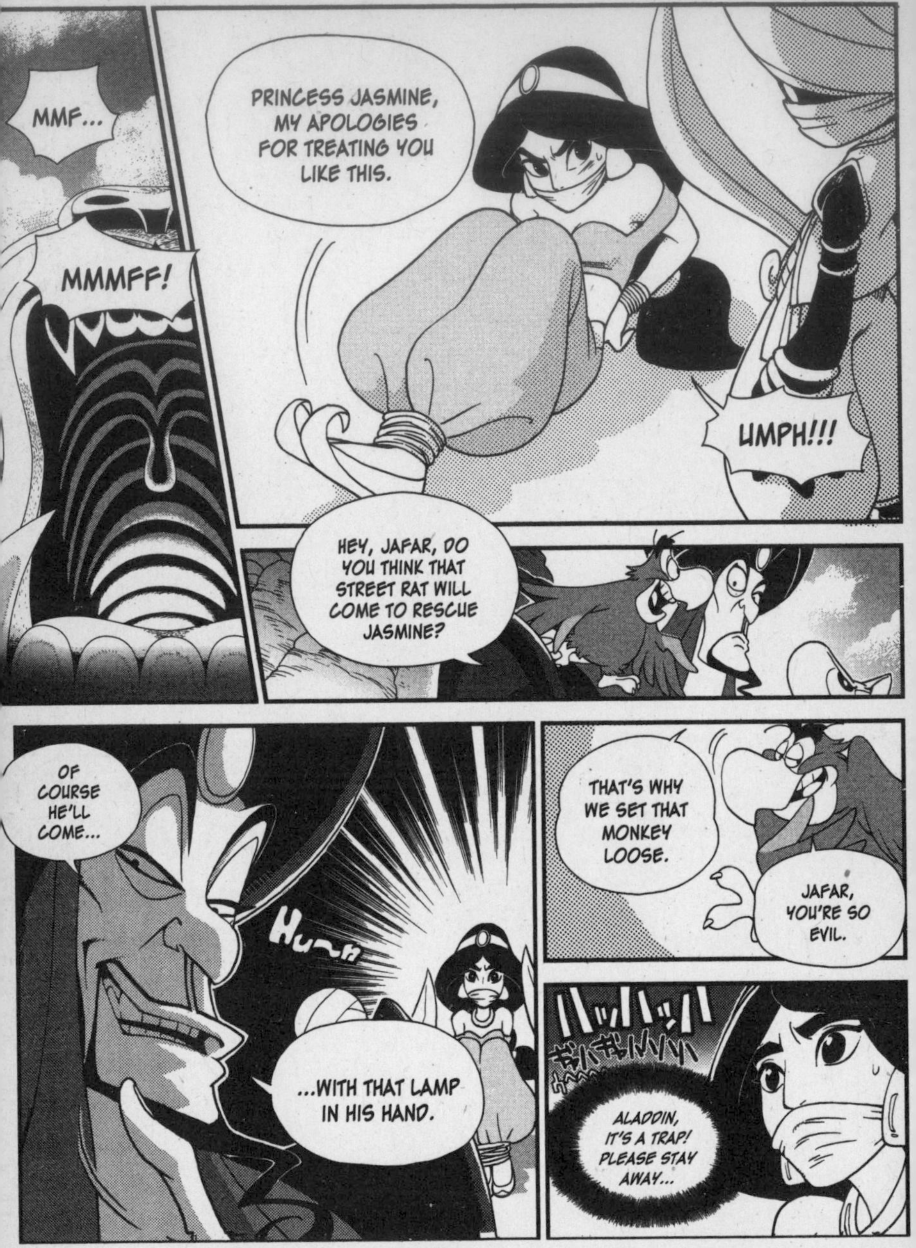
MMF...
MMMFF!
PRINCESS JASMINE, MY APOLOGIES FOR TREATING YOU LIKE THIS.
UMPH!!!
HEY, JAFAR, DO YOU THINK THAT STREET RAT WILL COME TO RESCUE JASMINE?
OF COURSE HE'LL COME...
Hu~n
...WITH THAT LAMP IN HIS HAND.
THAT'S WHY WE SET THAT MONKEY LOOSE.
JAFAR, YOU'RE SO EVIL.
ALADDIN, IT'S A TRAP! PLEASE STAY AWAY...

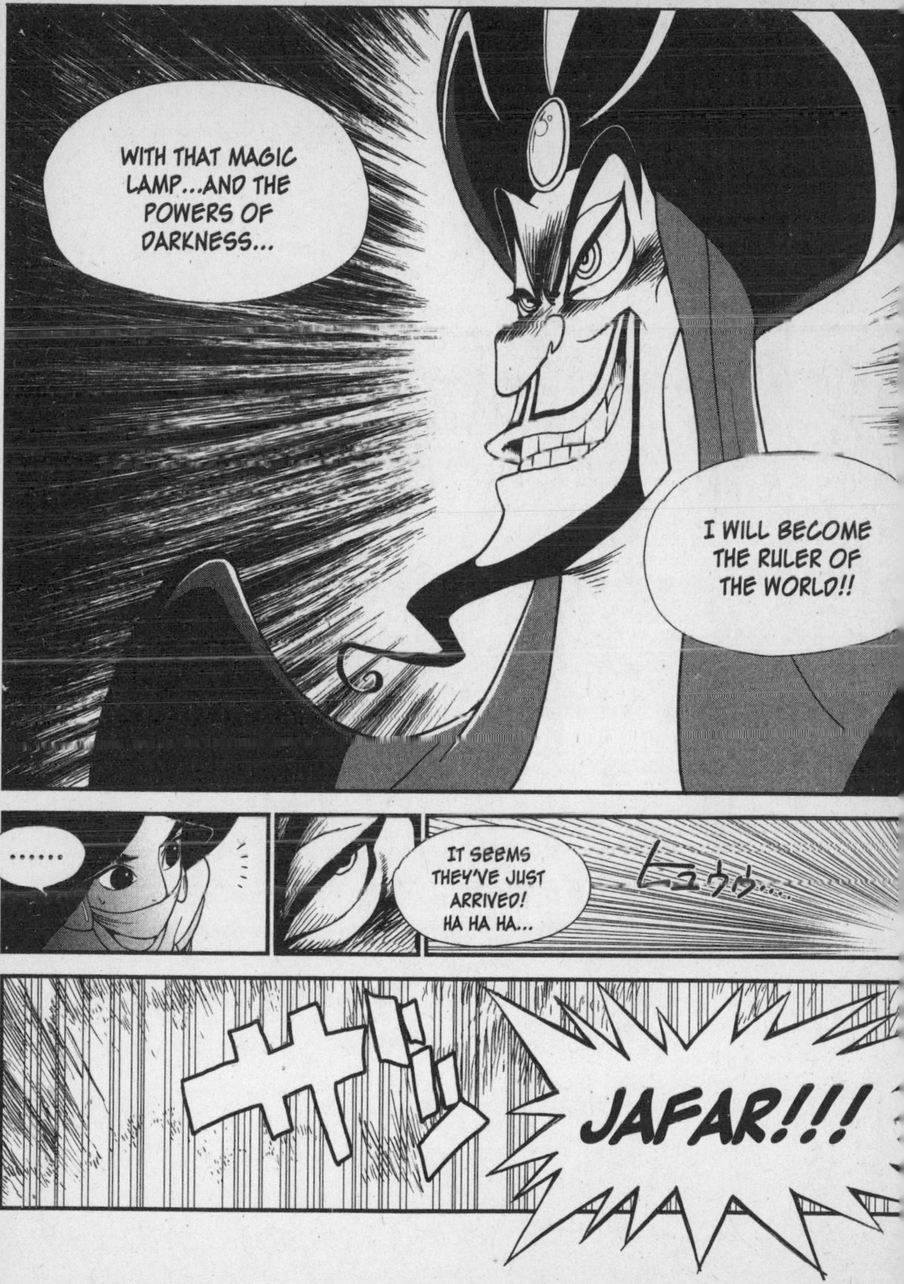
WITH THAT MAGIC LAMP...AND THE POWERS OF DARKNESS...
I WILL BECOME THE RULER OF THE WORLD!!
......
IT SEEMS THEY'VE JUST ARRIVED! HA HA HA...
ヒュウウ...
JAFAR!!!

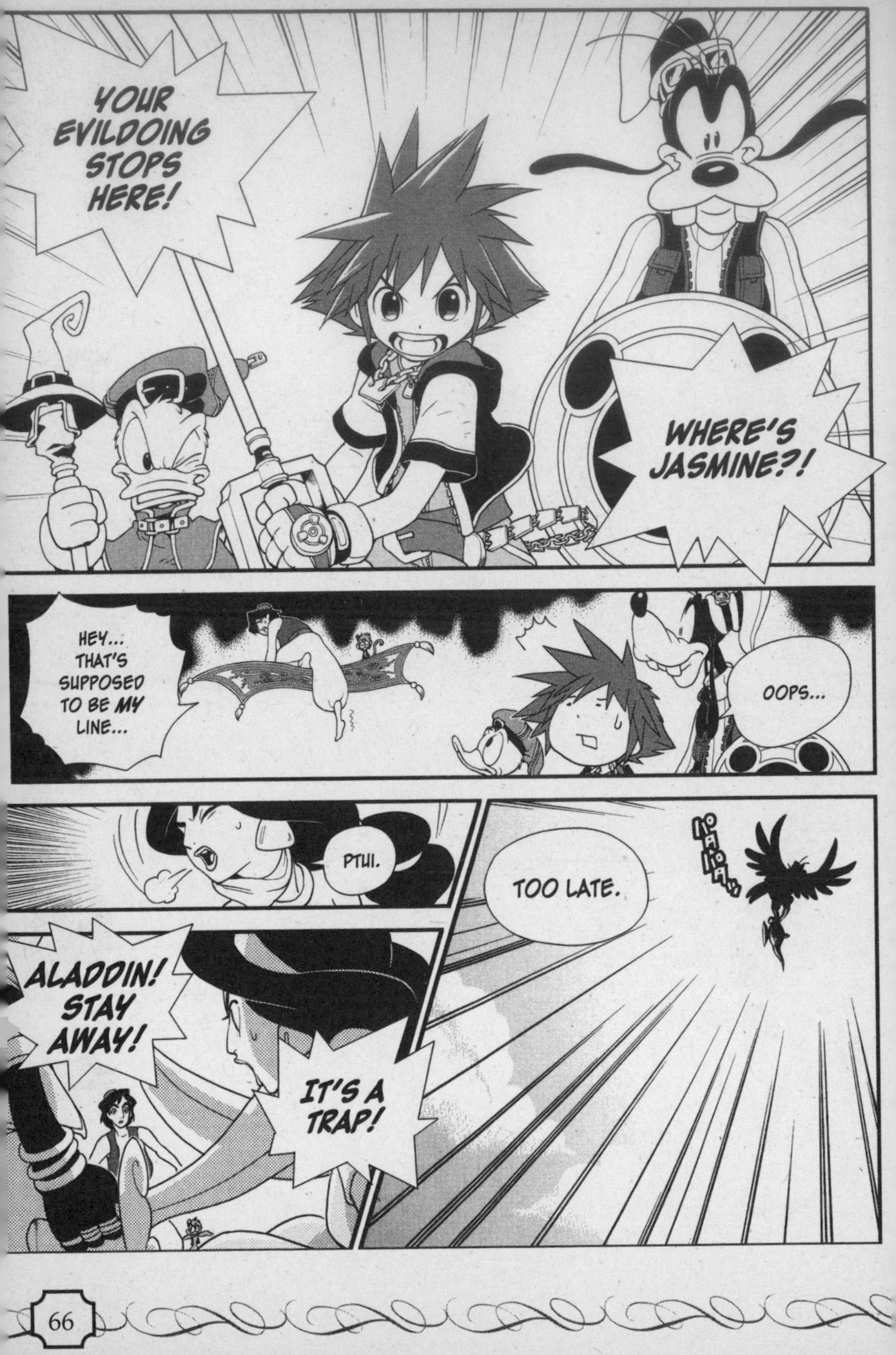
YOUR EVILDOING STOPS HERE!
WHERE'S JASMINE?!
HEY... THAT'S SUPPOSED TO BE MY LINE...
OOPS...
PTUI.
ALADDIN! STAY AWAY!
IT'S A TRAP!
TOO LATE.

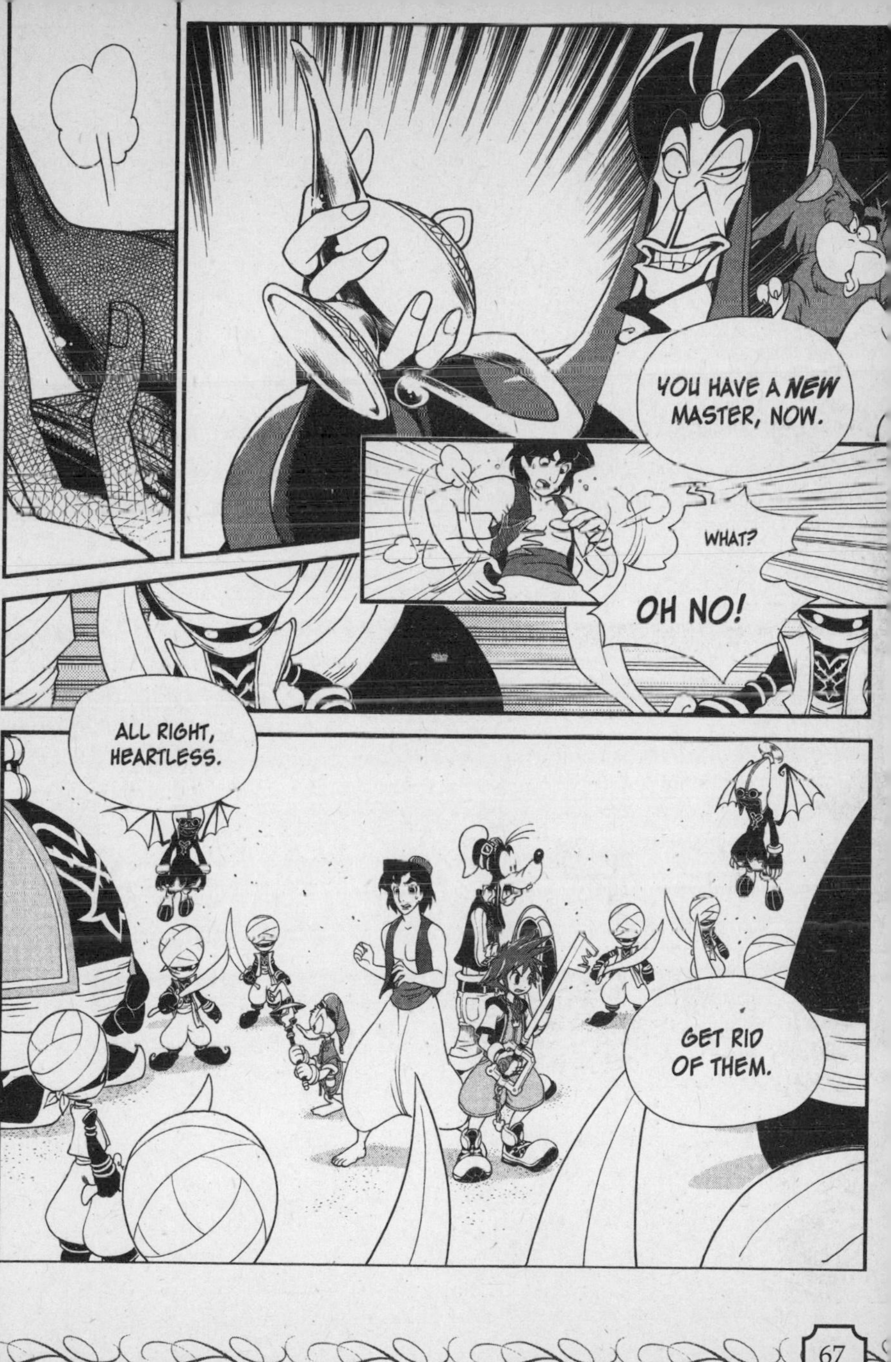
YOU HAVE A *NEW* MASTER, NOW.
WHAT?
OH NO!
ALL RIGHT, HEARTLESS.
GET RID OF THEM.

Episode 22

Endless Greed

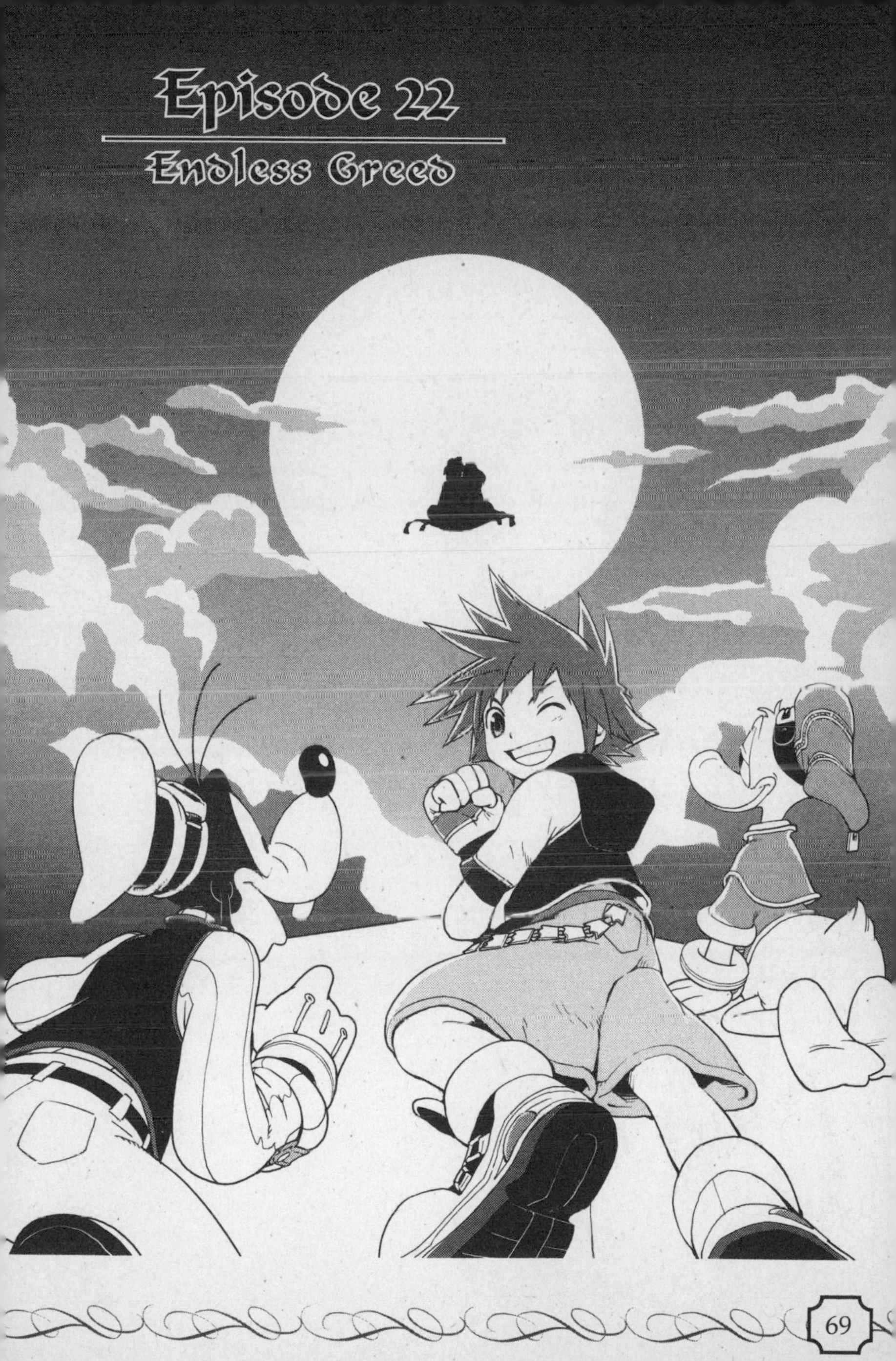

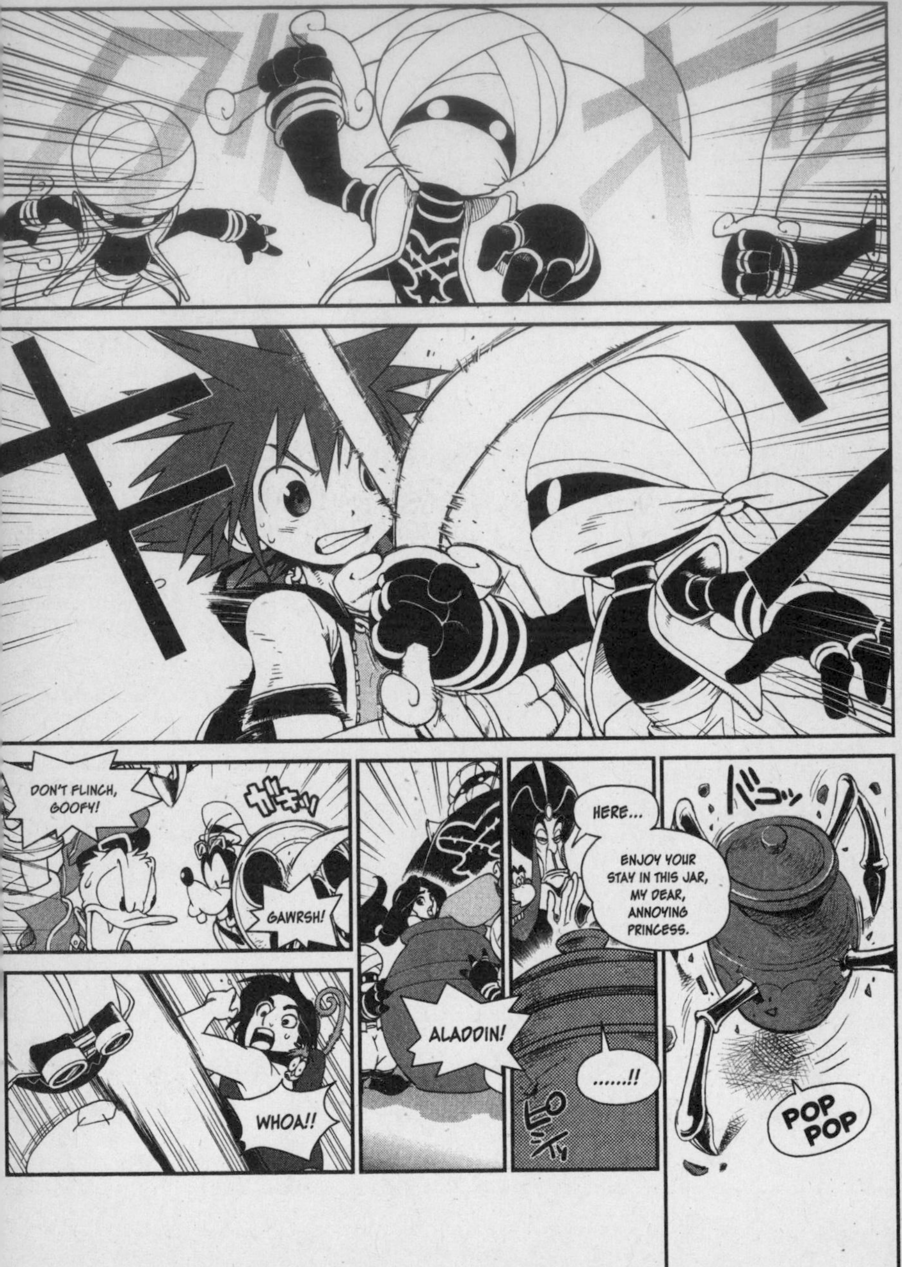
DON'T FLINCH, GOOFY!
GAWRSH!
WHOA!!
ALADDIN!
HERE...
ENJOY YOUR STAY IN THIS JAR, MY DEAR, ANNOYING PRINCESS.
......!!
POP POP

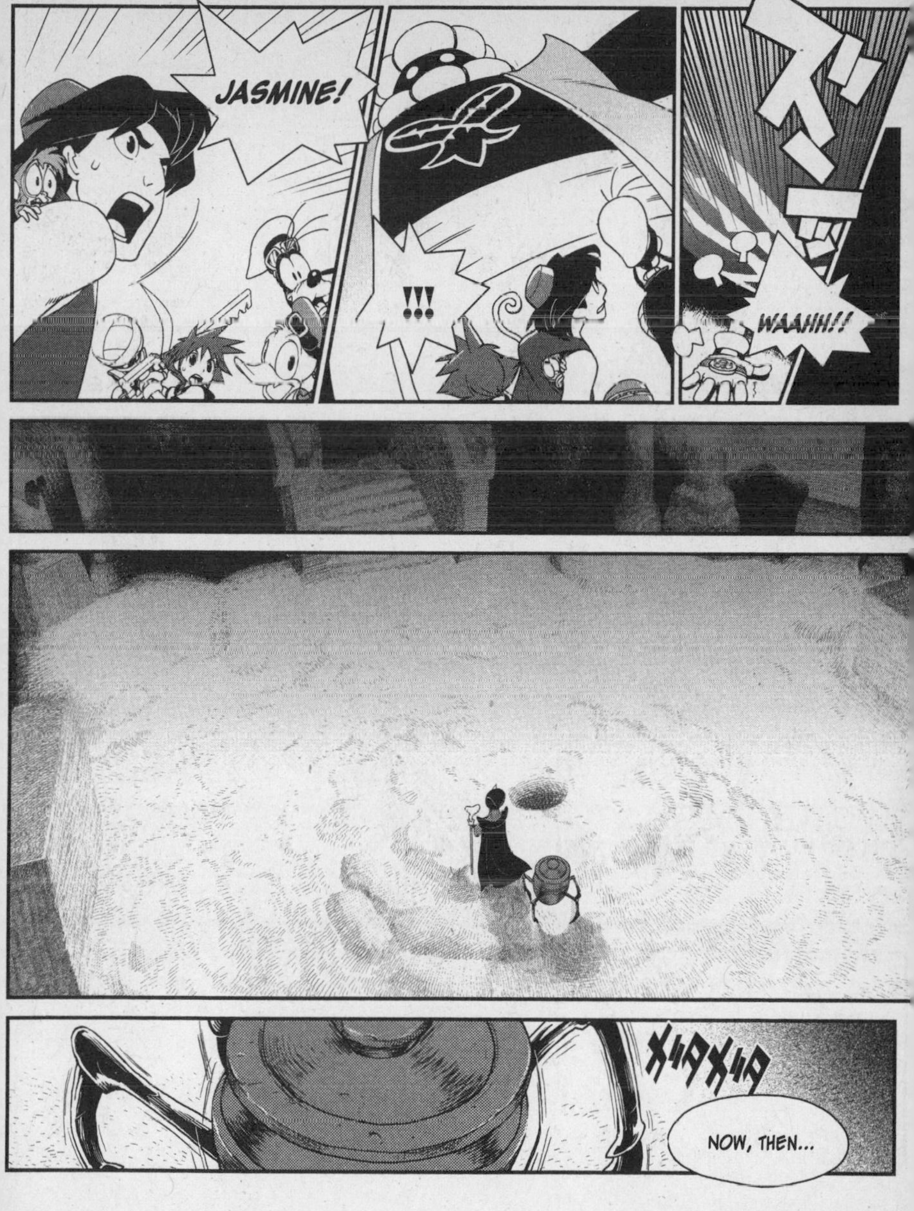
JASMINE!
!!!
WAANH!!
NOW, THEN...

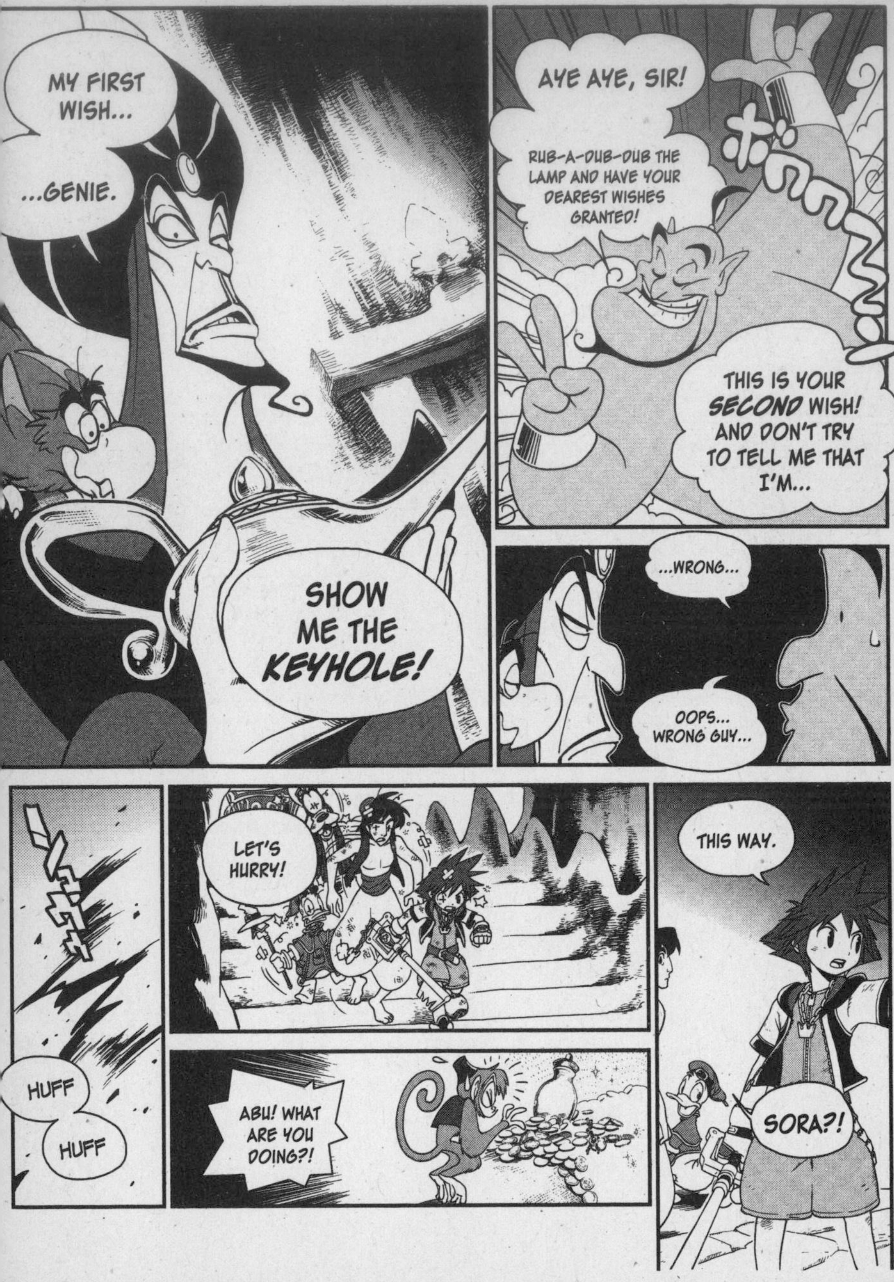
MY FIRST WISH...
...GENIE.
SHOW ME THE KEYHOLE!
AYE AYE, SIR!
RUB-A-DUB-DUB THE LAMP AND HAVE YOUR DEAREST WISHES GRANTED!
THIS IS YOUR SECOND WISH! AND DON'T TRY TO TELL ME THAT I'M...
...WRONG...
OOPS... WRONG GUY...
HUFF
HUFF
LET'S HURRY!
ABU! WHAT ARE YOU DOING?!
THIS WAY.
SORA?!

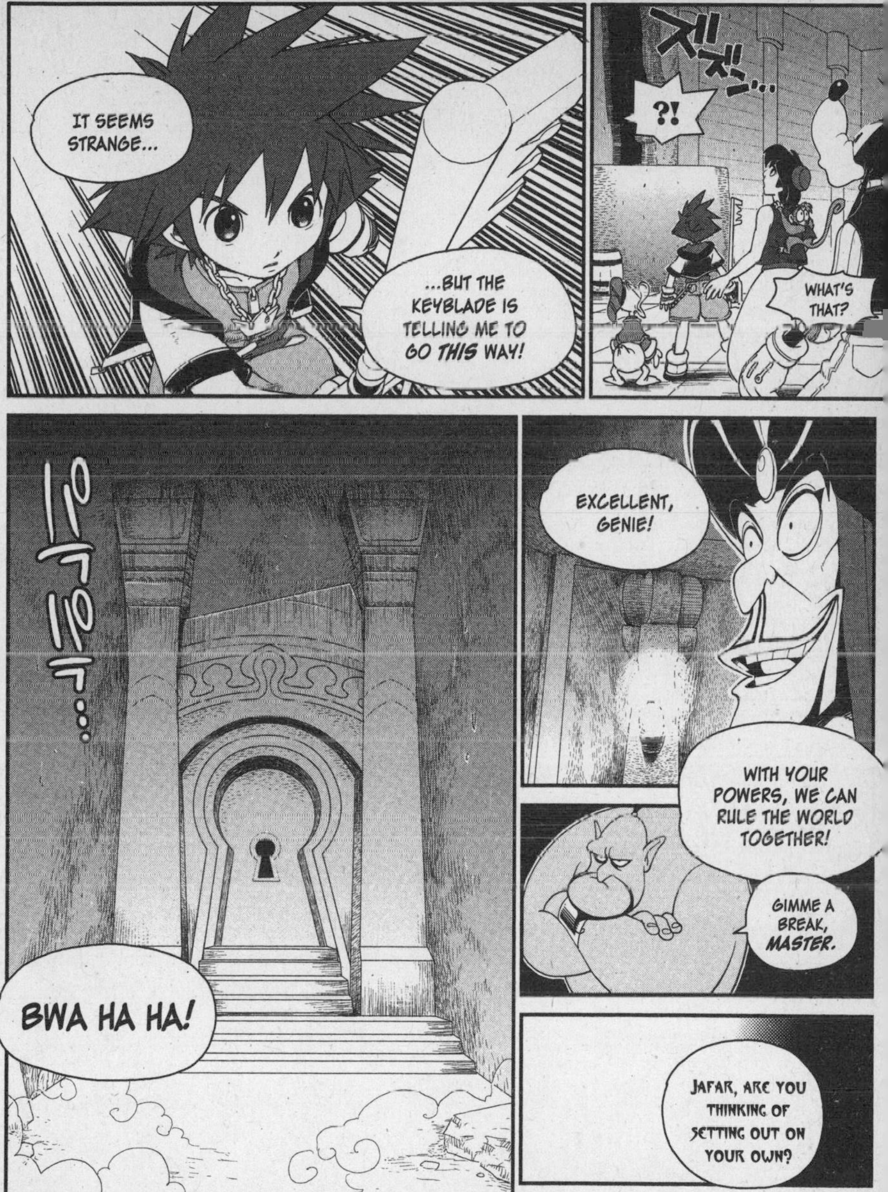
IT SEEMS STRANGE...
...BUT THE KEYBLADE IS TELLING ME TO GO *THIS* WAY!
?!
WHAT'S THAT?
BWA HA HA!
EXCELLENT, GENIE!
WITH YOUR POWERS, WE CAN RULE THE WORLD TOGETHER!
GIMME A BREAK, ***MASTER.***
JAFAR, ARE YOU THINKING OF SETTING OUT ON YOUR OWN?

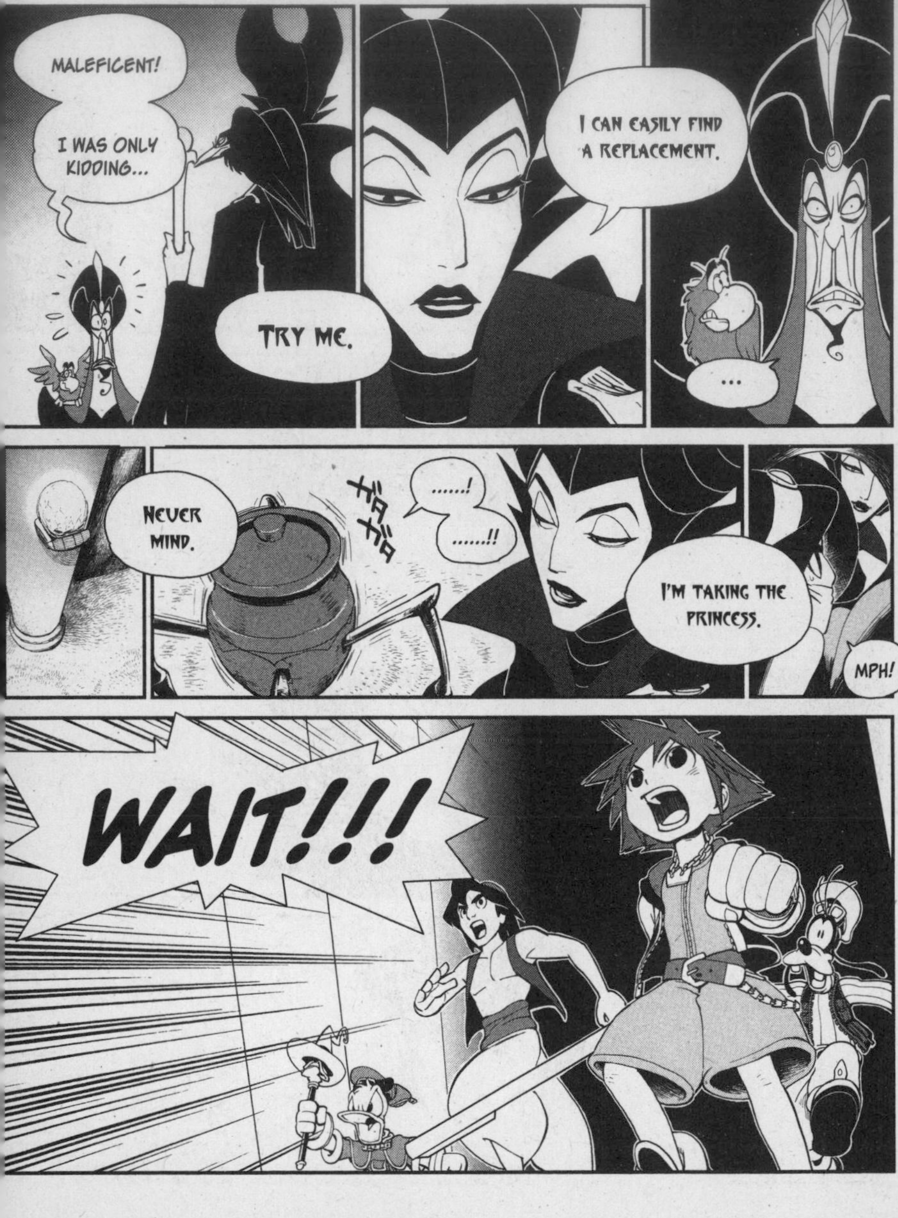
MALEFICENT!
I WAS ONLY KIDDING...
I CAN EASILY FIND A REPLACEMENT.
TRY ME.
...
NEVER MIND.
ガタ ガタ
......!
......!!
I'M TAKING THE PRINCESS.
MPH!
WAIT!!!

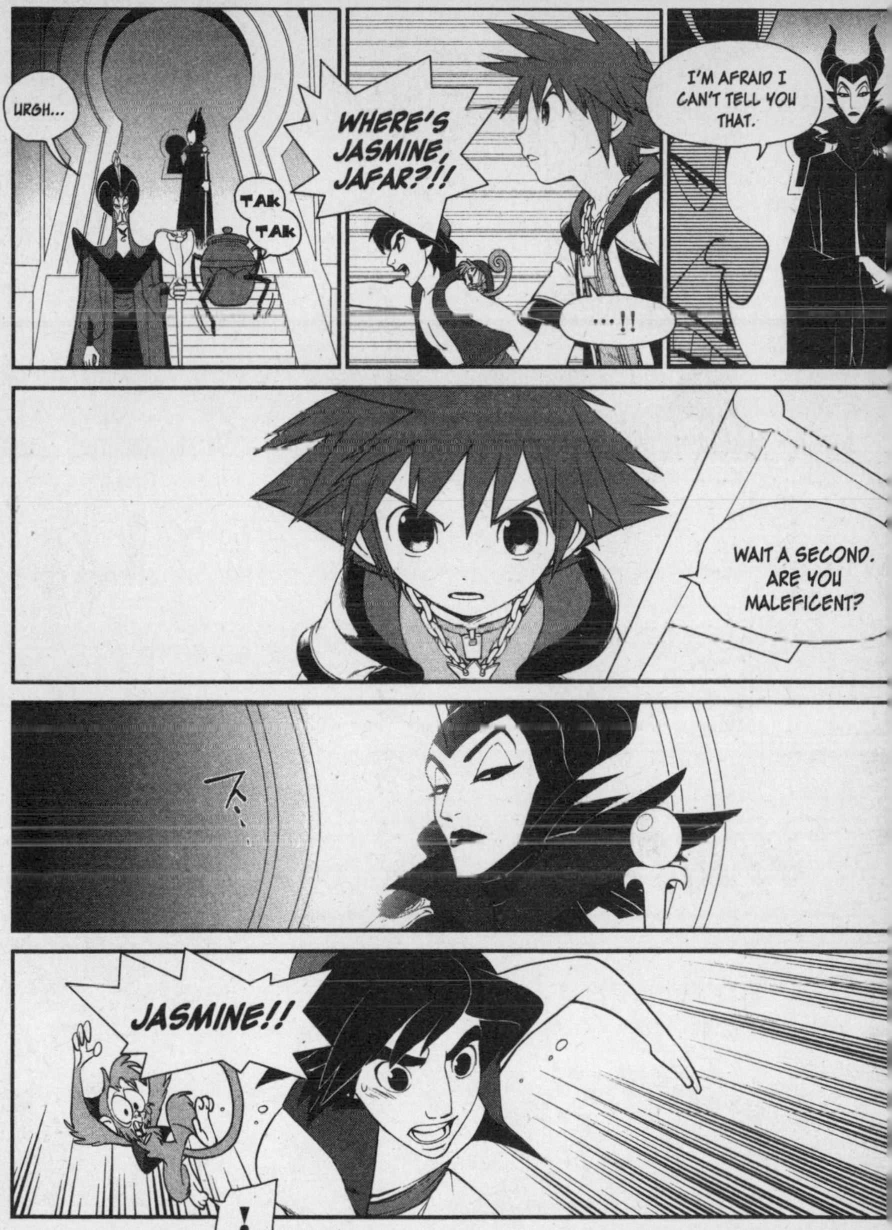
URGH...
TAK
TAK
WHERE'S JASMINE, JAFAR?!!
...!!
I'M AFRAID I CAN'T TELL YOU THAT.
WAIT A SECOND. ARE YOU MALEFICENT?
JASMINE!!
!

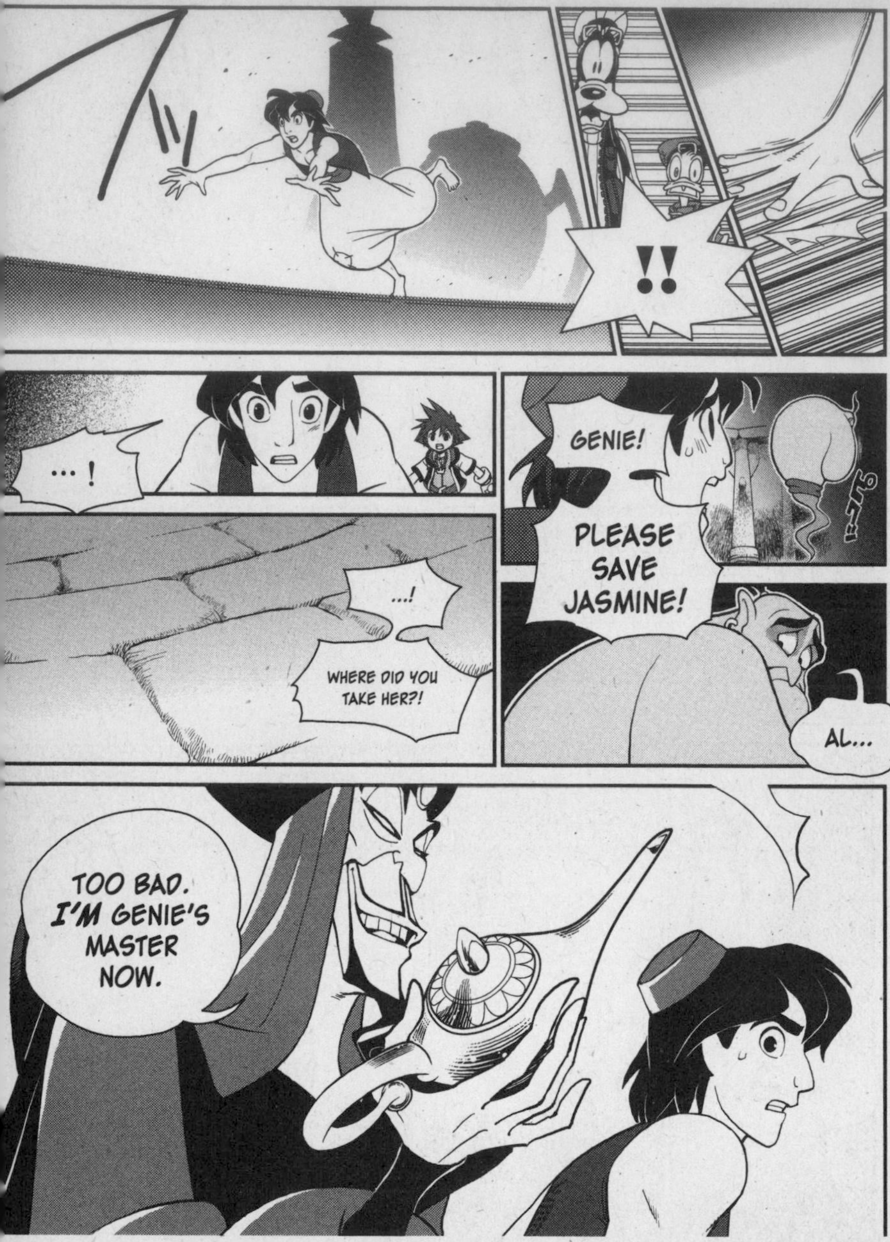

!!
...!
...!
WHERE DID YOU TAKE HER?!
GENIE!
PLEASE SAVE JASMINE!
AL...
TOO BAD. I'M GENIE'S MASTER NOW.

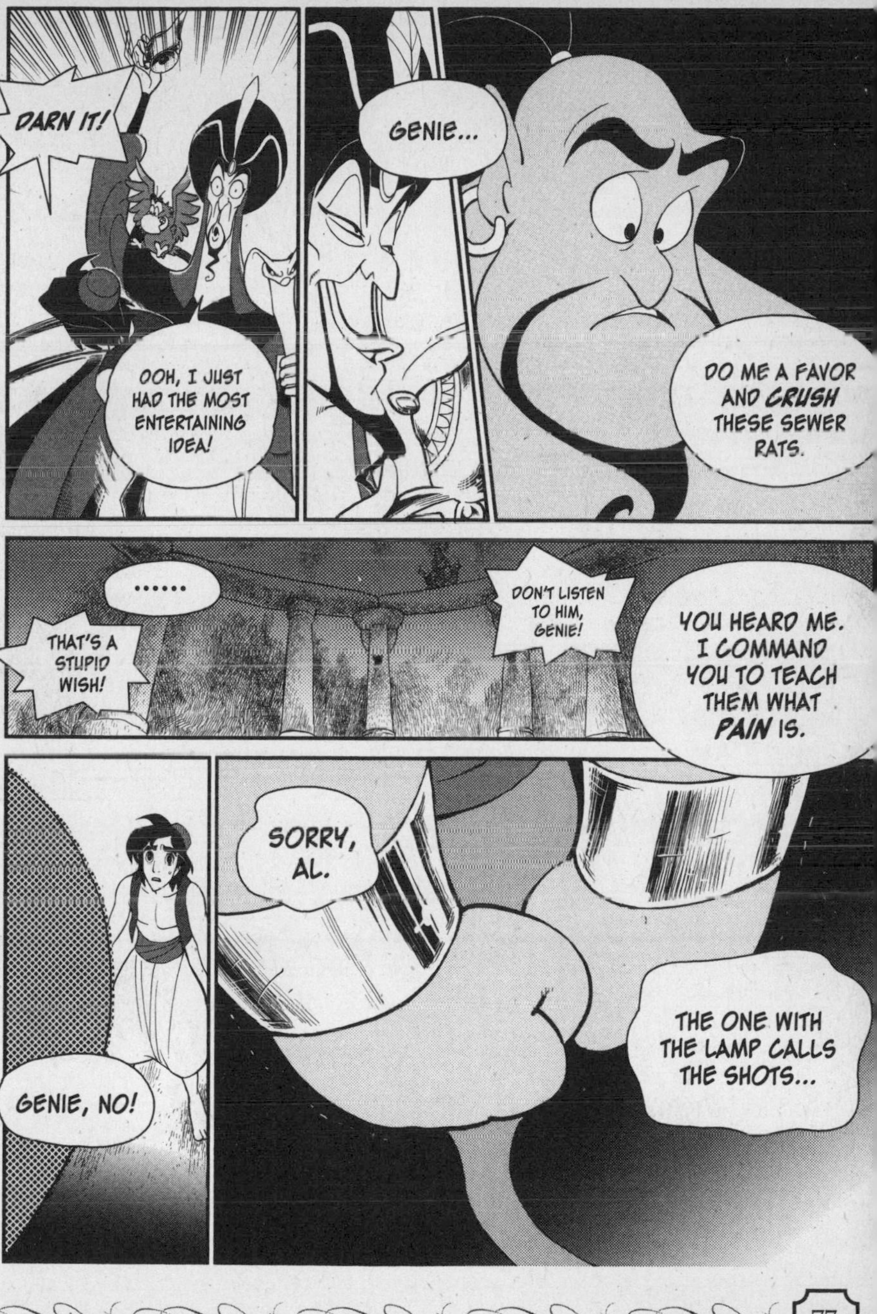
DARN IT!
OOH, I JUST HAD THE MOST ENTERTAINING IDEA!
GENIE...
DO ME A FAVOR AND CRUSH THESE SEWER RATS.
......
THAT'S A STUPID WISH!
DON'T LISTEN TO HIM, GENIE!
YOU HEARD ME. I COMMAND YOU TO TEACH THEM WHAT PAIN IS.
GENIE, NO!
SORRY, AL.
THE ONE WITH THE LAMP CALLS THE SHOTS...

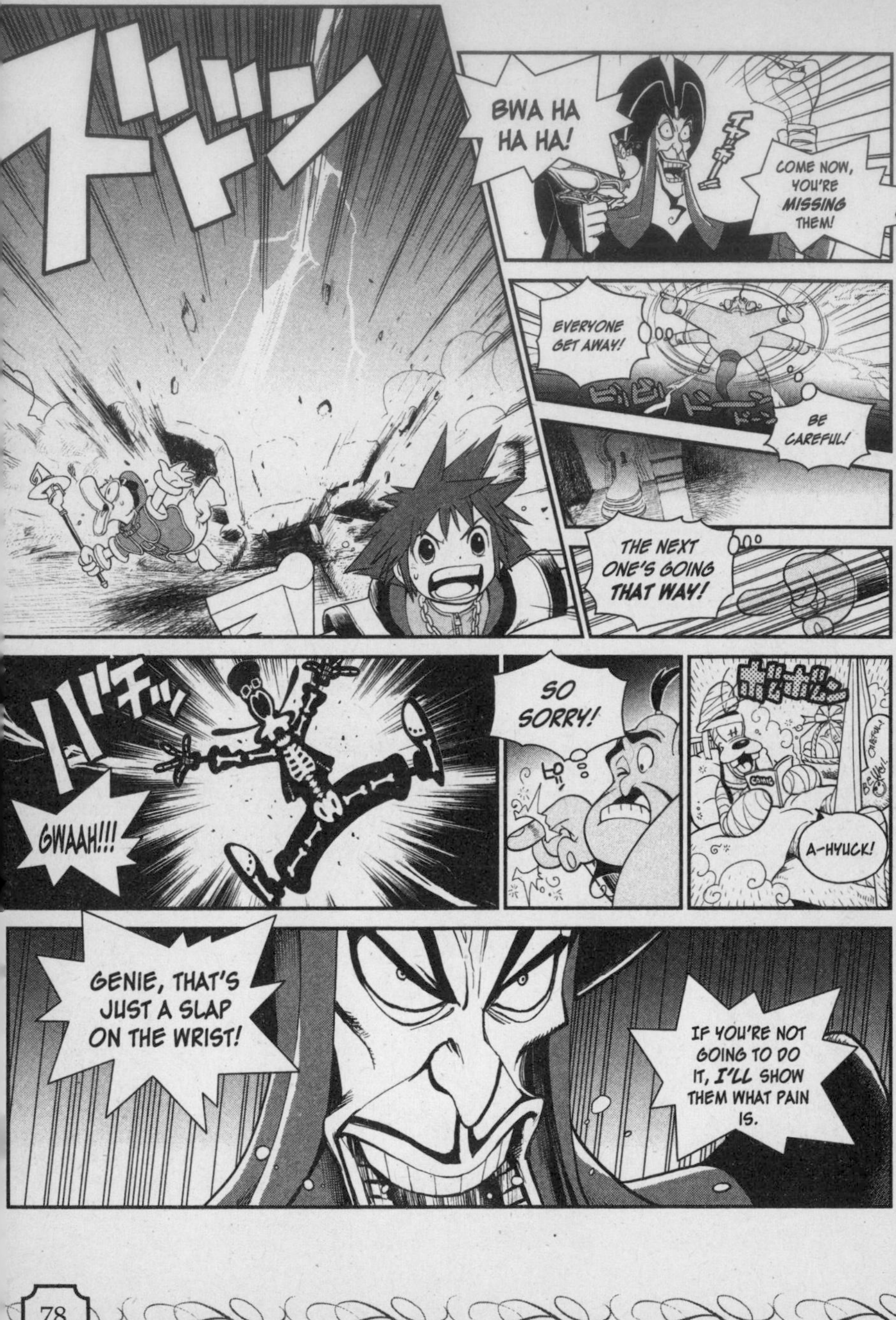
BWA HA HA HA!
COME NOW, YOU'RE MISSING THEM!
EVERYONE GET AWAY!
BE CAREFUL!
THE NEXT ONE'S GOING THAT WAY!
GWAAH!!!
SO SORRY!
A-HYUCK!
GENIE, THAT'S JUST A SLAP ON THE WRIST!
IF YOU'RE NOT GOING TO DO IT, I'LL SHOW THEM WHAT PAIN IS.

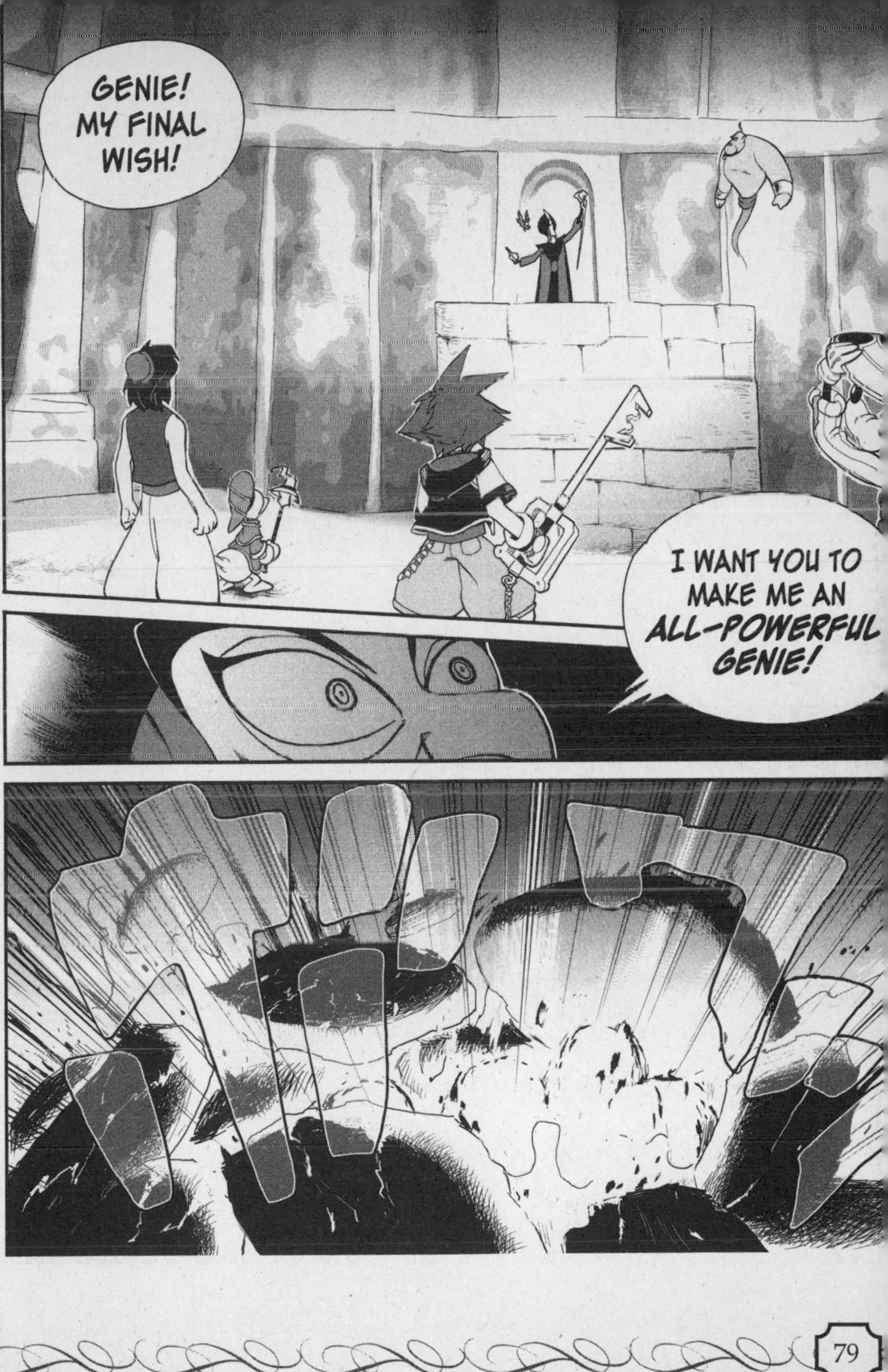
GENIE! MY FINAL WISH!
I WANT YOU TO MAKE ME AN ALL-POWERFUL GENIE!

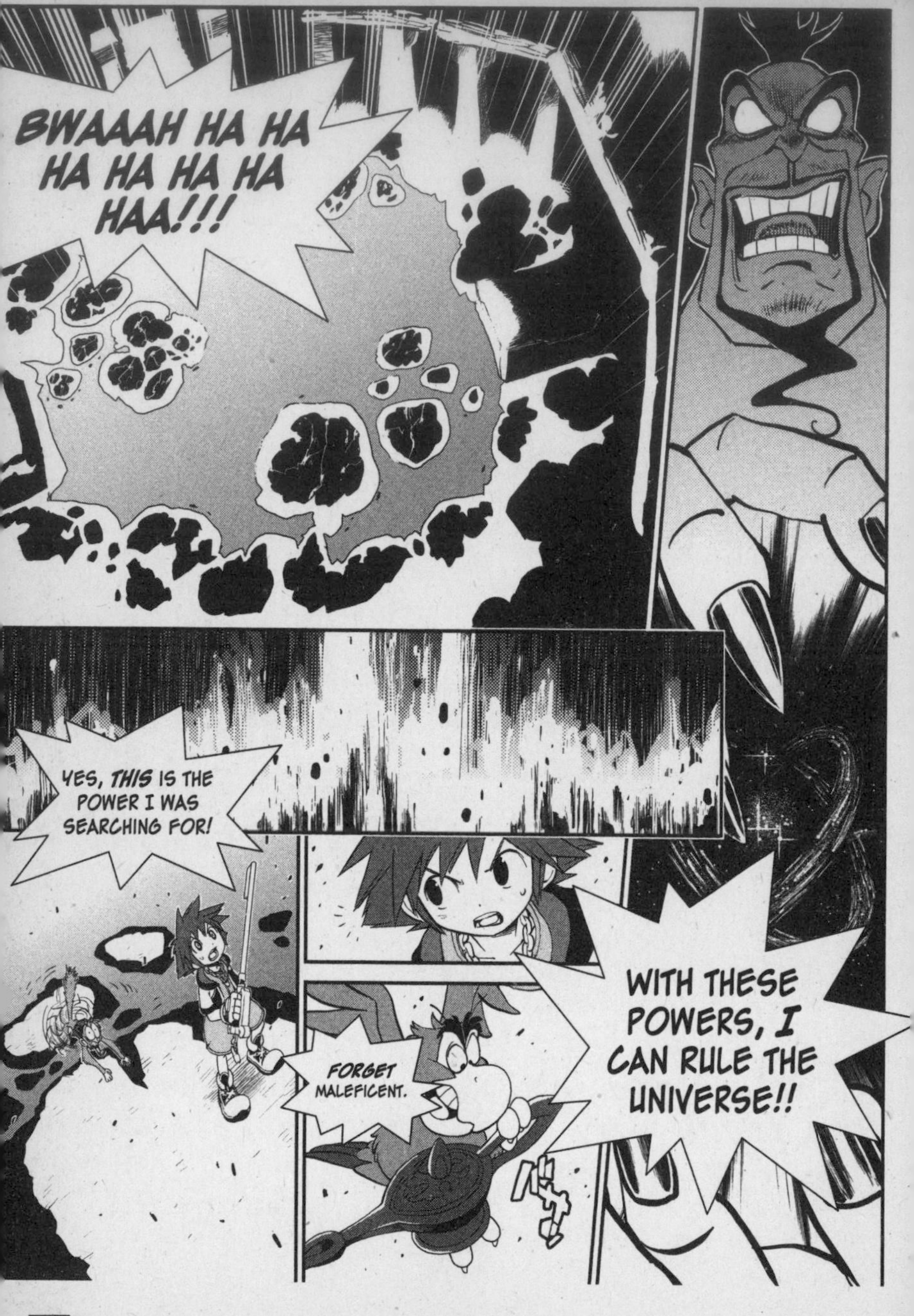
BWAAAH HA HA HA HA HA HA HAA!!!
YES, THIS IS THE POWER I WAS SEARCHING FOR!
FORGET MALEFICENT.
WITH THESE POWERS, I CAN RULE THE UNIVERSE!!

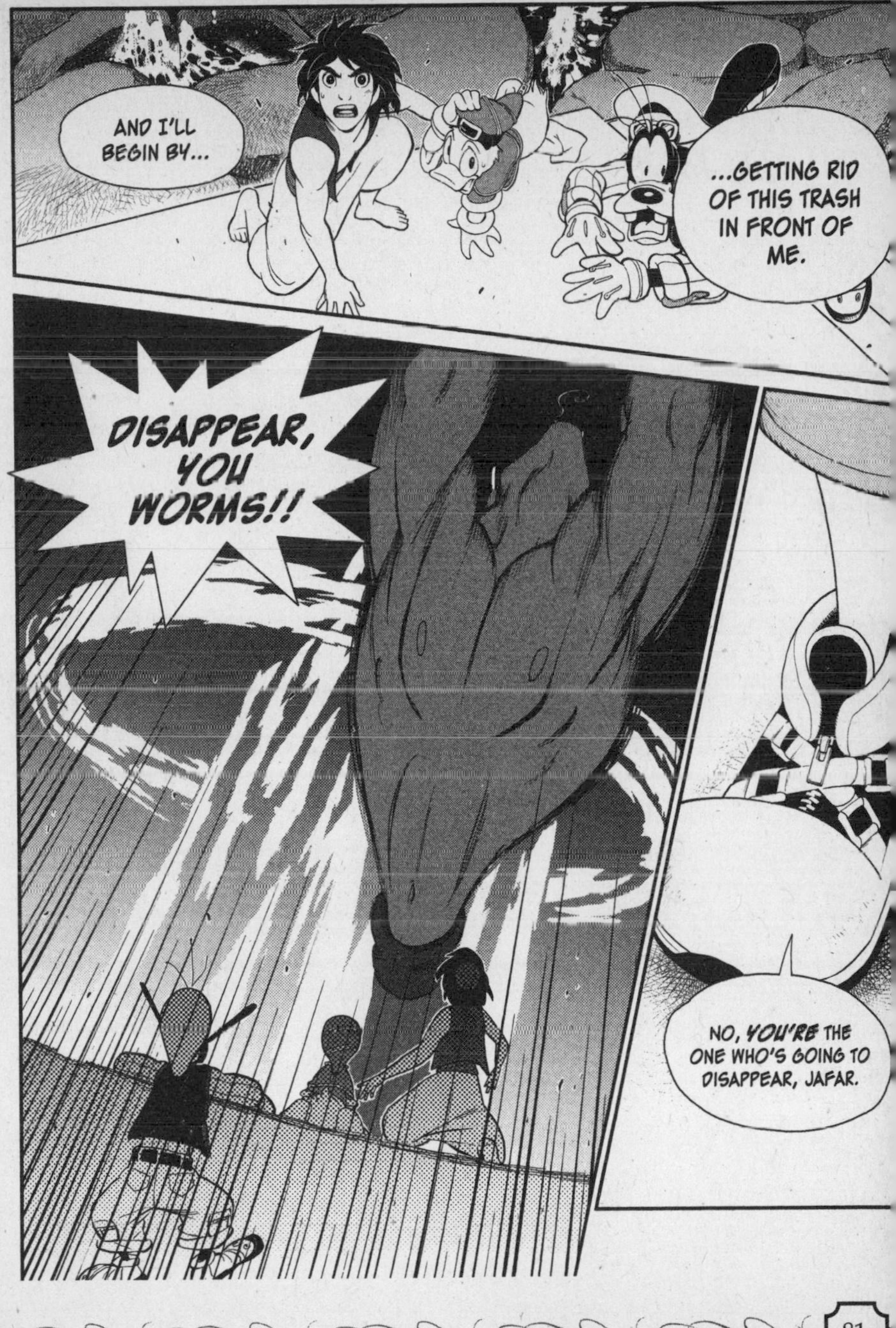
AND I'LL BEGIN BY...
...GETTING RID OF THIS TRASH IN FRONT OF ME.
DISAPPEAR, YOU WORMS!!
NO, *YOU'RE* THE ONE WHO'S GOING TO DISAPPEAR, JAFAR.

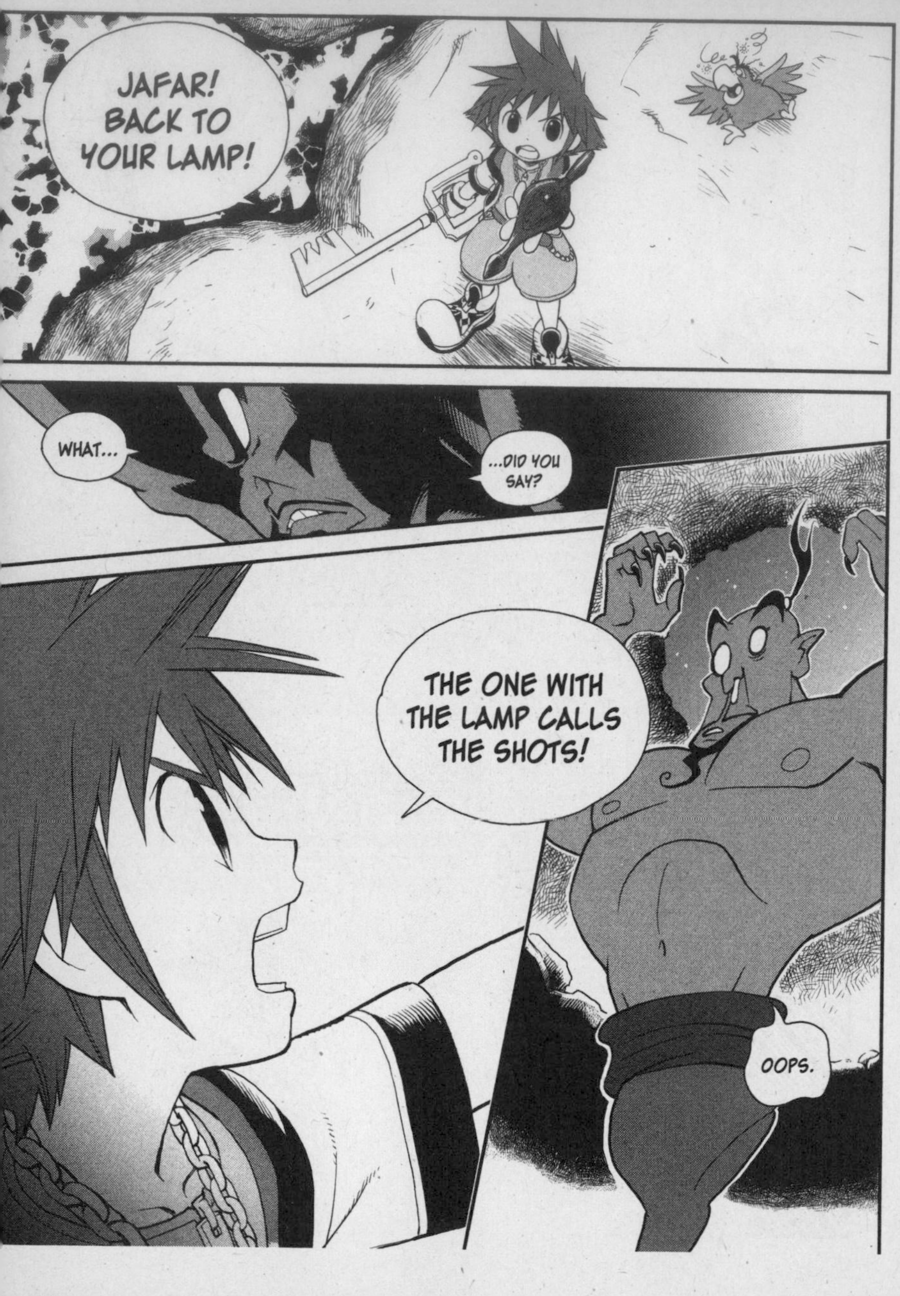
JAFAR! BACK TO YOUR LAMP!
WHAT...
...DID YOU SAY?
THE ONE WITH THE LAMP CALLS THE SHOTS!
OOPS.

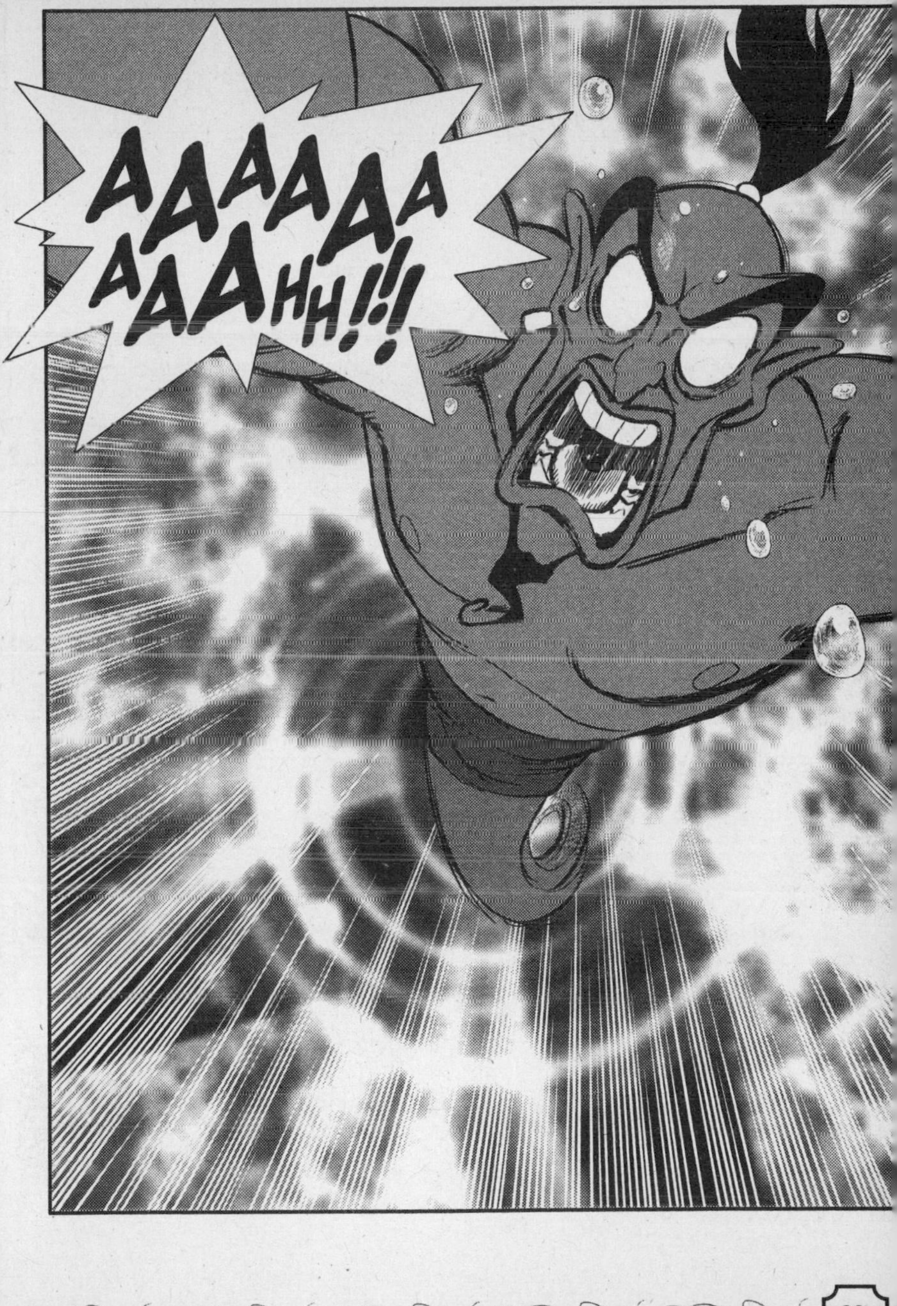
AAAAAAAAAHH!!!

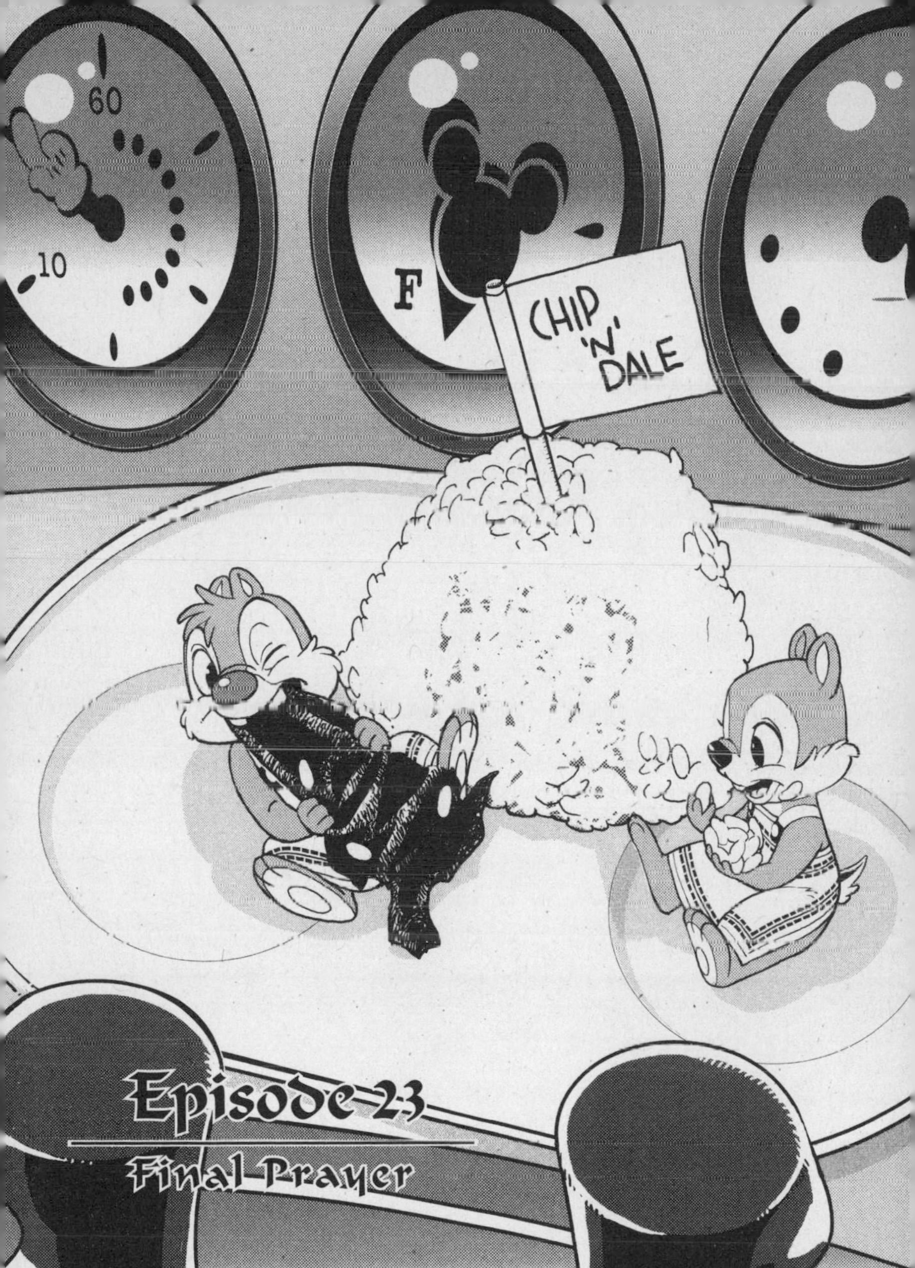
60
10
F
CHIP 'N' DALE

Episode 23

Final Prayer

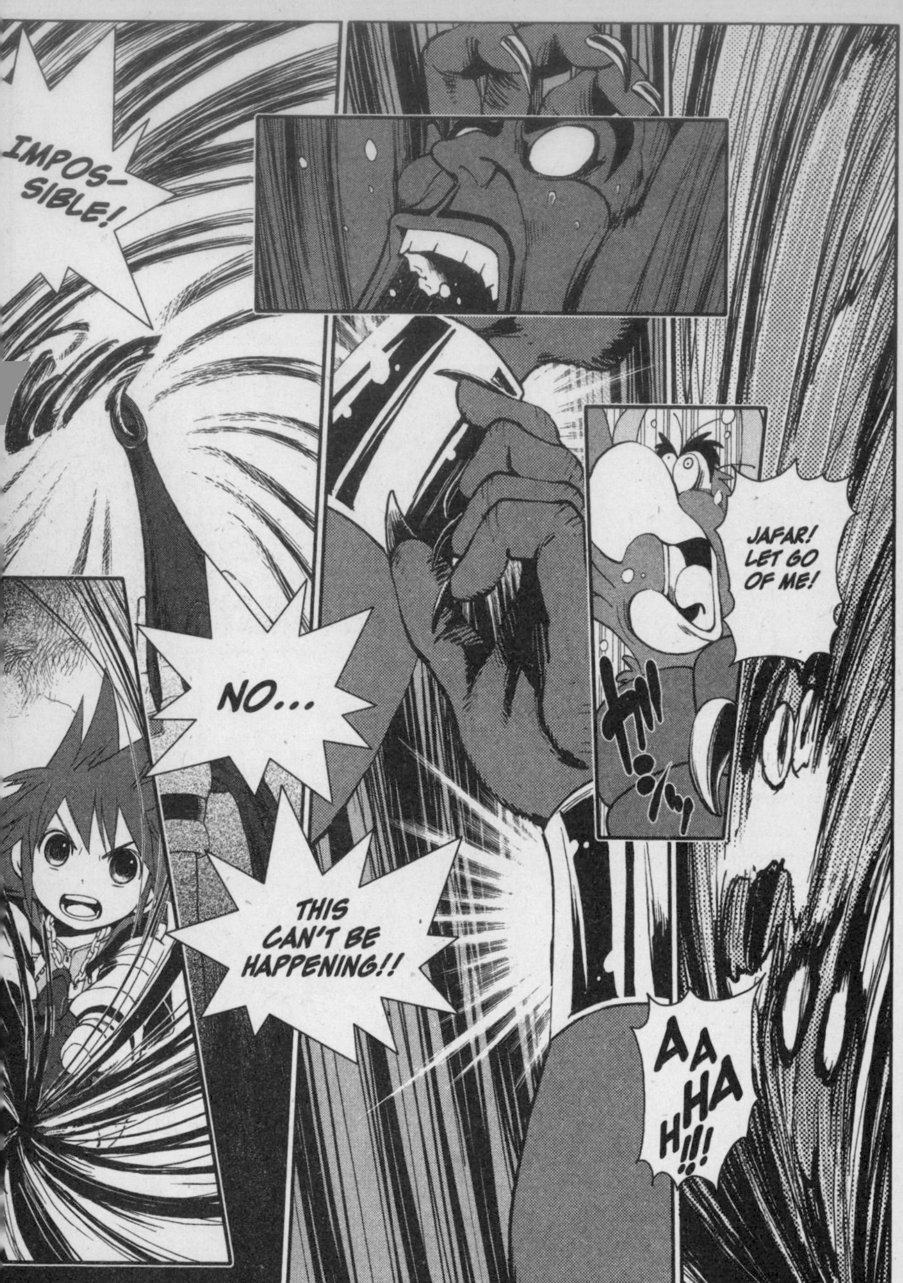
IMPOS-
SIBLE!
JAFAR! LET GO OF ME!
NO...
THIS CAN'T BE HAPPENING!!
AAHAHH!!!

LIKE YOUR NEW HOME?

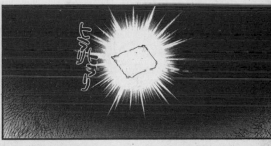

WAAH! HOW DID THIS HAPPEN?!

GET OUT OF HERE, IAGO!

HUH?

THIS IS...

...PART OF ANSEM'S REPORT!

SORA!

ARGH!

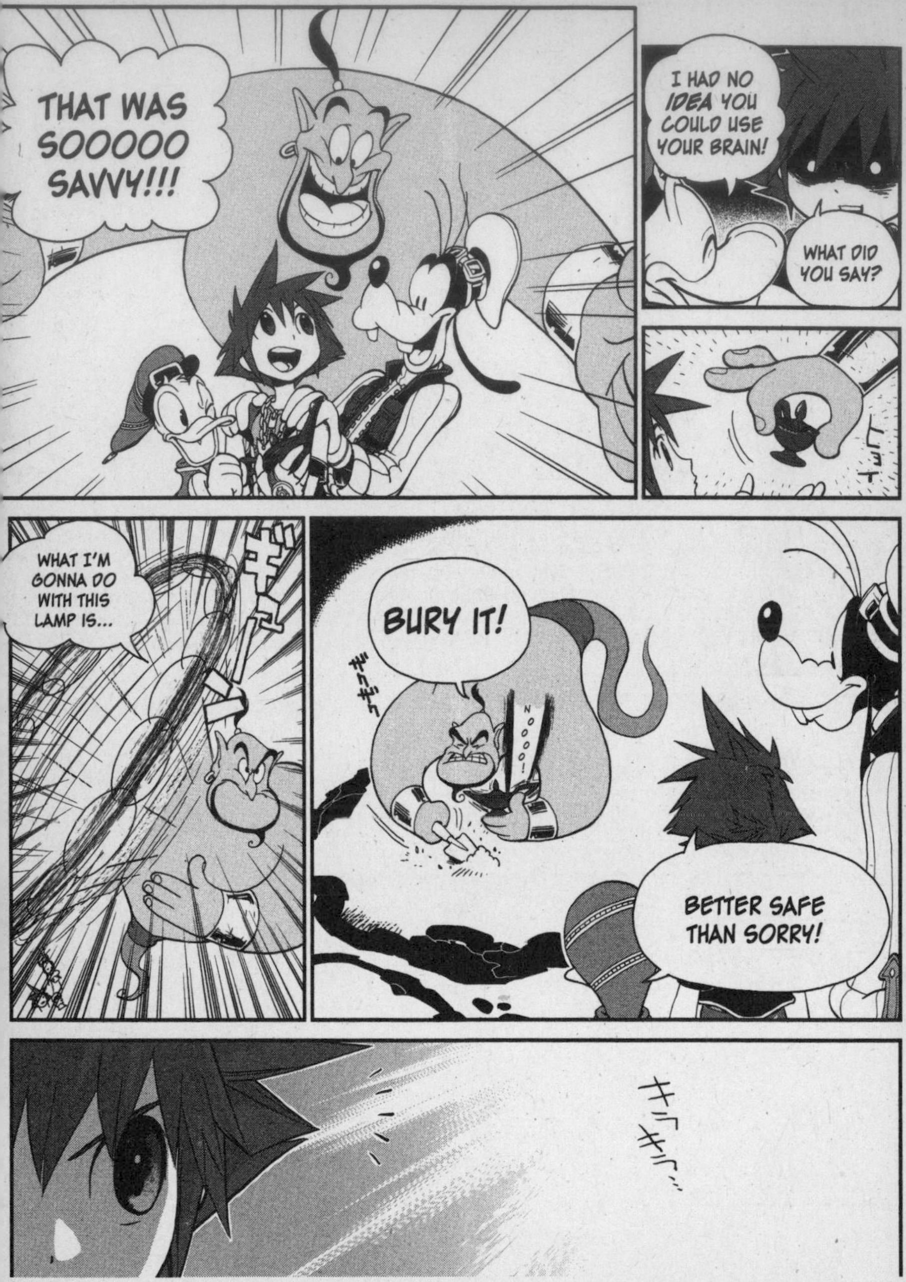
THAT WAS SOOOOO SAVVY!!!
I HAD NO IDEA YOU COULD USE YOUR BRAIN!
WHAT DID YOU SAY?
WHAT I'M GONNA DO WITH THIS LAMP IS...
BURY IT!
NOOOO!
BETTER SAFE THAN SORRY!
キラ キラ…

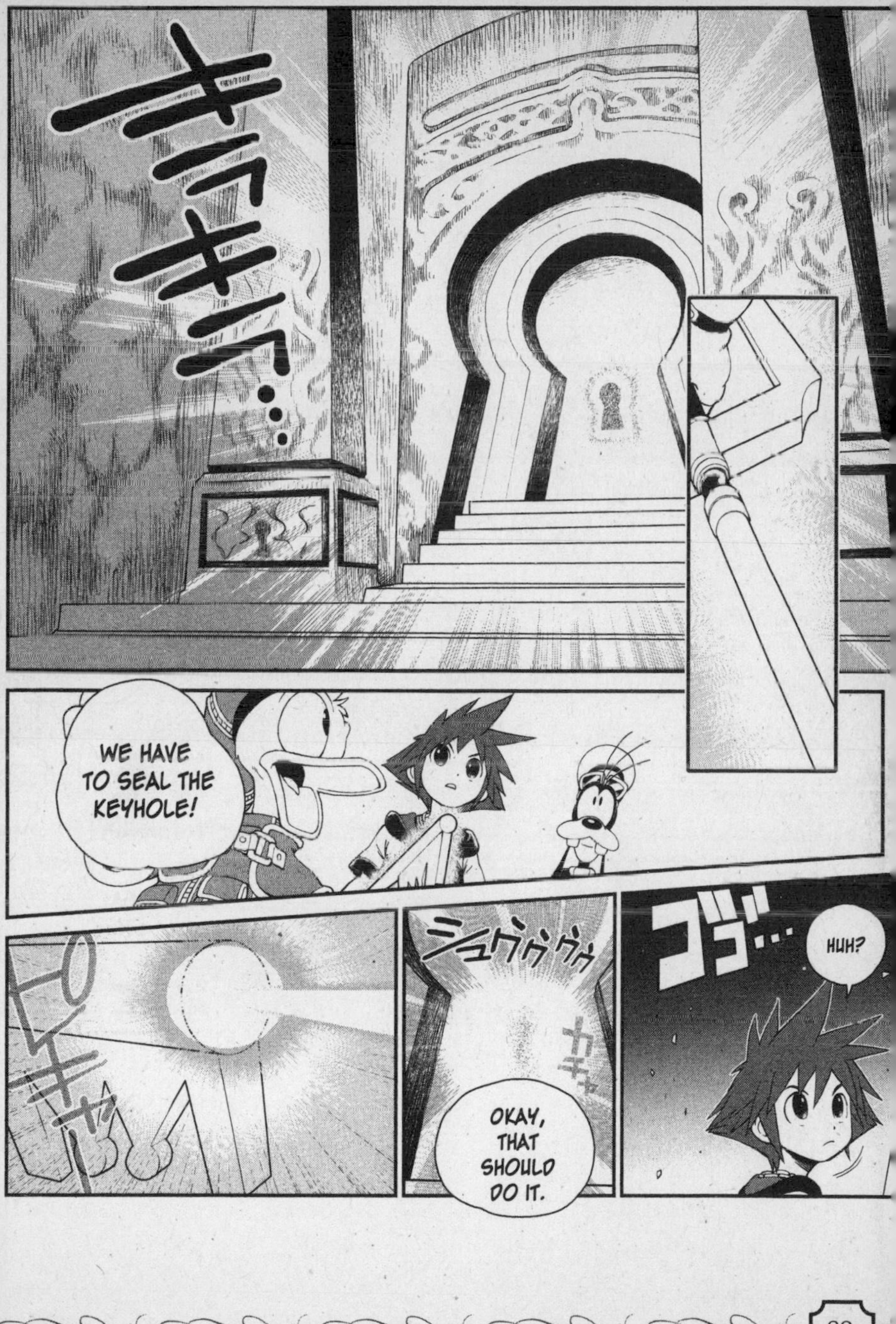
キラキラ…
WE HAVE TO SEAL THE KEYHOLE!
シュウウウウ
カチャ
OKAY, THAT SHOULD DO IT.
ゴゴ…
HUH?

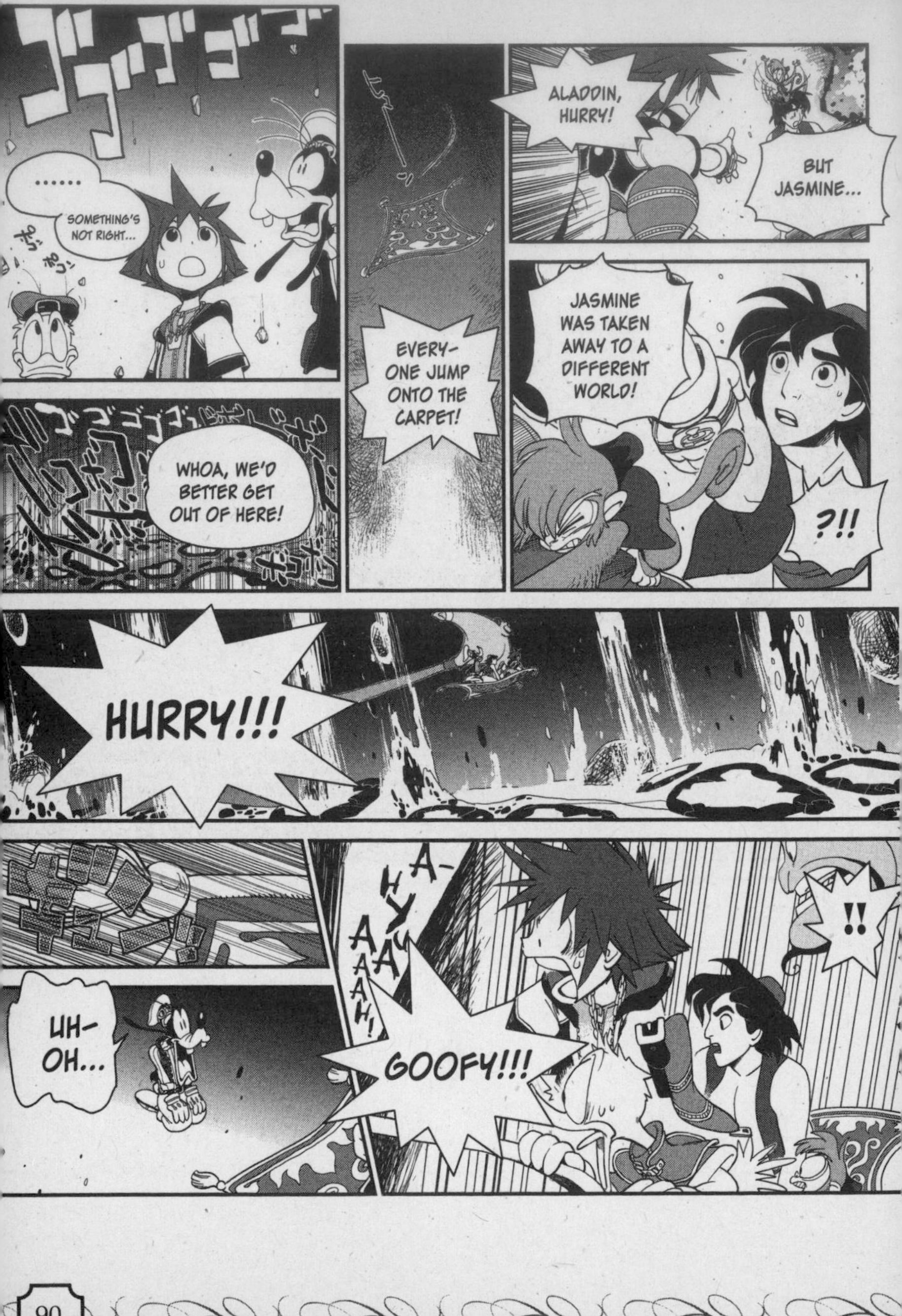
......
SOMETHING'S NOT RIGHT...
WHOA, WE'D BETTER GET OUT OF HERE!
EVERY-ONE JUMP ONTO THE CARPET!
ALADDIN, HURRY!
BUT JASMINE...
JASMINE WAS TAKEN AWAY TO A DIFFERENT WORLD!
?!!
HURRY!!!
UH-OH...
A-HYAAAAAH!
GOOFY!!!
!!

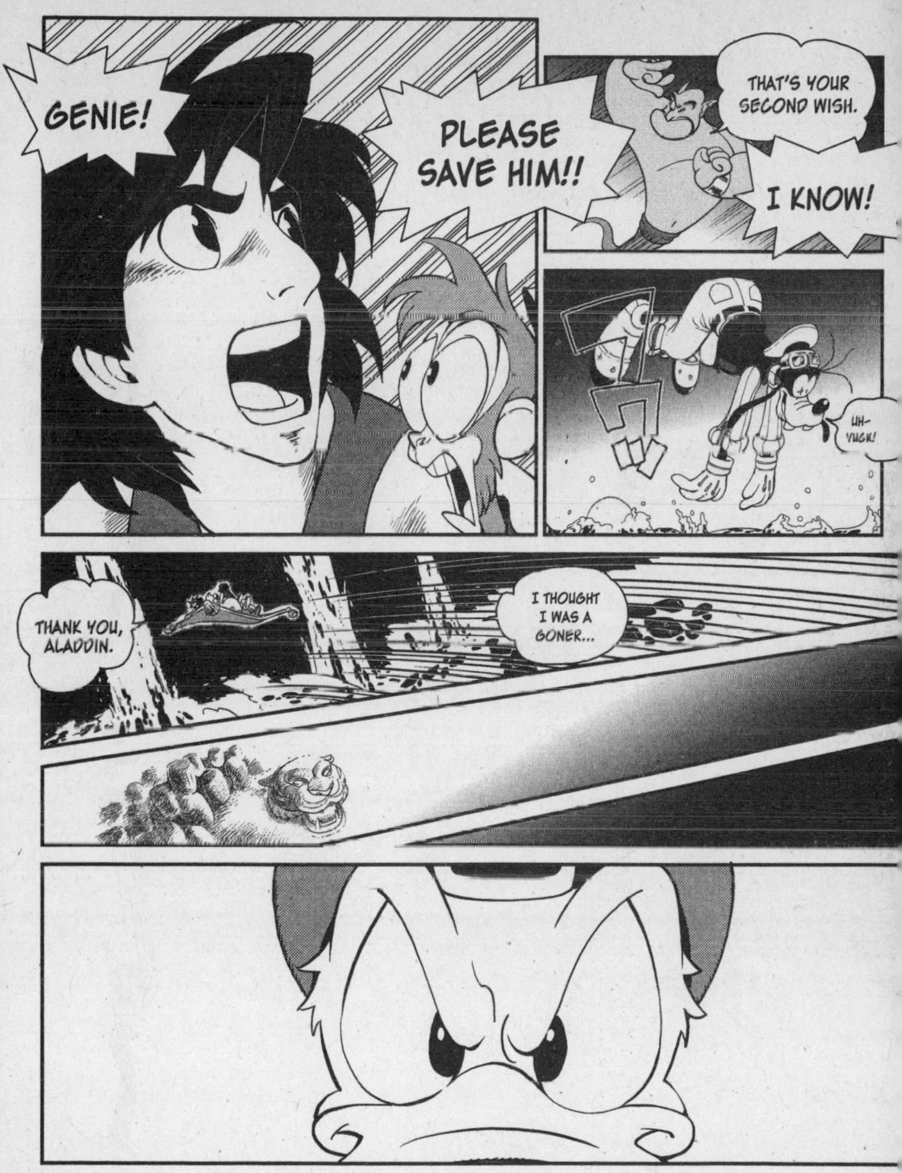
GENIE!
PLEASE SAVE HIM!!
THAT'S YOUR SECOND WISH.
I KNOW!
UH-YUCK!
THANK YOU, ALADDIN.
I THOUGHT I WAS A GONER...

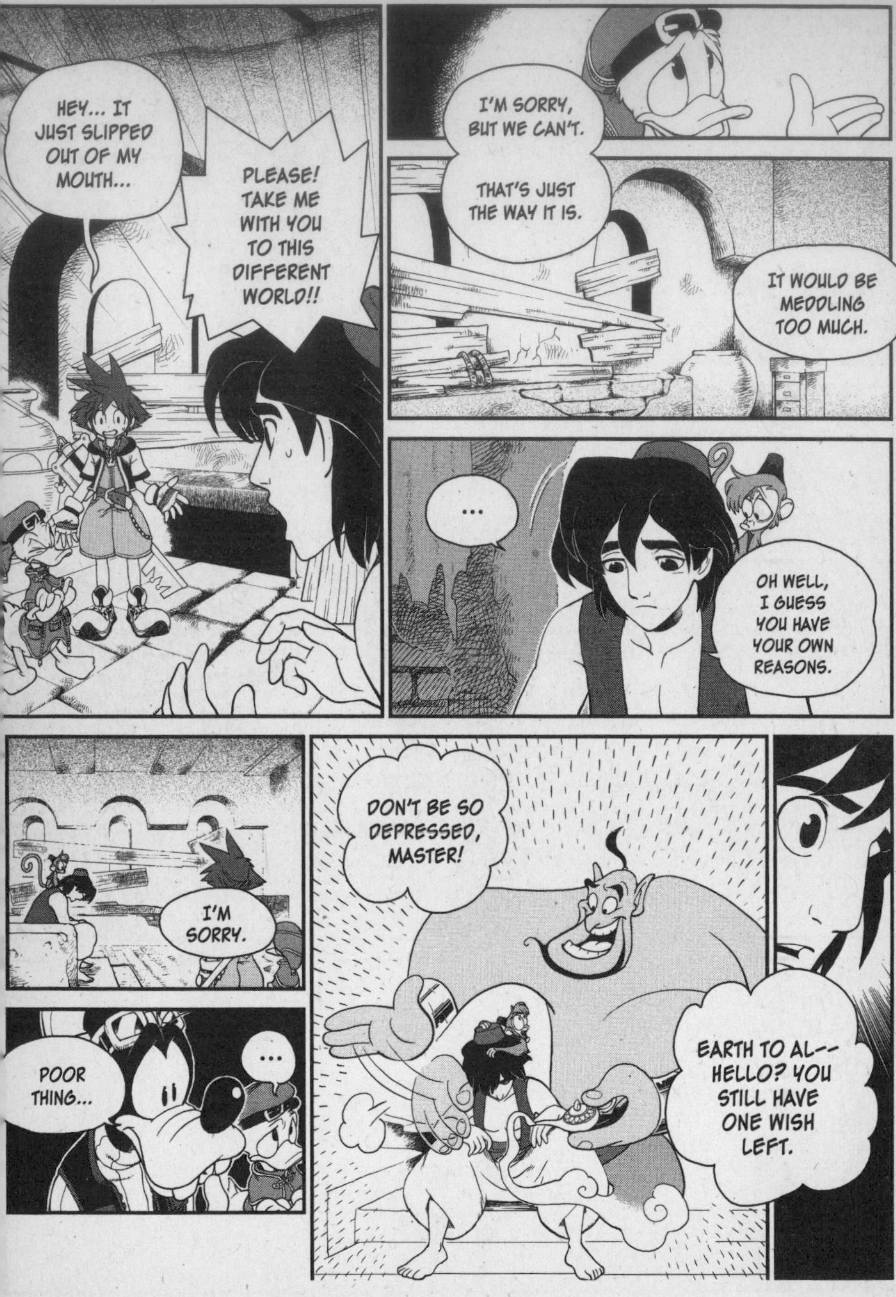
HEY... IT JUST SLIPPED OUT OF MY MOUTH...
PLEASE! TAKE ME WITH YOU TO THIS DIFFERENT WORLD!!
I'M SORRY, BUT WE CAN'T.
THAT'S JUST THE WAY IT IS.
IT WOULD BE MEDDLING TOO MUCH.
...
OH WELL, I GUESS YOU HAVE YOUR OWN REASONS.
I'M SORRY.
POOR THING...
...
DON'T BE SO DEPRESSED, MASTER!
EARTH TO AL-- HELLO? YOU STILL HAVE ONE WISH LEFT.

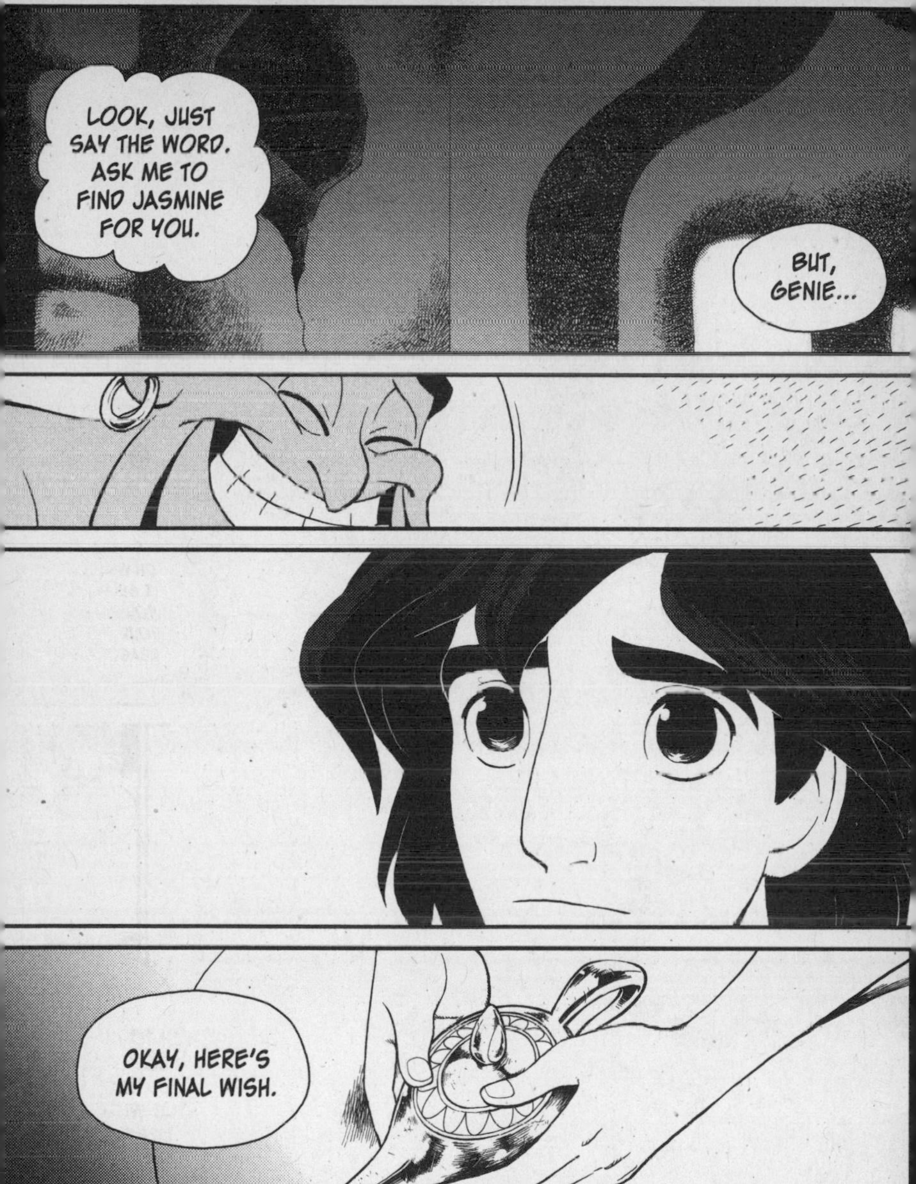
LOOK, JUST SAY THE WORD. ASK ME TO FIND JASMINE FOR YOU.
BUT, GENIE...
OKAY, HERE'S MY FINAL WISH.

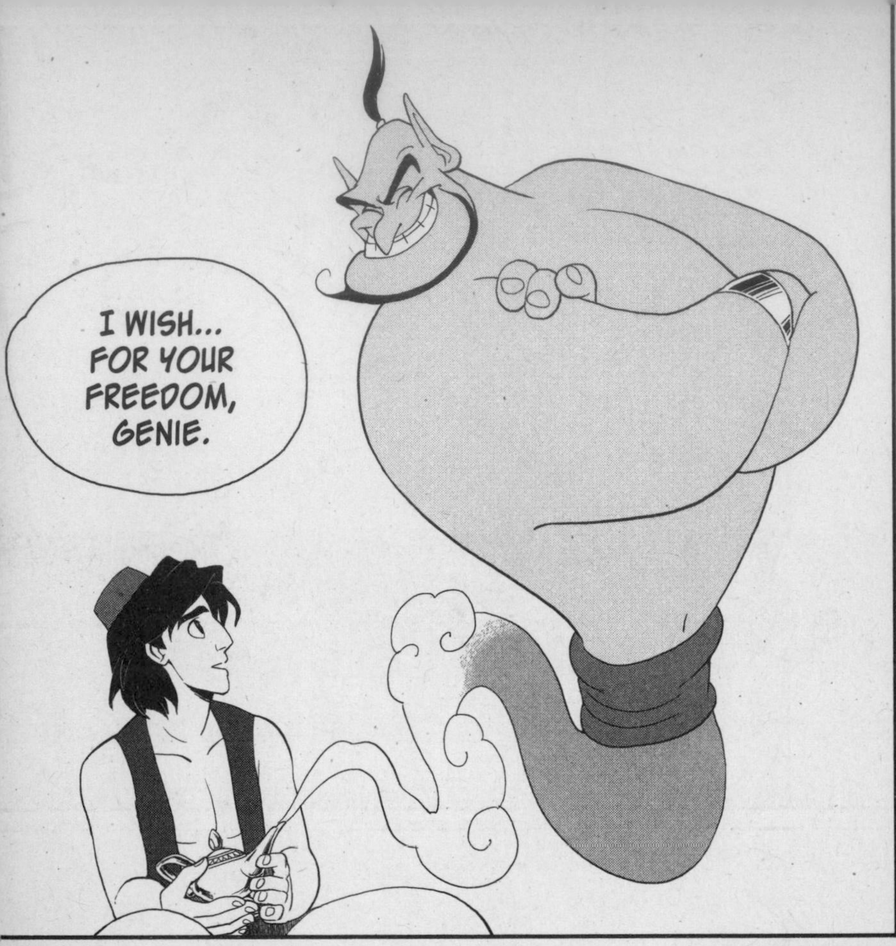
I WISH... FOR YOUR FREEDOM, GENIE.

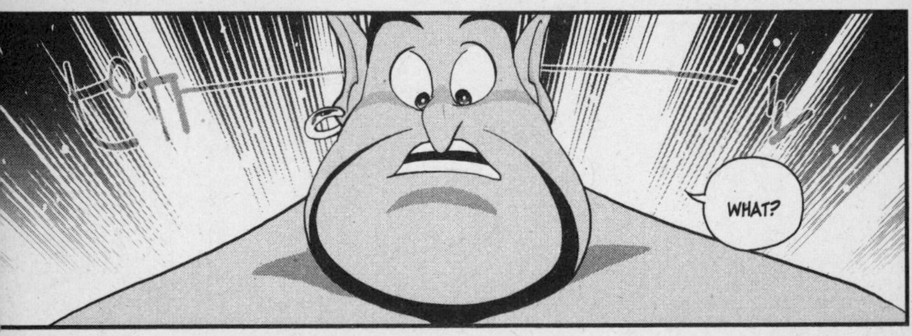
WHAT?

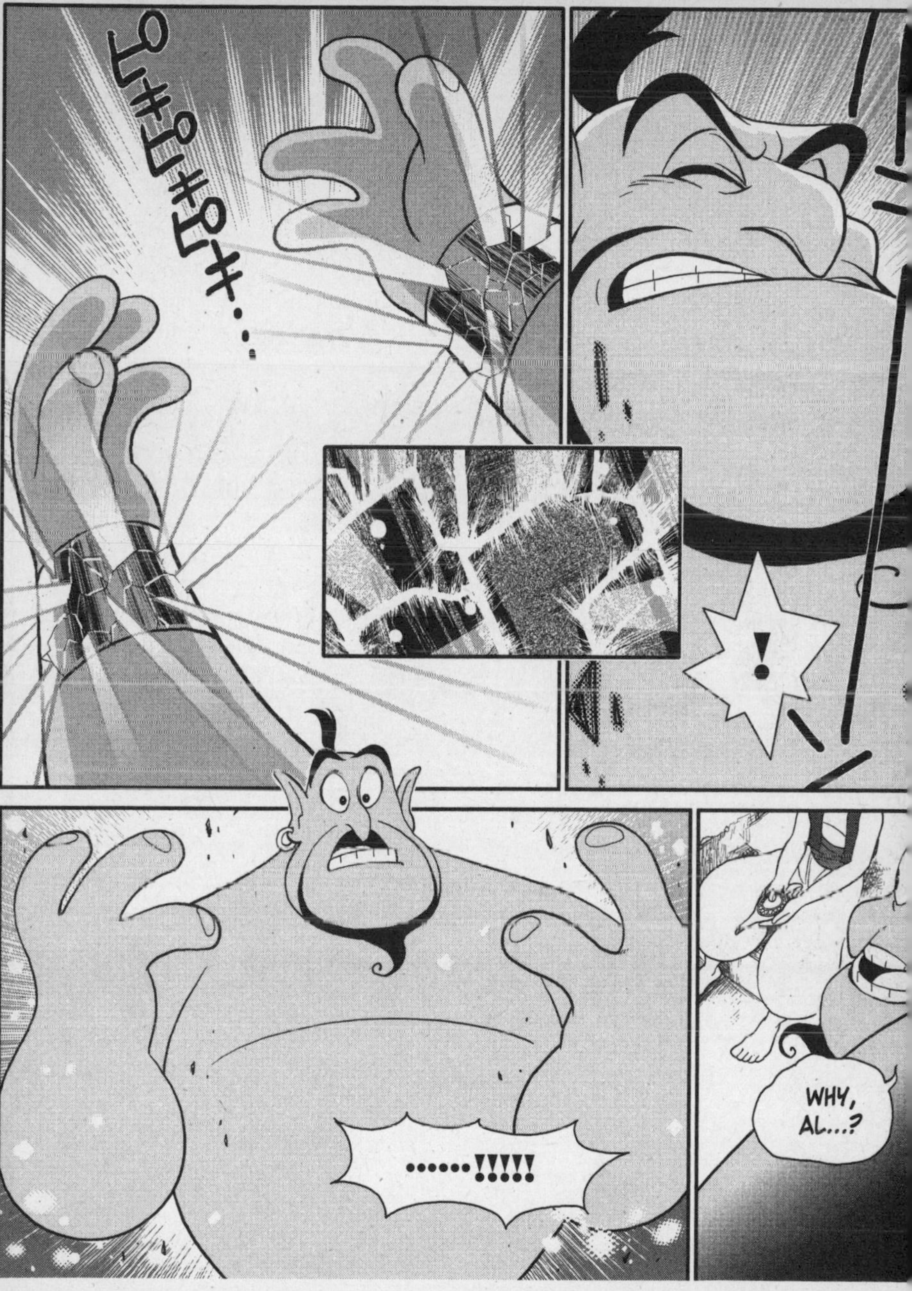
ピキピキピキ…
!
......!!!!!
WHY, AL...?

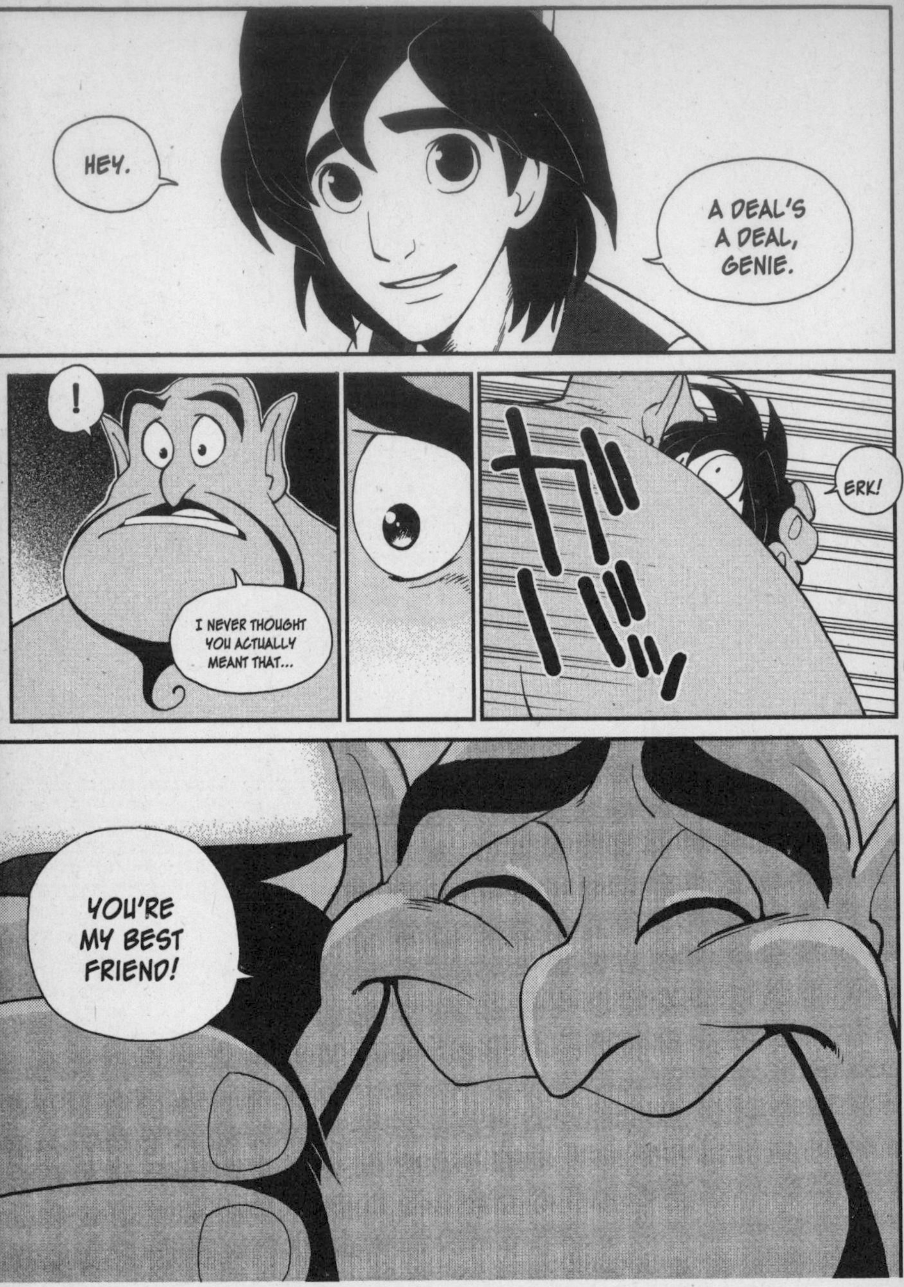
HEY.
A DEAL'S A DEAL, GENIE.
!
I NEVER THOUGHT YOU ACTUALLY MEANT THAT...
ERK!
YOU'RE MY BEST FRIEND!

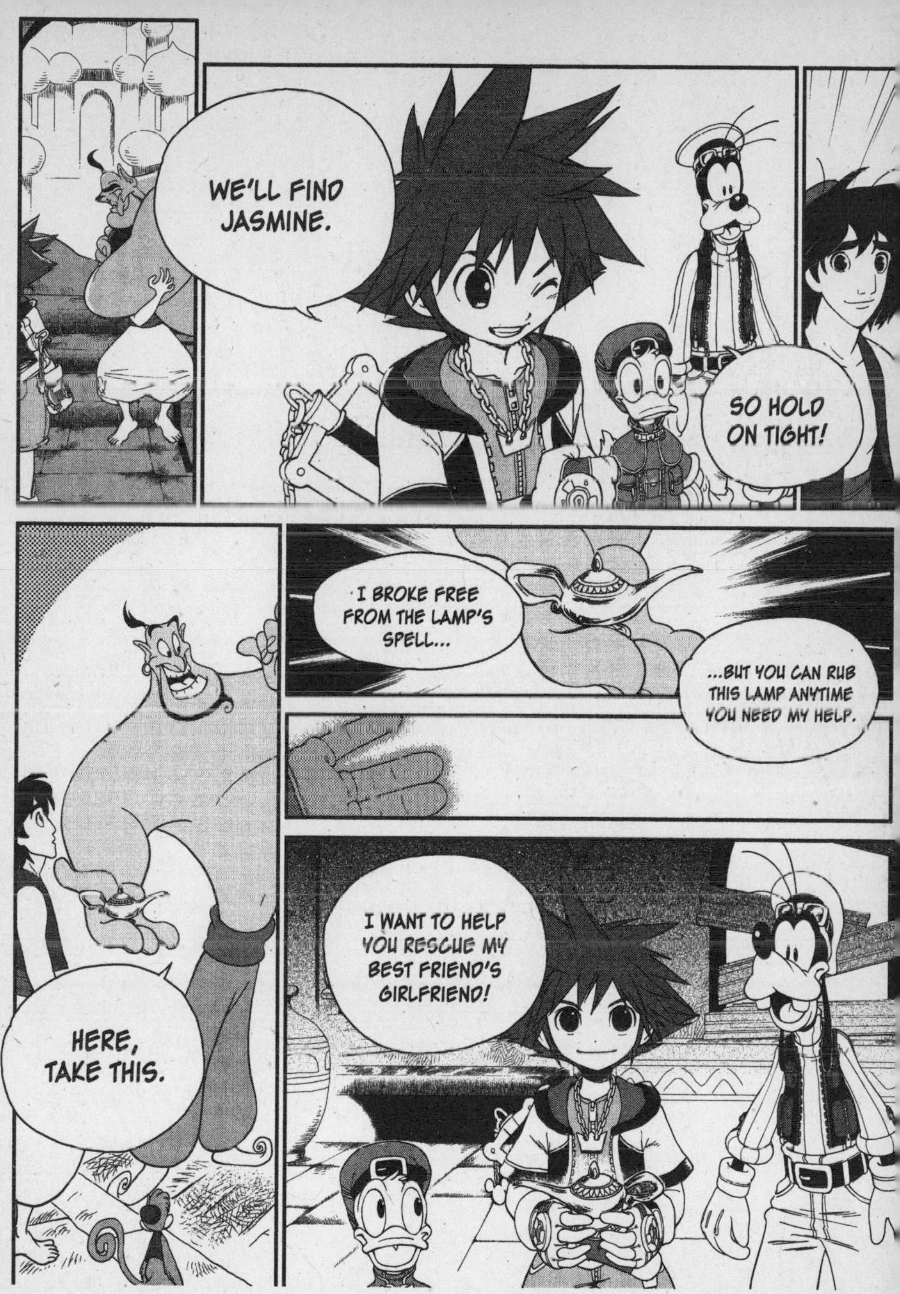
WE'LL FIND JASMINE.
SO HOLD ON TIGHT!
HERE, TAKE THIS.
I BROKE FREE FROM THE LAMP'S SPELL...
...BUT YOU CAN RUB THIS LAMP ANYTIME YOU NEED MY HELP.
I WANT TO HELP YOU RESCUE MY BEST FRIEND'S GIRLFRIEND!

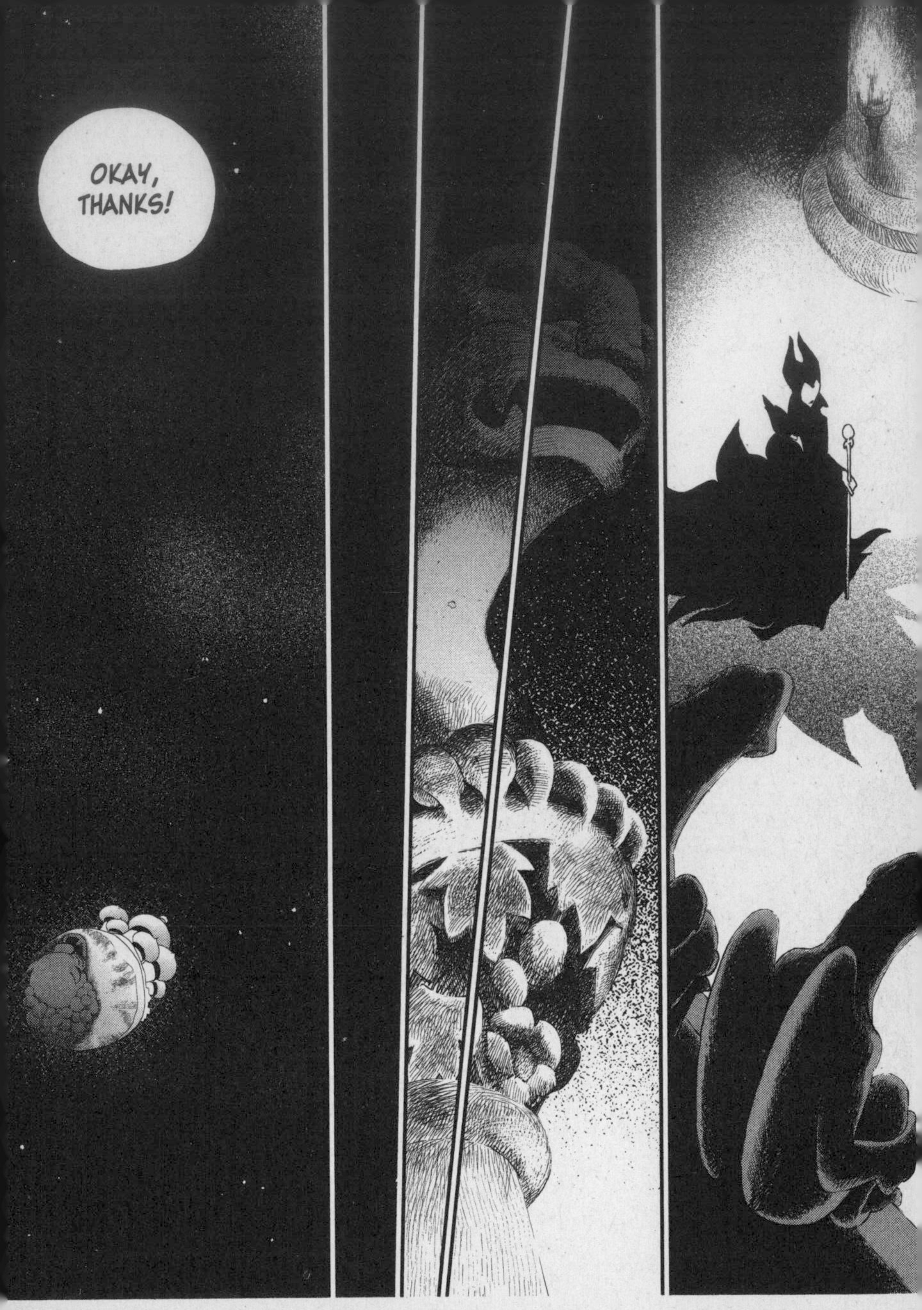
OKAY, THANKS!

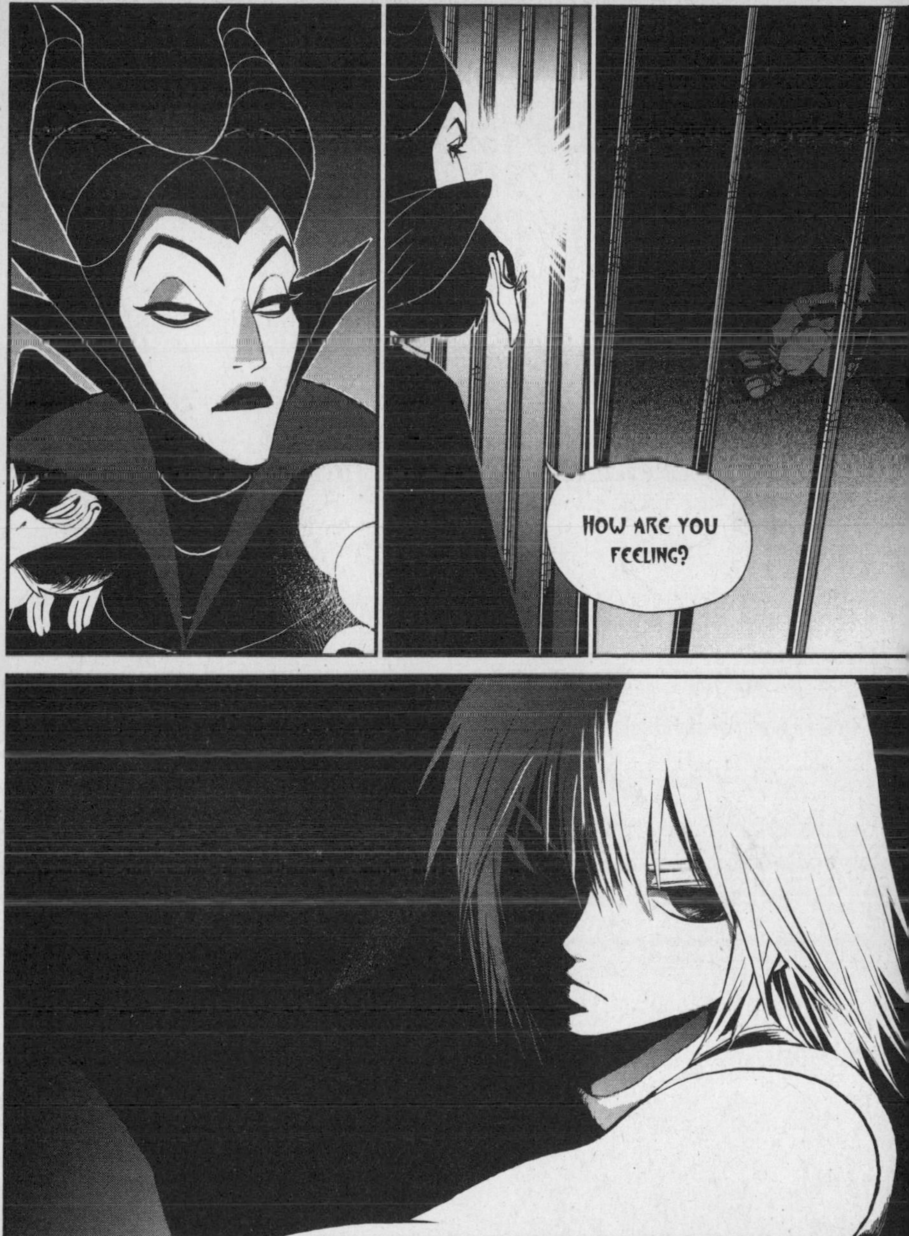
HOW ARE YOU FEELING?

Episode 24

Olympus Coliseum

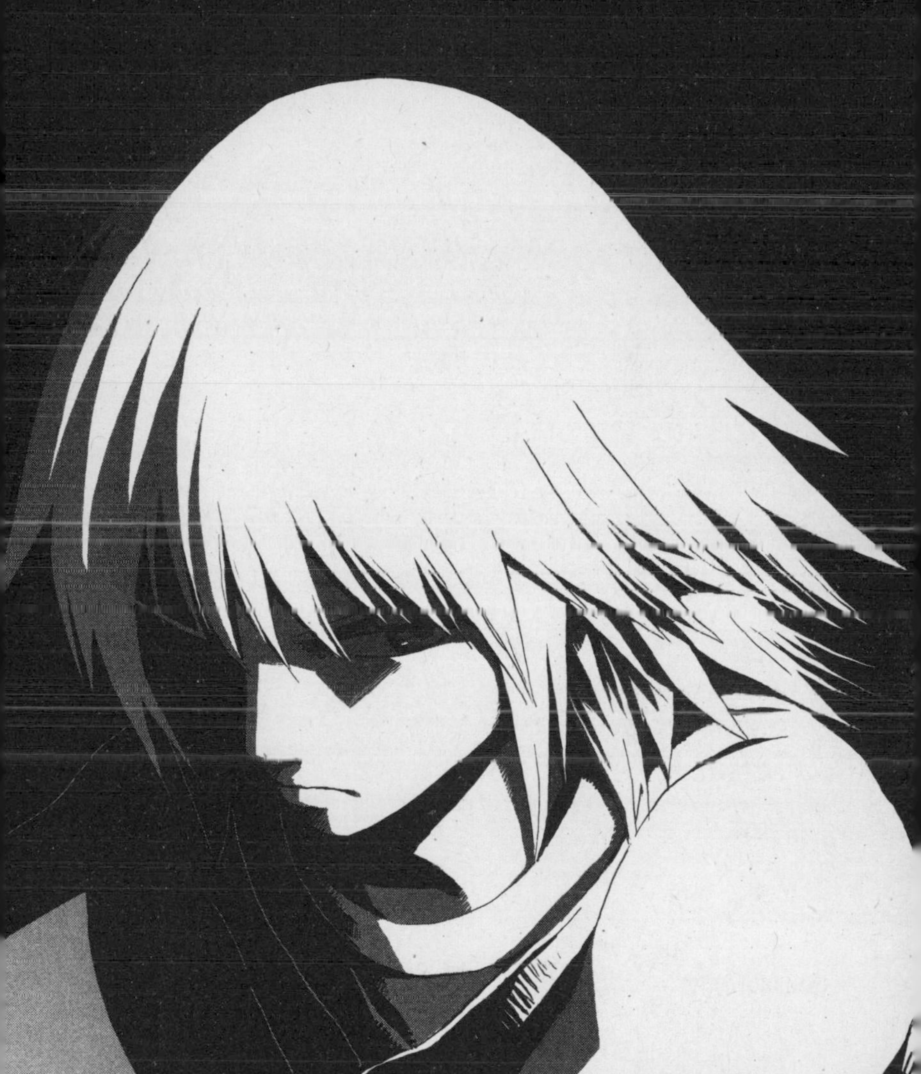

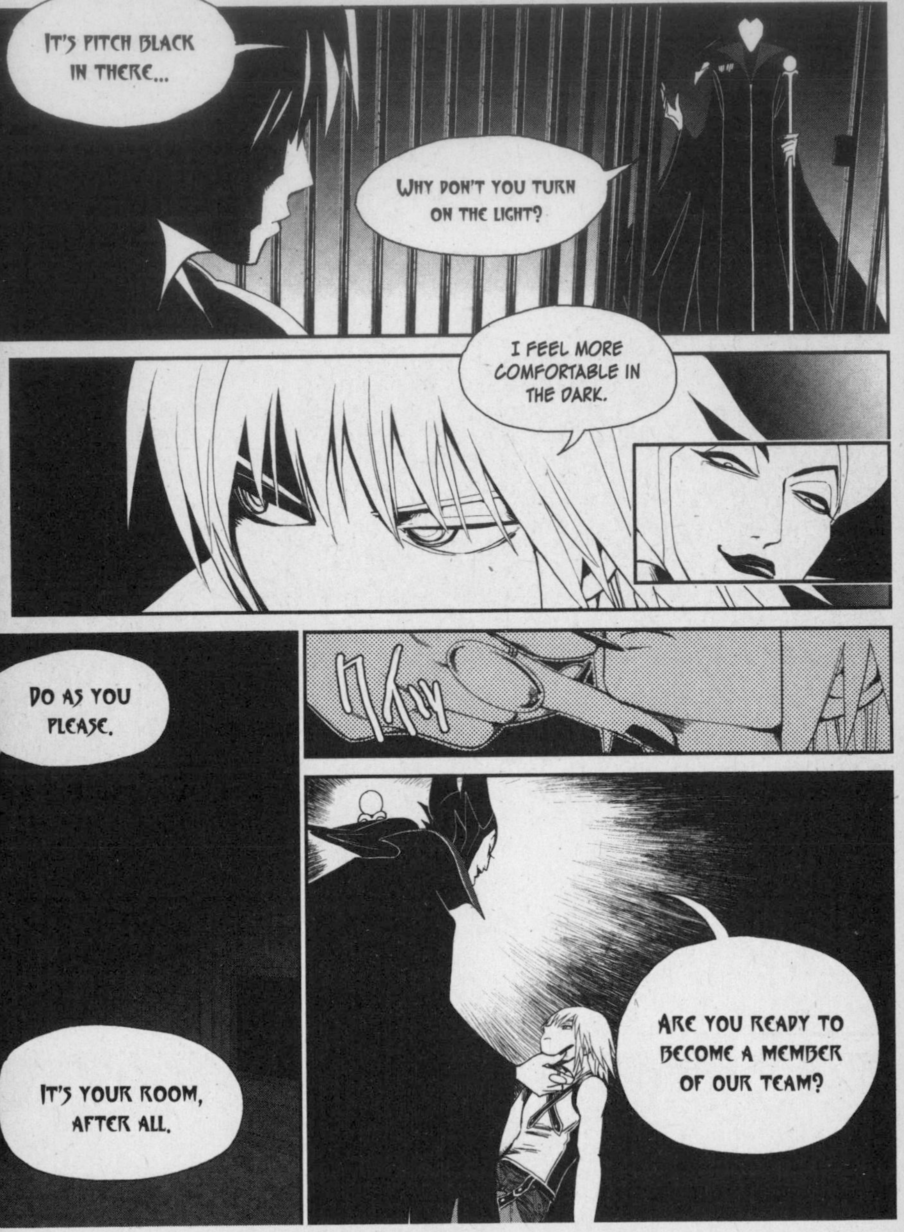
IT'S PITCH BLACK IN THERE...
WHY DON'T YOU TURN ON THE LIGHT?
I FEEL MORE COMFORTABLE IN THE DARK.
DO AS YOU PLEASE.
IT'S YOUR ROOM, AFTER ALL.
ARE YOU READY TO BECOME A MEMBER OF OUR TEAM?

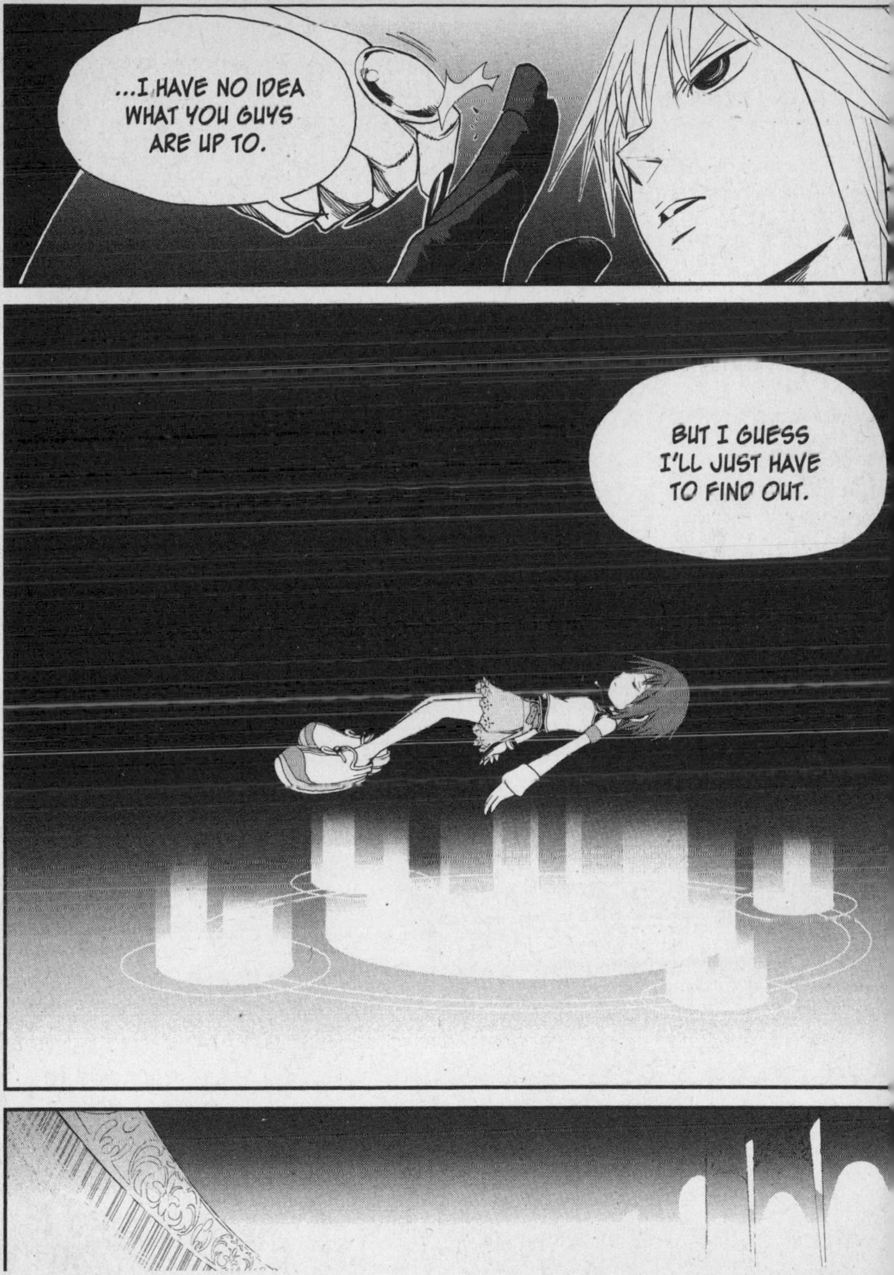
...I HAVE NO IDEA WHAT YOU GUYS ARE UP TO.
BUT I GUESS I'LL JUST HAVE TO FIND OUT.

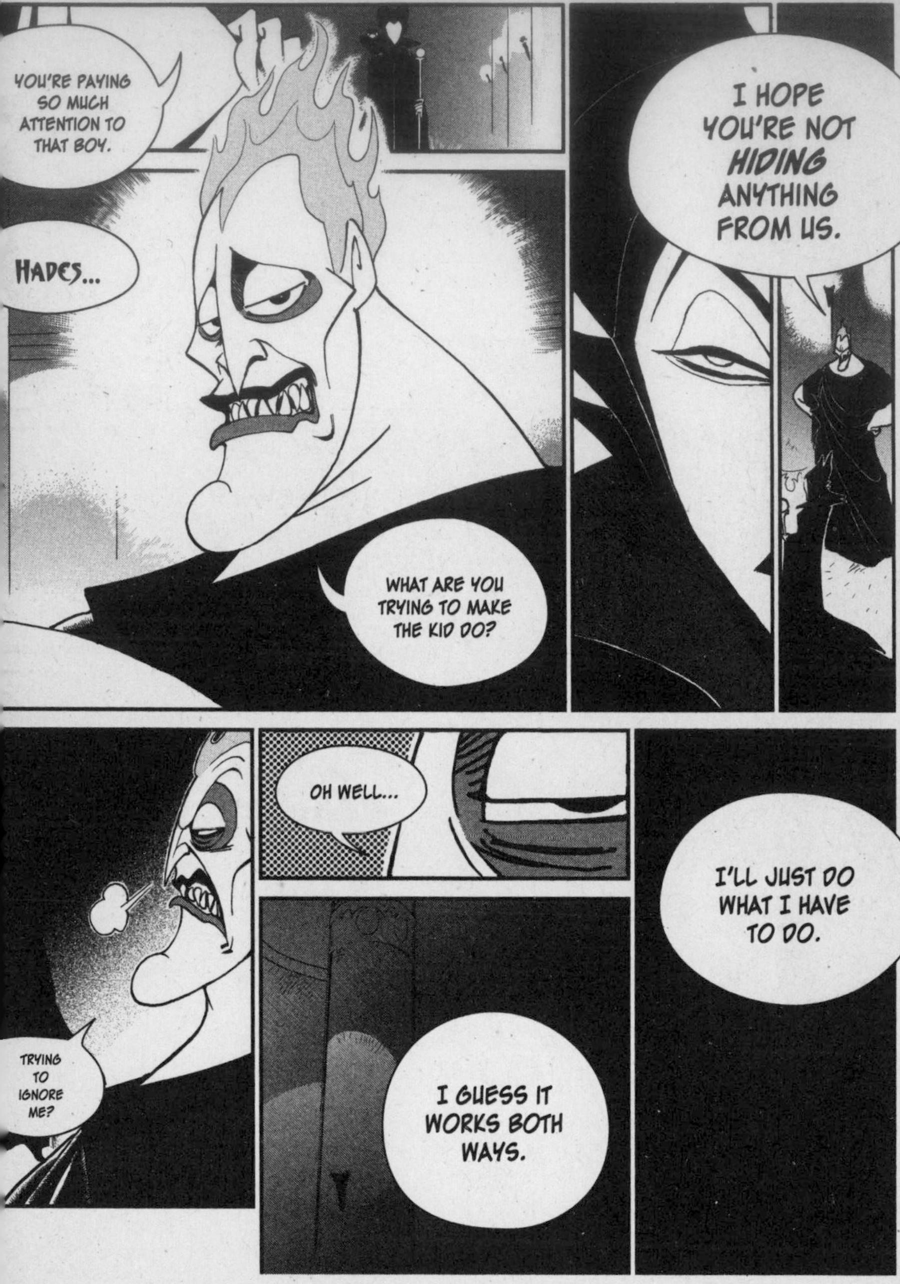
YOU'RE PAYING SO MUCH ATTENTION TO THAT BOY.
HADES...
WHAT ARE YOU TRYING TO MAKE THE KID DO?
I HOPE YOU'RE NOT *HIDING* ANYTHING FROM US.
TRYING TO IGNORE ME?
OH WELL...
I GUESS IT WORKS BOTH WAYS.
I'LL JUST DO WHAT I HAVE TO DO.

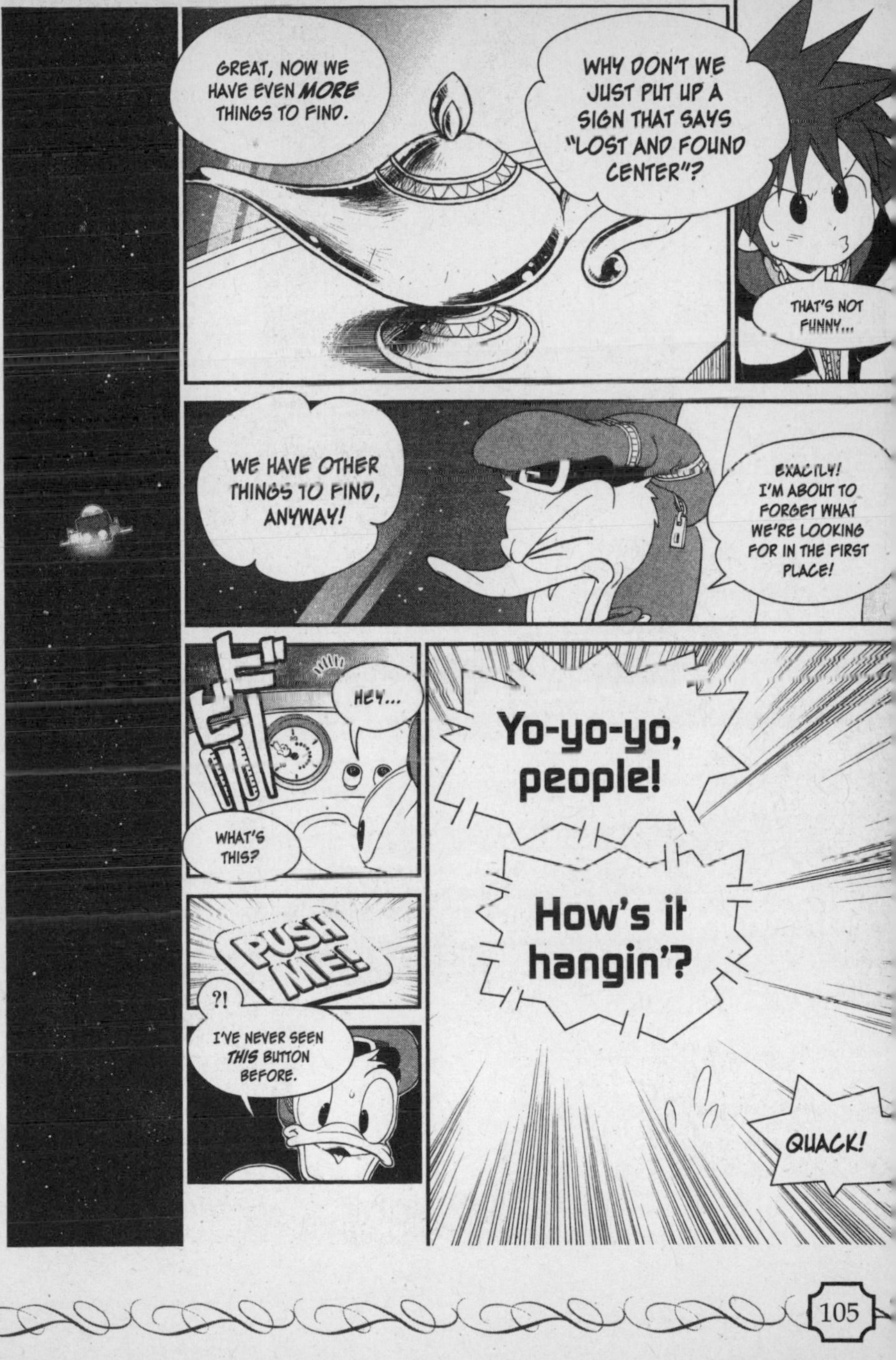
GREAT, NOW WE HAVE EVEN *MORE* THINGS TO FIND.
WHY DON'T WE JUST PUT UP A SIGN THAT SAYS "LOST AND FOUND CENTER"?
THAT'S NOT FUNNY...
WE HAVE OTHER THINGS TO FIND, ANYWAY!
EXACTLY! I'M ABOUT TO FORGET WHAT WE'RE LOOKING FOR IN THE FIRST PLACE!
HEY...
WHAT'S THIS?
PUSH ME!
?!
I'VE NEVER SEEN *THIS* BUTTON BEFORE.
Yo-yo-yo, people!
How's it hangin'?
QUACK!

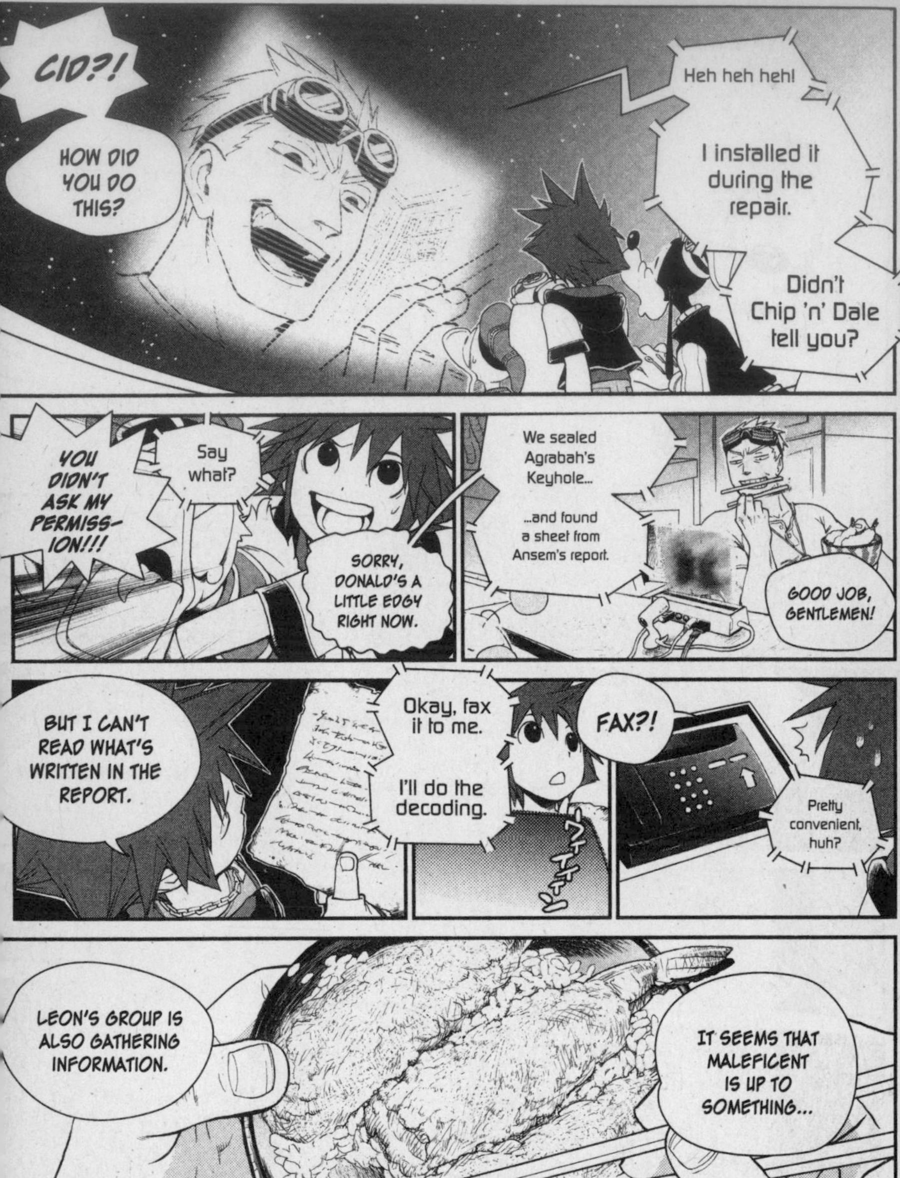
CID?!
HOW DID YOU DO THIS?
Heh heh heh!
I installed it during the repair.
Didn't Chip 'n' Dale tell you?
Say what?
YOU DIDN'T ASK MY PERMISS-ION!!!
SORRY, DONALD'S A LITTLE EDGY RIGHT NOW.
We sealed Agrabah's Keyhole...
...and found a sheet from Ansem's report.
GOOD JOB, GENTLEMEN!
BUT I CAN'T READ WHAT'S WRITTEN IN THE REPORT.
Okay, fax it to me.
I'll do the decoding.
FAX?!
Pretty convenient, huh?
LEON'S GROUP IS ALSO GATHERING INFORMATION.
IT SEEMS THAT MALEFICENT IS UP TO SOMETHING...

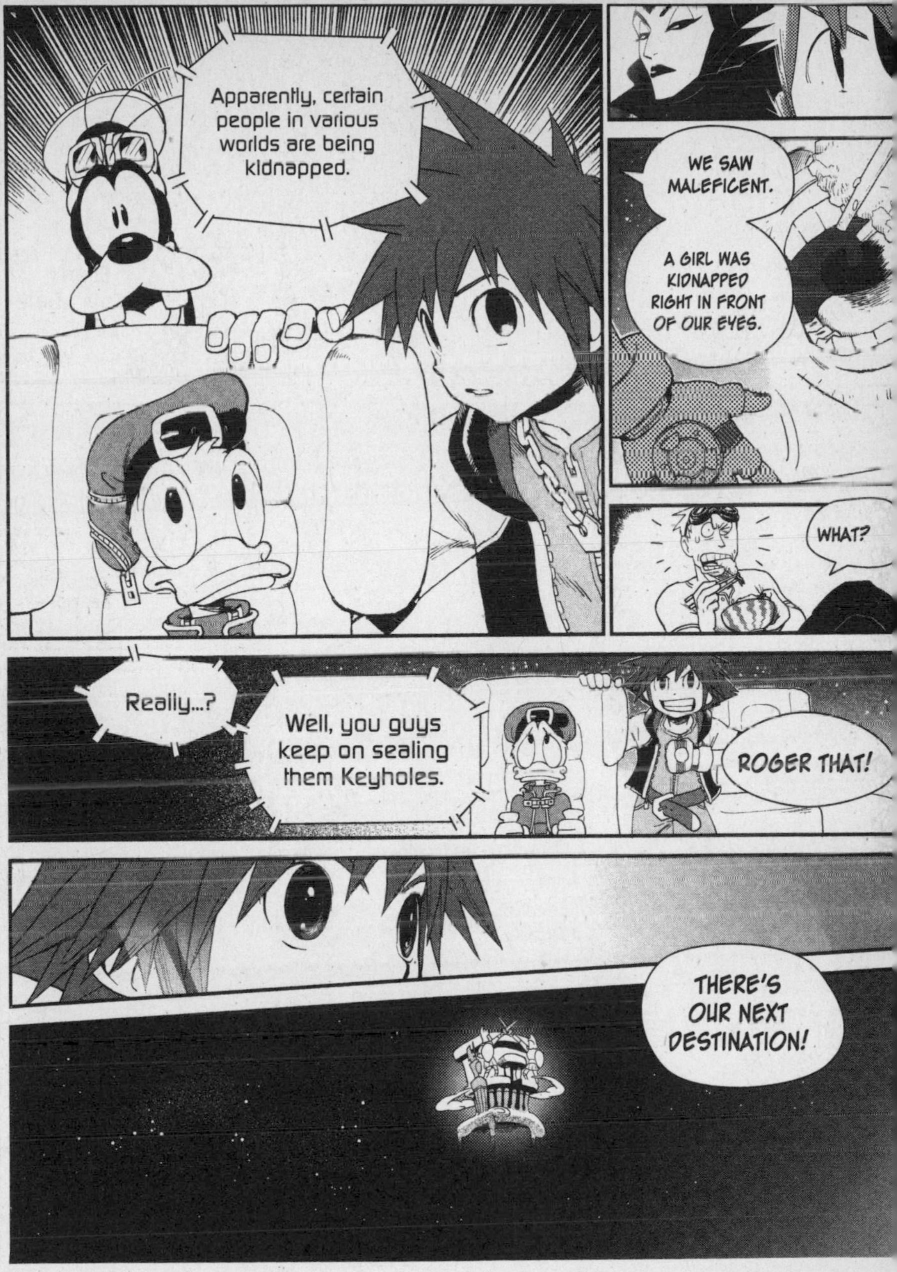
Apparently, certain people in various worlds are being kidnapped.
WE SAW MALEFICENT.
A GIRL WAS KIDNAPPED RIGHT IN FRONT OF OUR EYES.
WHAT?
Really...?
Well, you guys keep on sealing them Keyholes.
ROGER THAT!
THERE'S OUR NEXT DESTINATION!

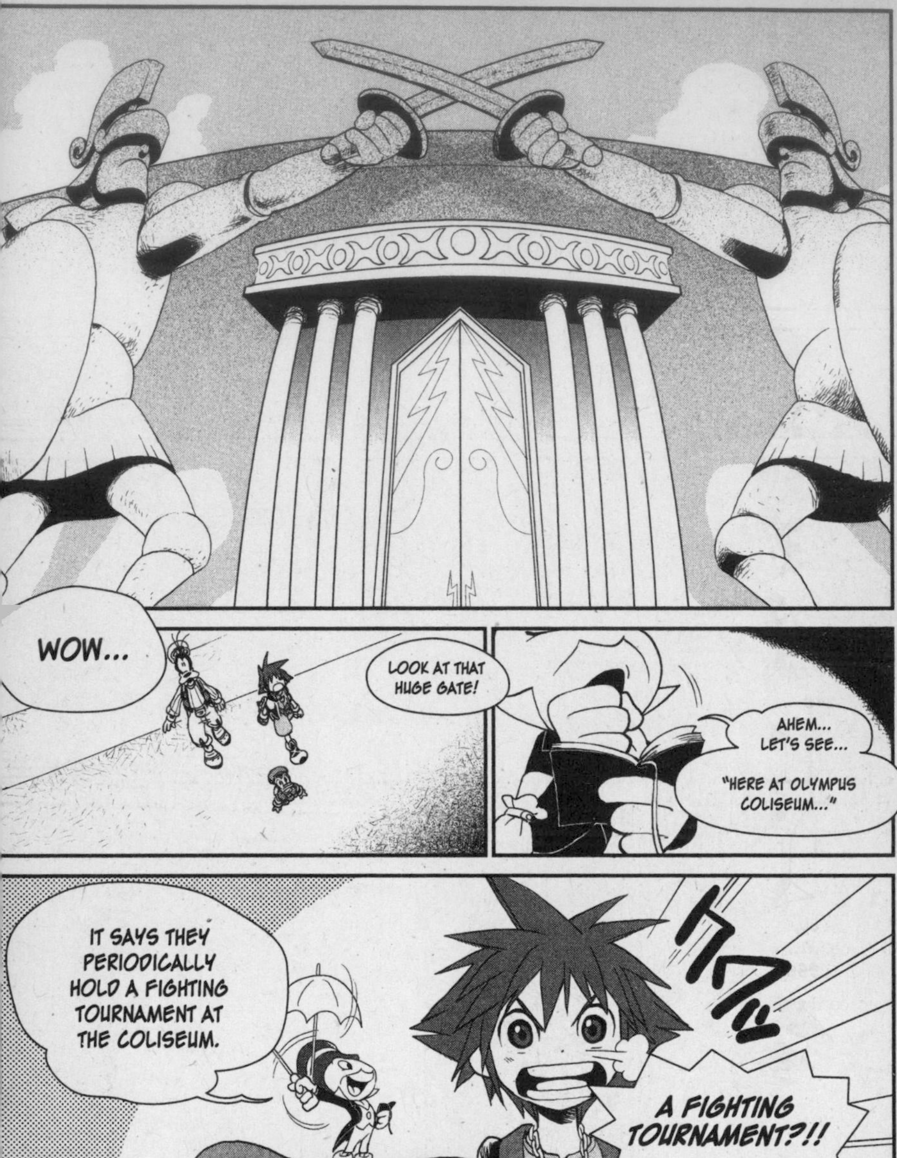
WOW...
LOOK AT THAT HUGE GATE!
AHEM... LET'S SEE...
"HERE AT OLYMPUS COLISEUM..."
IT SAYS THEY PERIODICALLY HOLD A FIGHTING TOURNAMENT AT THE COLISEUM.
A FIGHTING TOURNAMENT?!!
?!

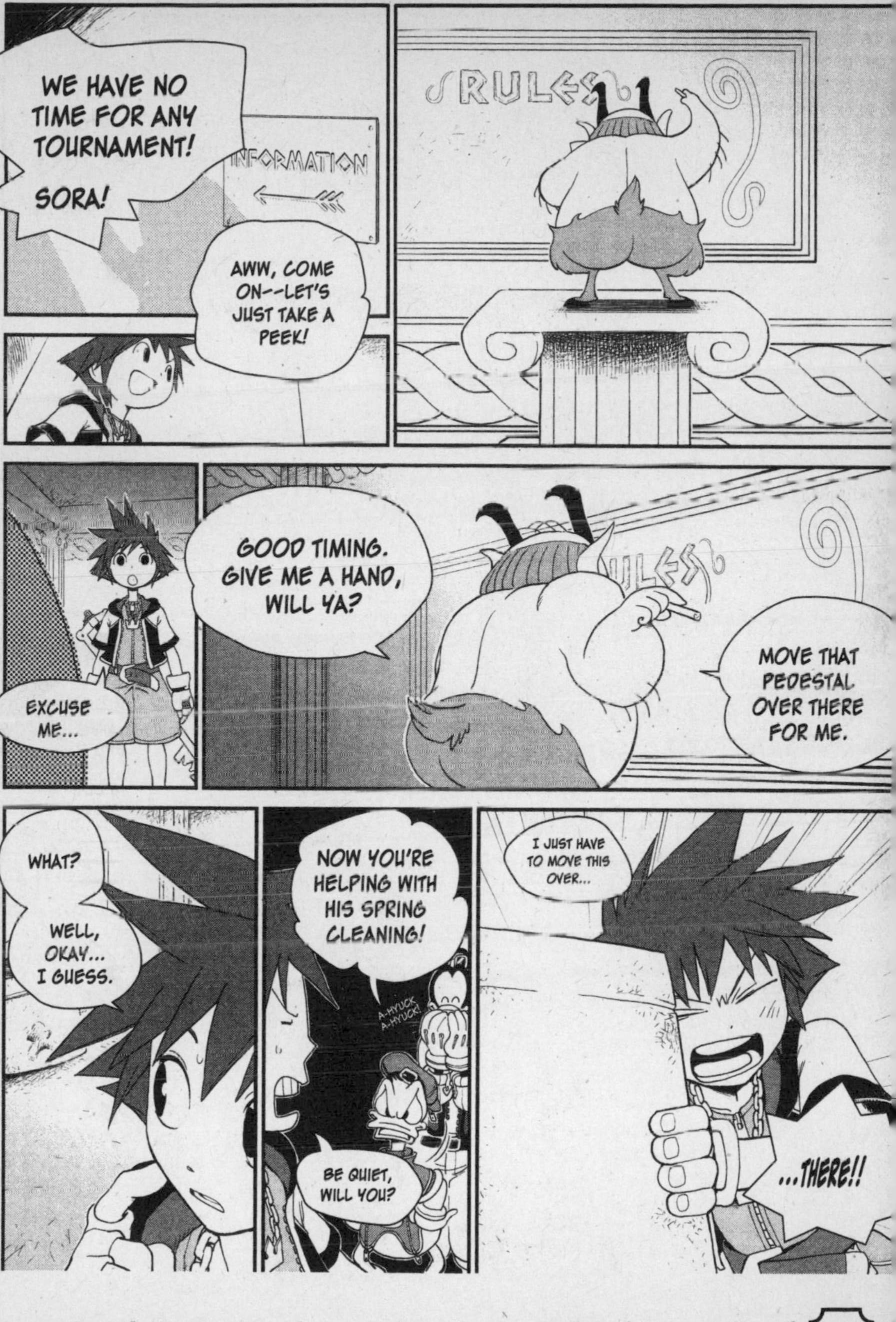

WE HAVE NO TIME FOR ANY TOURNAMENT!
SORA!
INFORMATION
AWW, COME ON--LET'S JUST TAKE A PEEK!
RULES
GOOD TIMING. GIVE ME A HAND, WILL YA?
EXCUSE ME...
RULES
MOVE THAT PEDESTAL OVER THERE FOR ME.
WHAT?
WELL, OKAY... I GUESS.
NOW YOU'RE HELPING WITH HIS SPRING CLEANING!
A-HYUCK A-HYUCK!
BE QUIET, WILL YOU?
I JUST HAVE TO MOVE THIS OVER...
...THERE!!

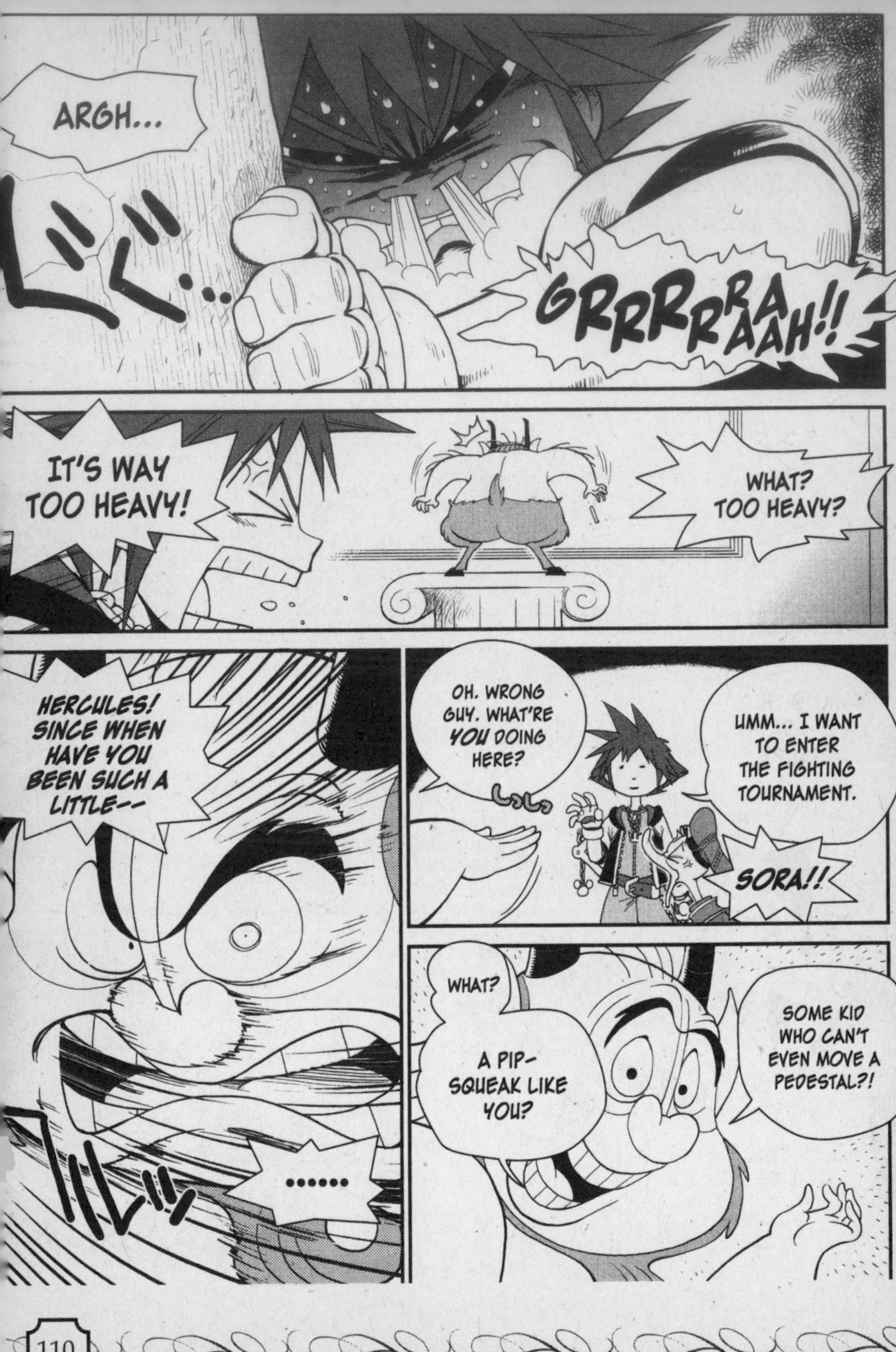
ARGH...
GRRRRRAAH!!
IT'S WAY TOO HEAVY!
WHAT? TOO HEAVY?
HERCULES! SINCE WHEN HAVE YOU BEEN SUCH A LITTLE--
......
OH. WRONG GUY. WHAT'RE *YOU* DOING HERE?
UMM... I WANT TO ENTER THE FIGHTING TOURNAMENT.
SORA!!
WHAT?
A PIP-SQUEAK LIKE YOU?
SOME KID WHO CAN'T EVEN MOVE A PEDESTAL?!

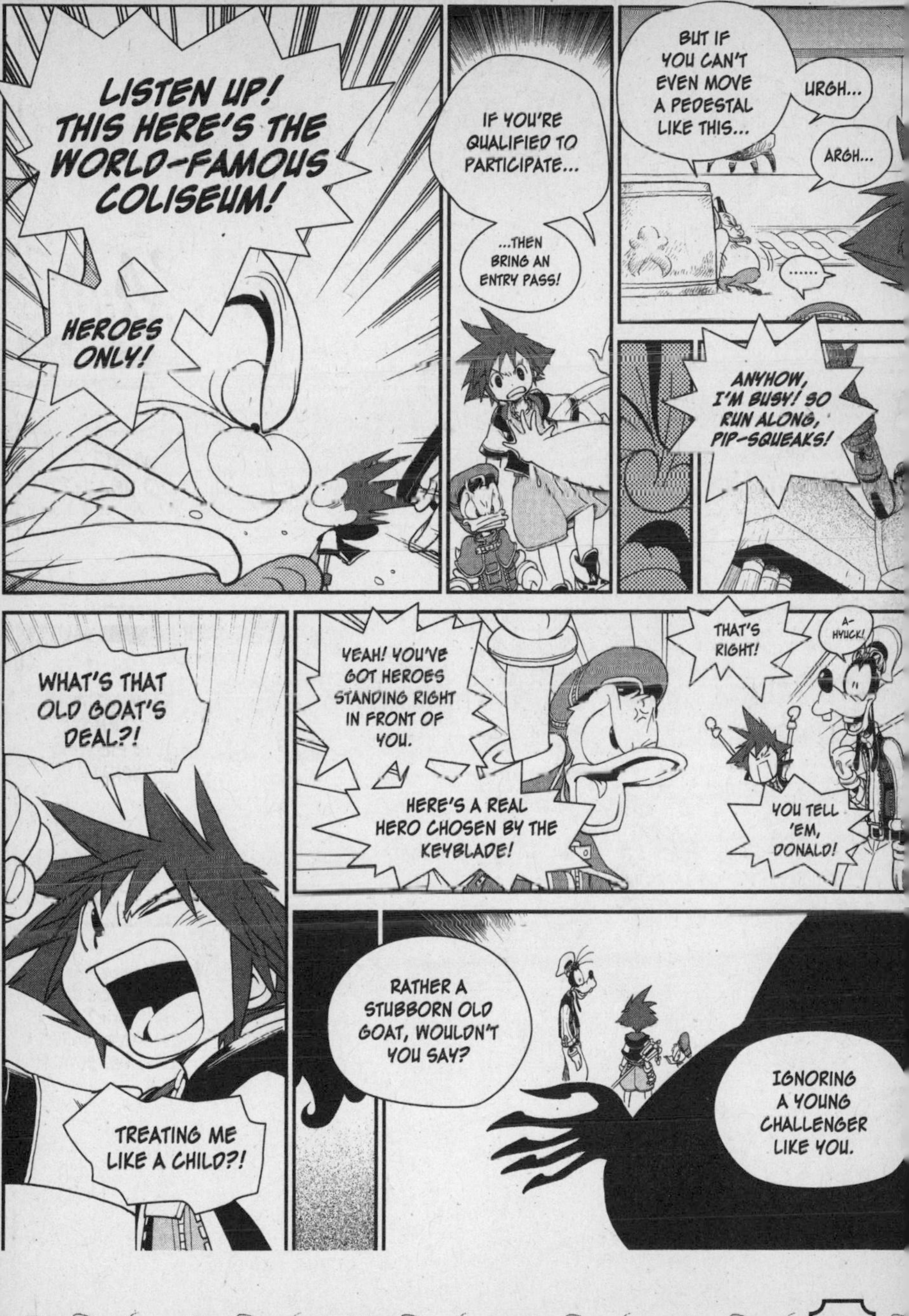
LISTEN UP! THIS HERE'S THE WORLD-FAMOUS COLISEUM!
HEROES ONLY!
IF YOU'RE QUALIFIED TO PARTICIPATE...
...THEN BRING AN ENTRY PASS!
BUT IF YOU CAN'T EVEN MOVE A PEDESTAL LIKE THIS...
URGH...
ARGH...
......
ANYHOW, I'M BUSY! SO RUN ALONG, PIP-SQUEAKS!
WHAT'S THAT OLD GOAT'S DEAL?!
TREATING ME LIKE A CHILD?!
YEAH! YOU'VE GOT HEROES STANDING RIGHT IN FRONT OF YOU.
HERE'S A REAL HERO CHOSEN BY THE KEYBLADE!
THAT'S RIGHT!
A-HYUCK!
YOU TELL 'EM, DONALD!
RATHER A STUBBORN OLD GOAT, WOULDN'T YOU SAY?
IGNORING A YOUNG CHALLENGER LIKE YOU.

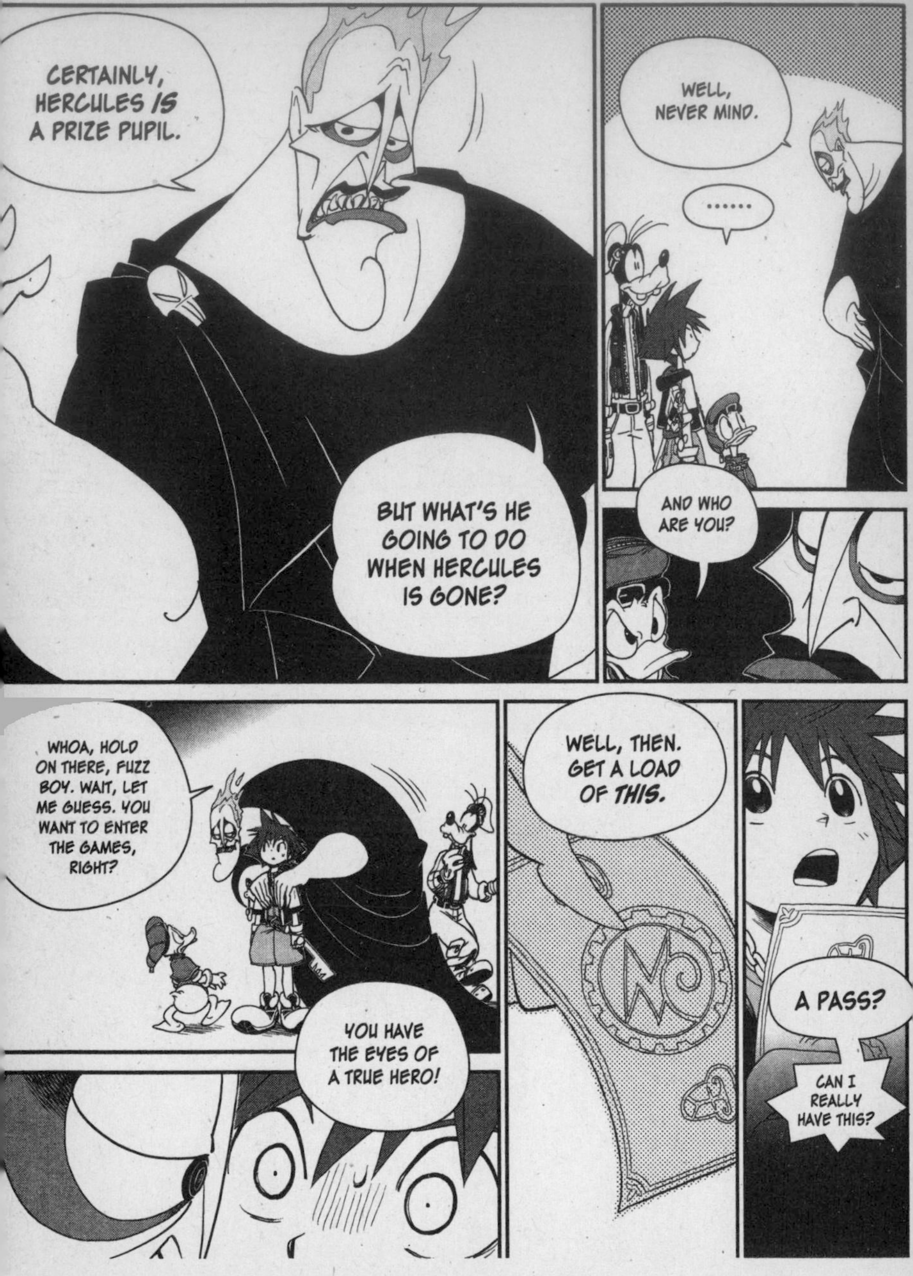
CERTAINLY, HERCULES *IS* A PRIZE PUPIL.
BUT WHAT'S HE GOING TO DO WHEN HERCULES IS GONE?
WELL, NEVER MIND.
......
AND WHO ARE YOU?
WHOA, HOLD ON THERE, FUZZ BOY. WAIT, LET ME GUESS. YOU WANT TO ENTER THE GAMES, RIGHT?
YOU HAVE THE EYES OF A TRUE HERO!
WELL, THEN. GET A LOAD OF *THIS.*
A PASS?
CAN I REALLY HAVE THIS?

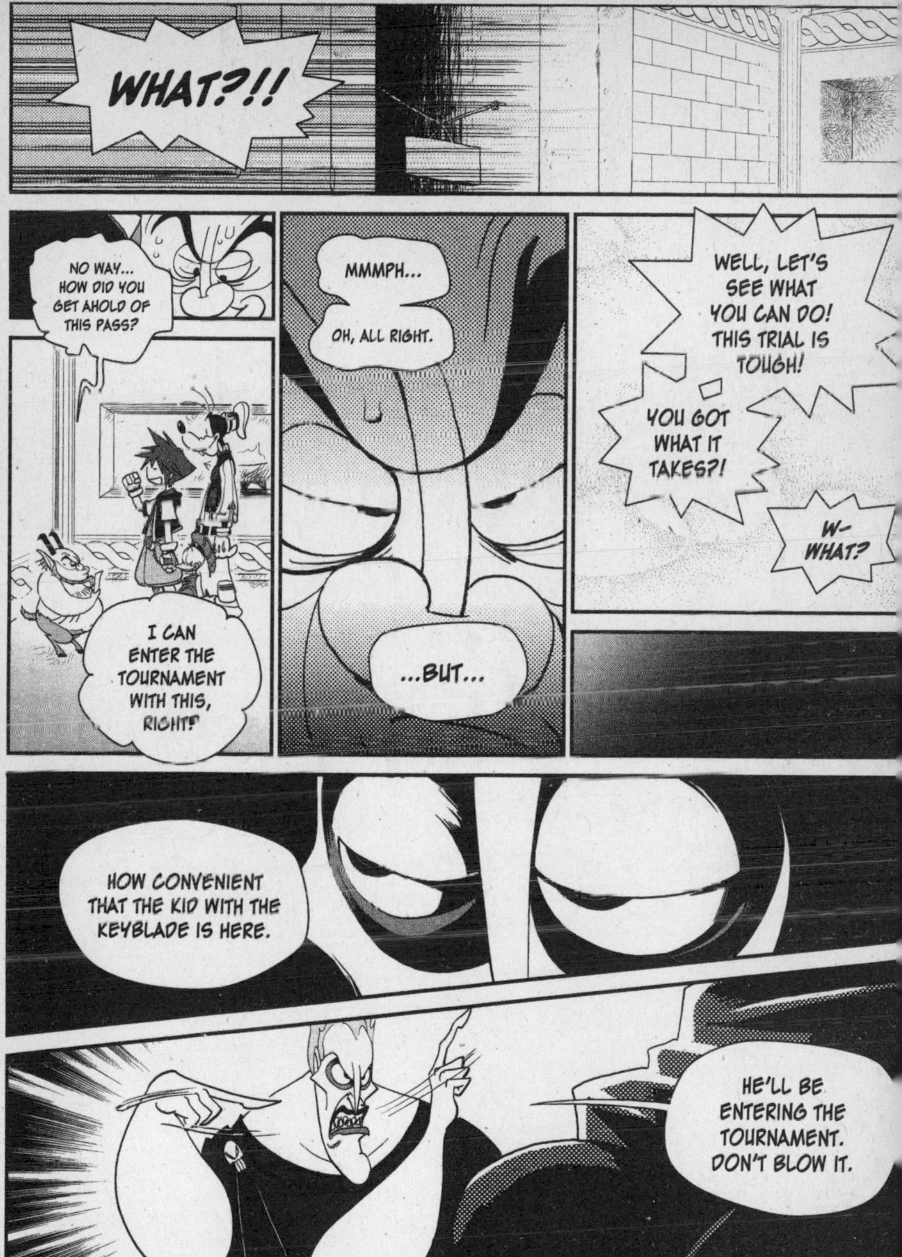
WHAT?!!
NO WAY... HOW DID YOU GET AHOLD OF THIS PASS?
I CAN ENTER THE TOURNAMENT WITH THIS, RIGHT?
MMMPH...
OH, ALL RIGHT.
...BUT...
WELL, LET'S SEE WHAT YOU CAN DO! THIS TRIAL IS TOUGH!
YOU GOT WHAT IT TAKES?!
W-WHAT?
HOW CONVENIENT THAT THE KID WITH THE KEYBLADE IS HERE.
HE'LL BE ENTERING THE TOURNAMENT. DON'T BLOW IT.

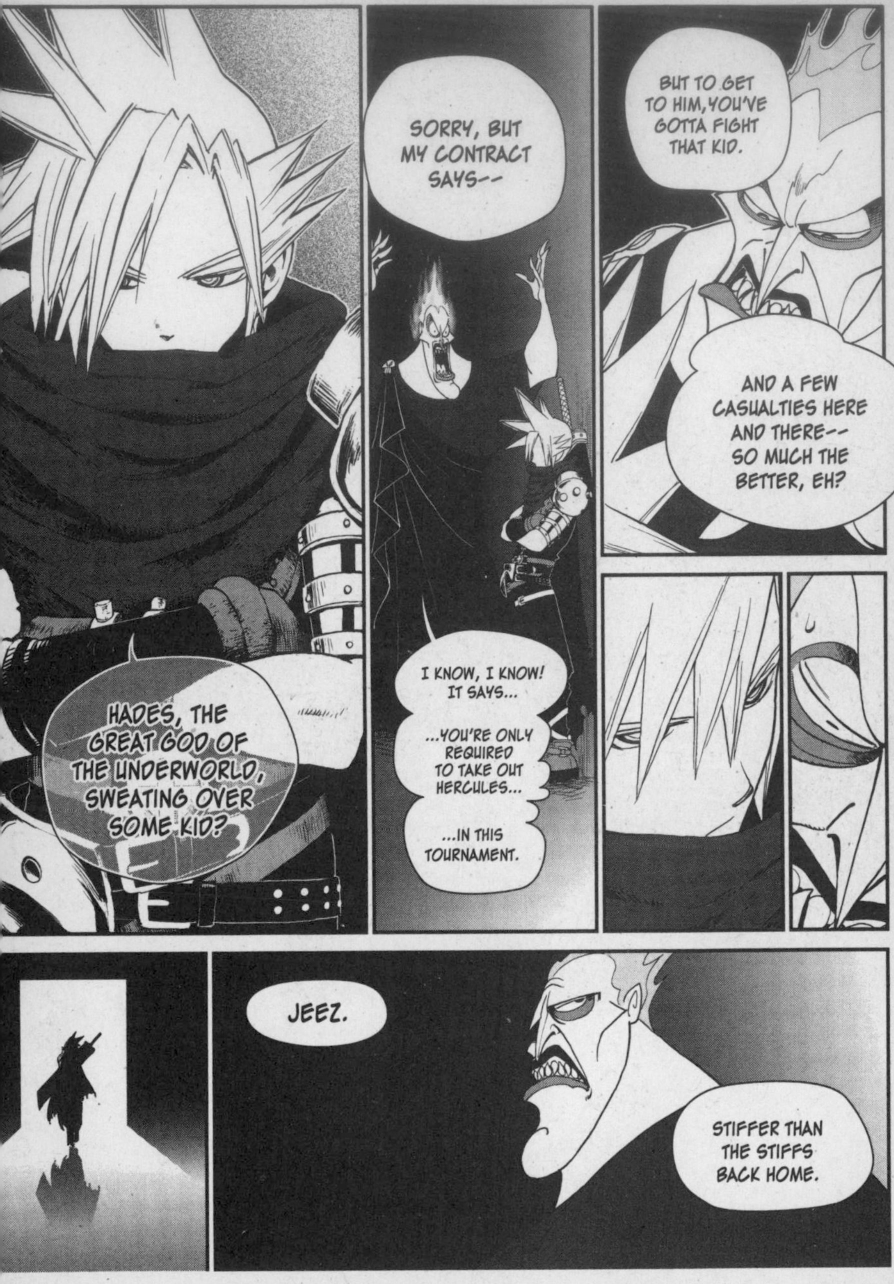
HADES, THE GREAT GOD OF THE UNDERWORLD, SWEATING OVER SOME KID?
SORRY, BUT MY CONTRACT SAYS--
I KNOW, I KNOW! IT SAYS...
...YOU'RE ONLY REQUIRED TO TAKE OUT HERCULES...
...IN THIS TOURNAMENT.
BUT TO GET TO HIM, YOU'VE GOTTA FIGHT THAT KID.
AND A FEW CASUALTIES HERE AND THERE-- SO MUCH THE BETTER, EH?
JEEZ.
STIFFER THAN THE STIFFS BACK HOME.

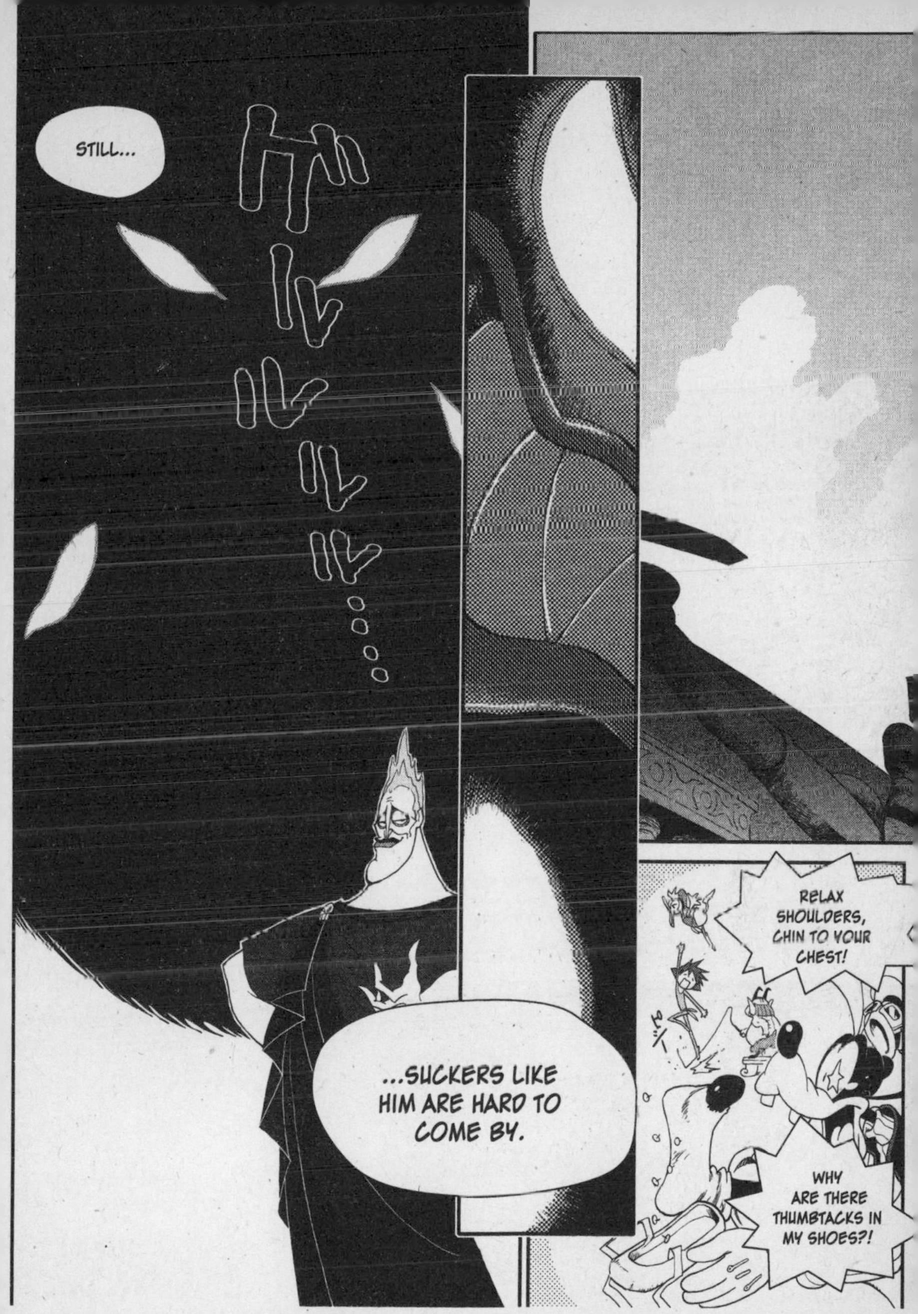

STILL...
ガルルルル...
...SUCKERS LIKE HIM ARE HARD TO COME BY.
RELAX SHOULDERS, CHIN TO YOUR CHEST!
WHY ARE THERE THUMBTACKS IN MY SHOES?!

Episode 25

That's What a Hero's All About

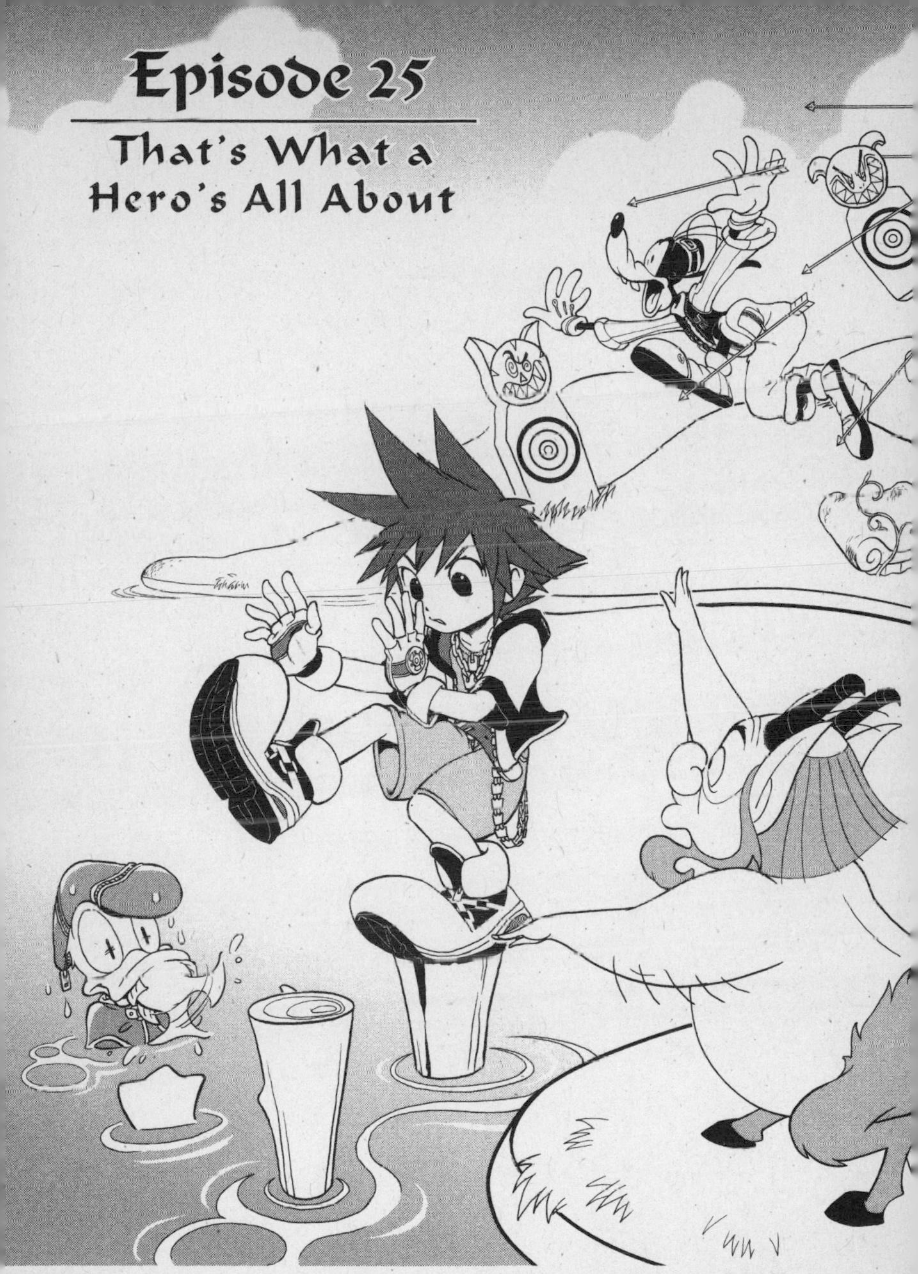

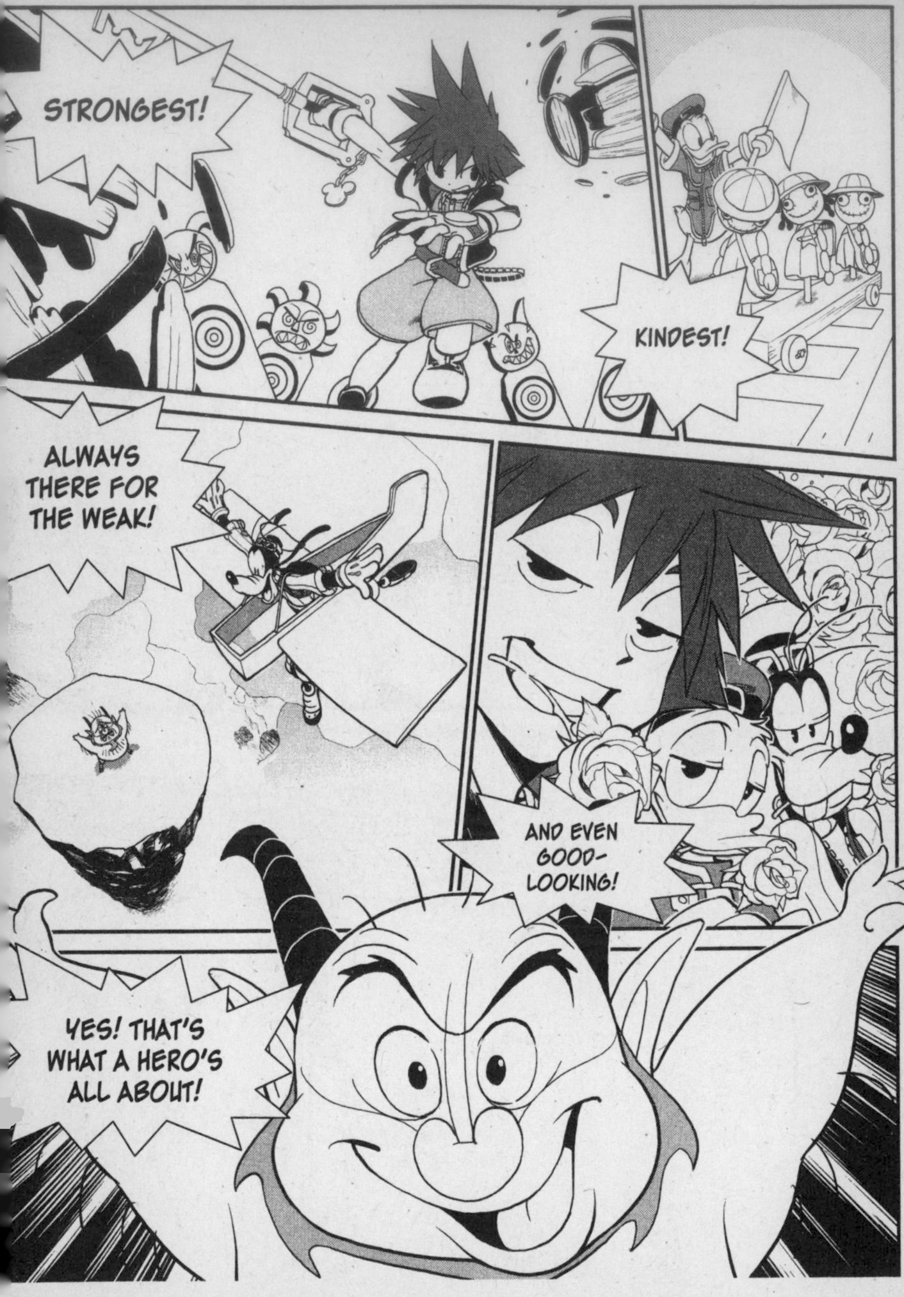
STRONGEST!
KINDEST!
ALWAYS THERE FOR THE WEAK!
AND EVEN GOOD-LOOKING!
YES! THAT'S WHAT A HERO'S ALL ABOUT!

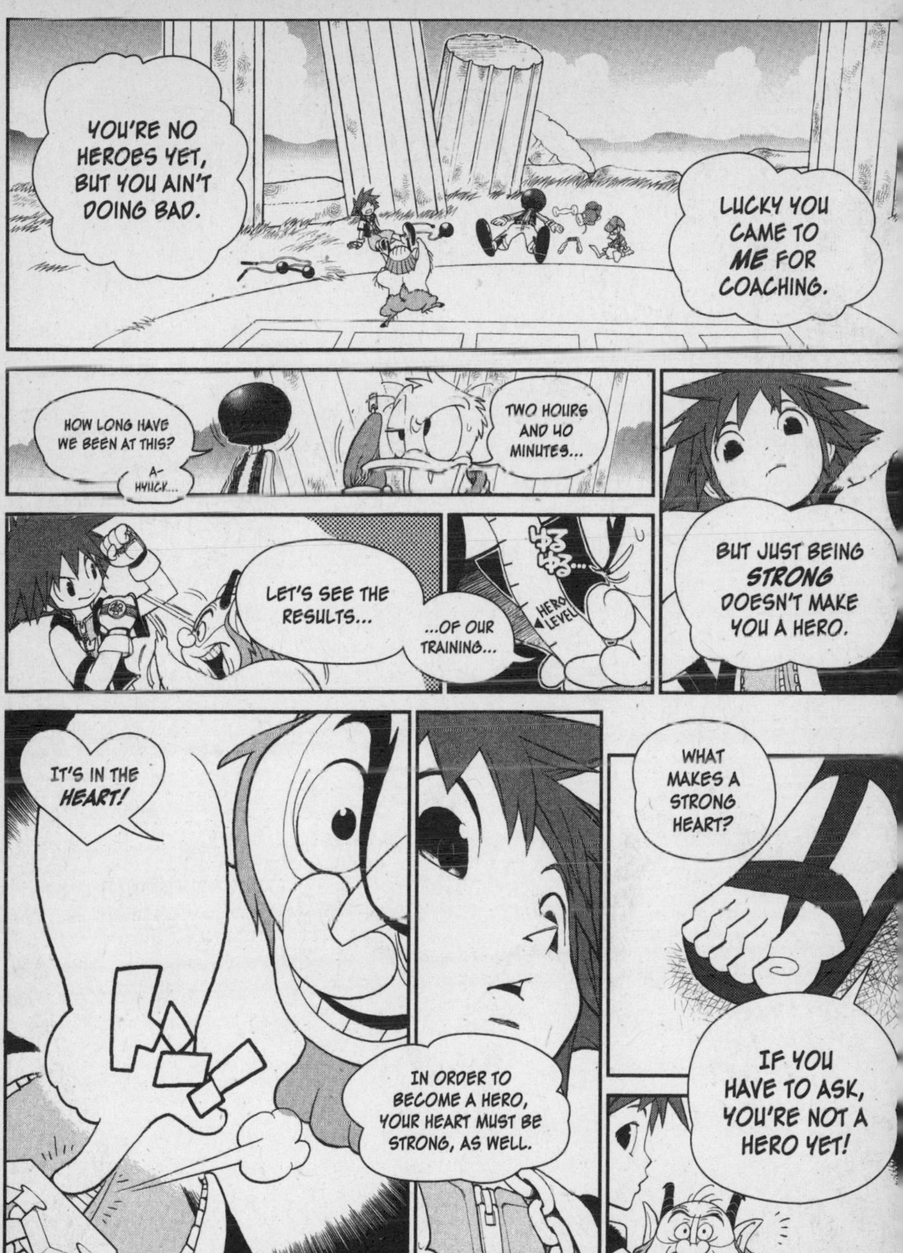
YOU'RE NO HEROES YET, BUT YOU AIN'T DOING BAD.
LUCKY YOU CAME TO *ME* FOR COACHING.
HOW LONG HAVE WE BEEN AT THIS?
A-HYUCK...
TWO HOURS AND 40 MINUTES...
LET'S SEE THE RESULTS...
...OF OUR TRAINING...
ゆるゆる...
HERO LEVEL
BUT JUST BEING *STRONG* DOESN'T MAKE YOU A HERO.
IT'S IN THE *HEART!*
IN ORDER TO BECOME A HERO, YOUR HEART MUST BE STRONG, AS WELL.
WHAT MAKES A STRONG HEART?
IF YOU HAVE TO ASK, YOU'RE NOT A HERO YET!

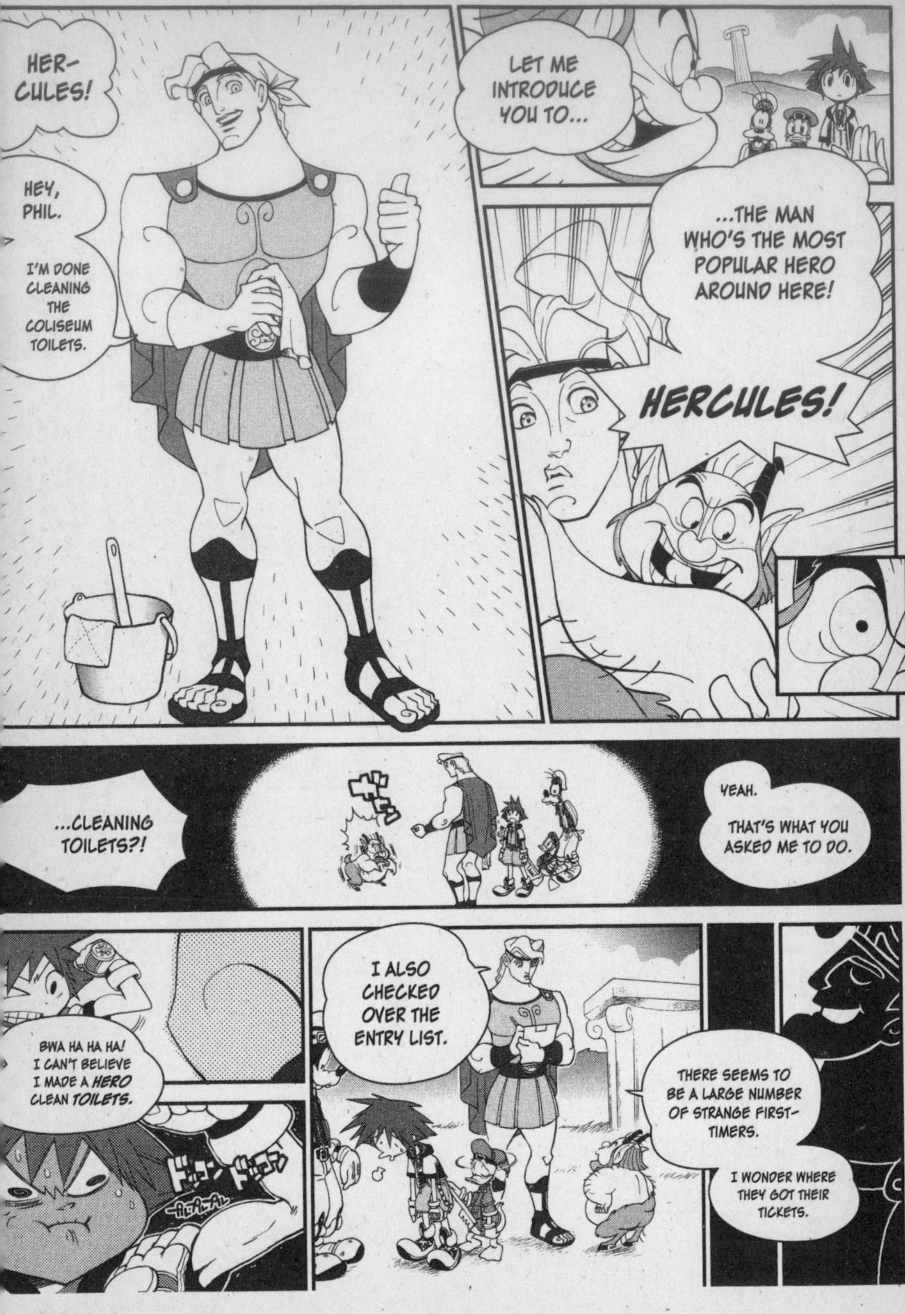
HER-CULES!
HEY, PHIL.
I'M DONE CLEANING THE COLISEUM TOILETS.
LET ME INTRODUCE YOU TO...
...THE MAN WHO'S THE MOST POPULAR HERO AROUND HERE!
HERCULES!
...CLEANING TOILETS?!
YEAH.
THAT'S WHAT YOU ASKED ME TO DO.
BWA HA HA HA! I CAN'T BELIEVE I MADE A *HERO* CLEAN *TOILETS*.
I ALSO CHECKED OVER THE ENTRY LIST.
THERE SEEMS TO BE A LARGE NUMBER OF STRANGE FIRST-TIMERS.
I WONDER WHERE THEY GOT THEIR TICKETS.

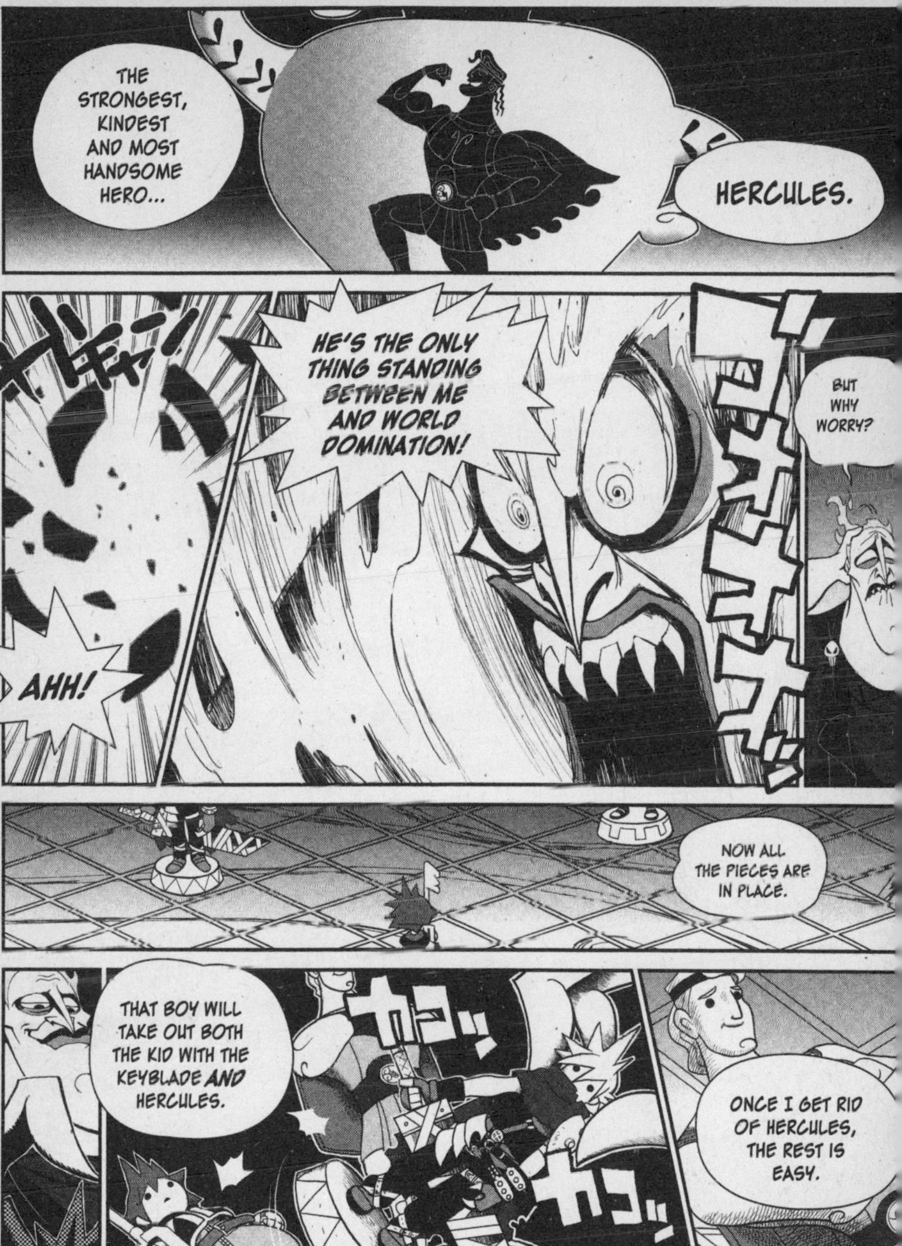
THE STRONGEST, KINDEST AND MOST HANDSOME HERO...
HERCULES.
HE'S THE ONLY THING STANDING BETWEEN ME AND WORLD DOMINATION!
AHH!
BUT WHY WORRY?
NOW ALL THE PIECES ARE IN PLACE.
THAT BOY WILL TAKE OUT BOTH THE KID WITH THE KEYBLADE *AND* HERCULES.
カコッ
カコッ
ONCE I GET RID OF HERCULES, THE REST IS EASY.

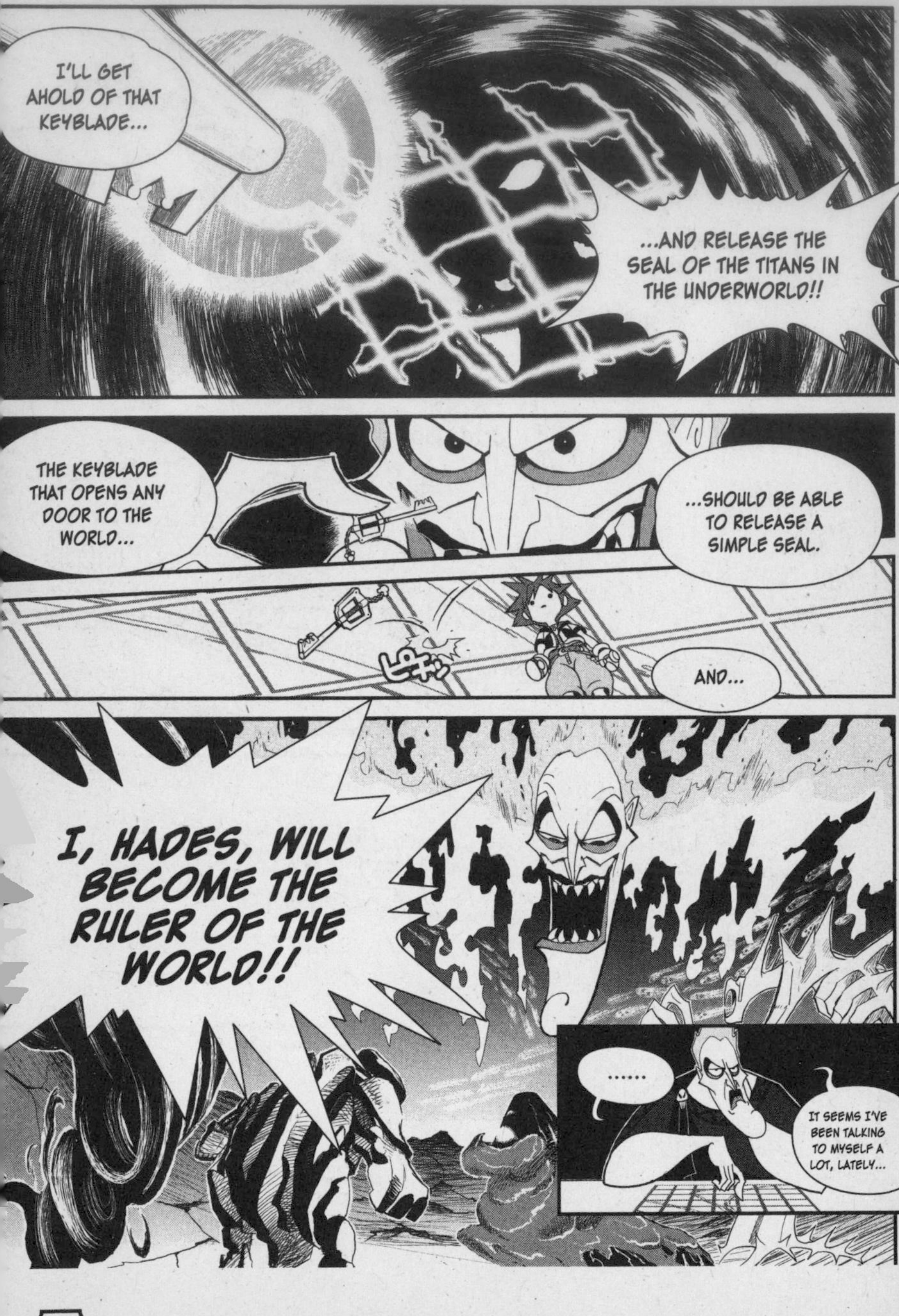
I'LL GET AHOLD OF THAT KEYBLADE...
...AND RELEASE THE SEAL OF THE TITANS IN THE UNDERWORLD!!
THE KEYBLADE THAT OPENS ANY DOOR TO THE WORLD...
...SHOULD BE ABLE TO RELEASE A SIMPLE SEAL.
AND...
I, HADES, WILL BECOME THE RULER OF THE WORLD!!
......
IT SEEMS I'VE BEEN TALKING TO MYSELF A LOT, LATELY...

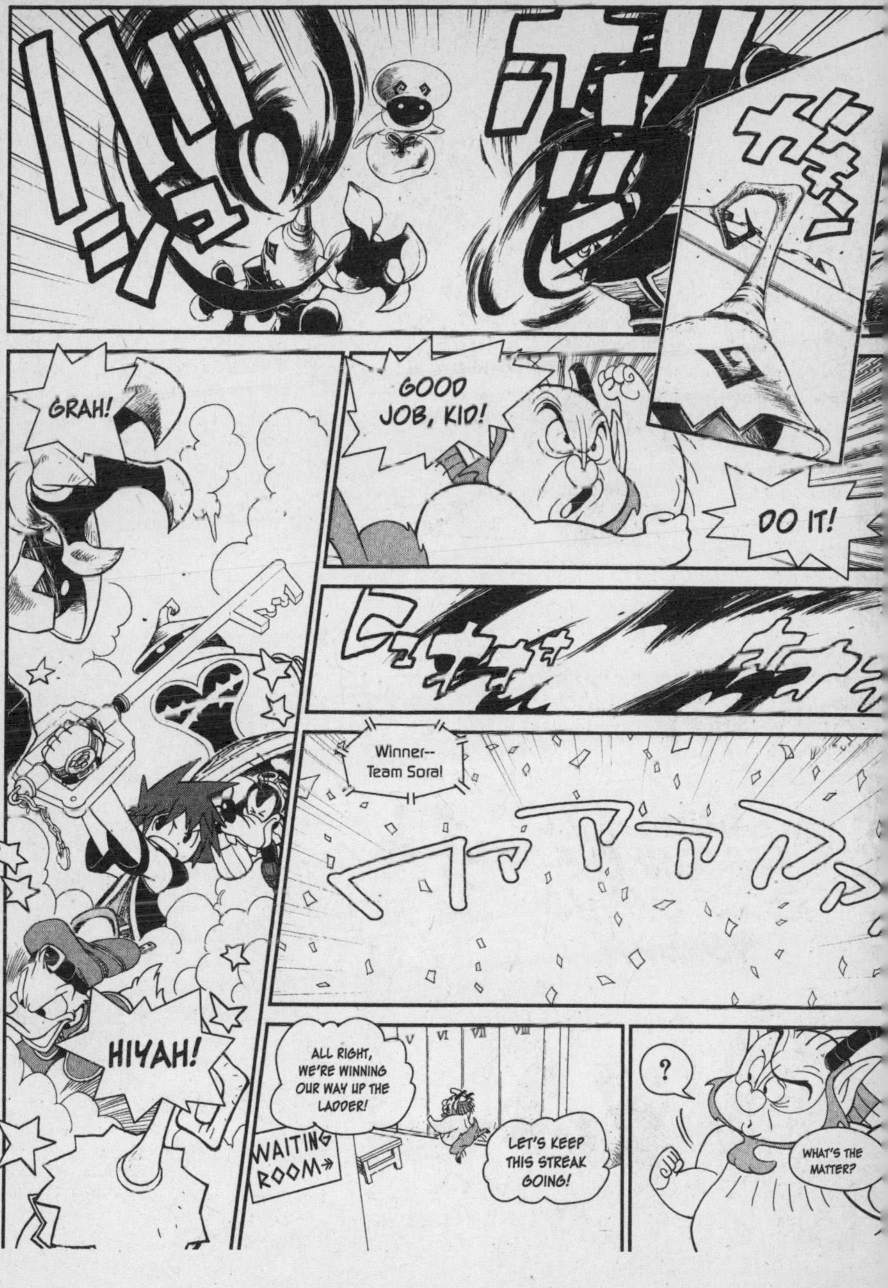
GRAH!
HIYAH!
GOOD JOB, KID!
DO IT!
Winner--Team Sora!
ALL RIGHT, WE'RE WINNING OUR WAY UP THE LADDER!
WAITING ROOM→
LET'S KEEP THIS STREAK GOING!
?
WHAT'S THE MATTER?

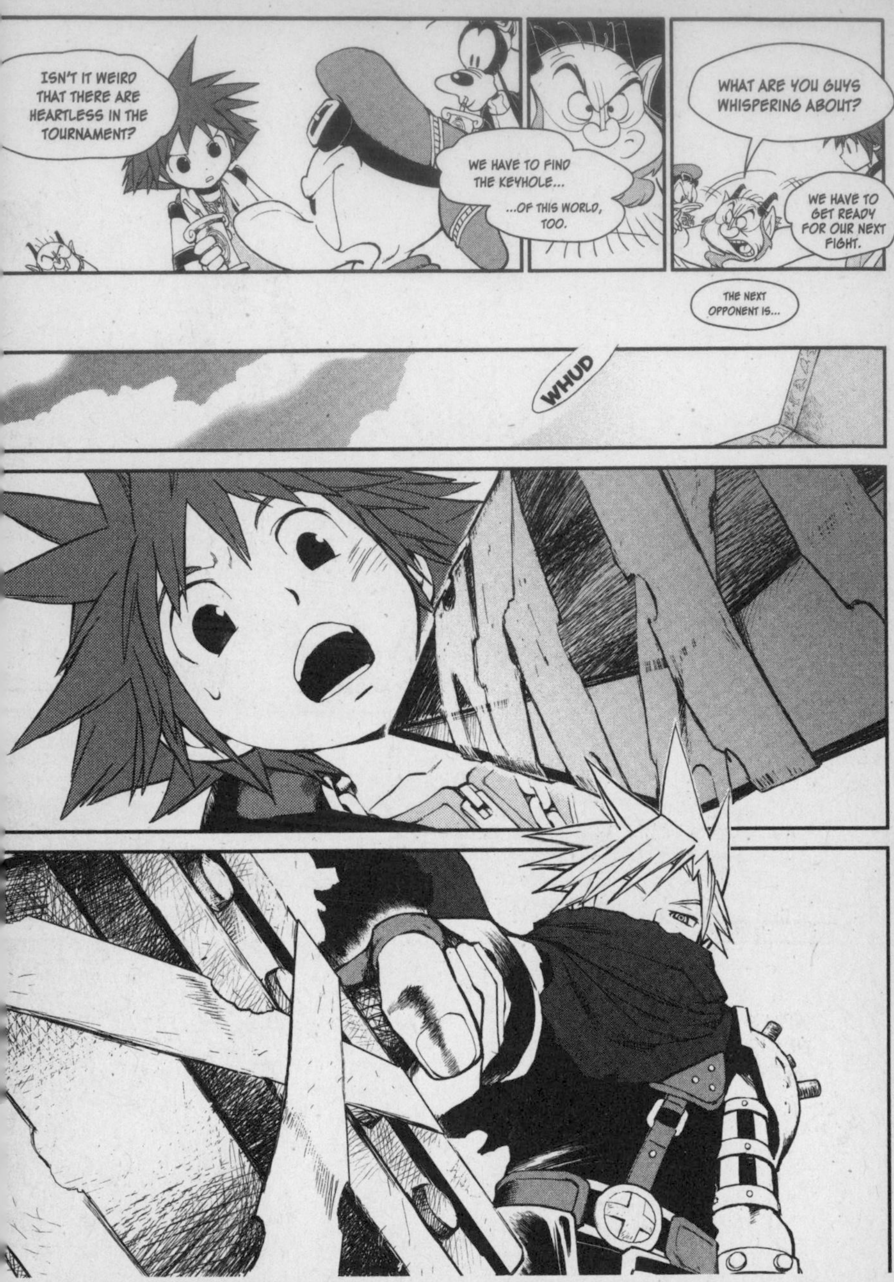
ISN'T IT WEIRD THAT THERE ARE HEARTLESS IN THE TOURNAMENT?
WE HAVE TO FIND THE KEYHOLE...
...OF THIS WORLD, TOO.
WHAT ARE YOU GUYS WHISPERING ABOUT?
WE HAVE TO GET READY FOR OUR NEXT FIGHT.
THE NEXT OPPONENT IS...
WHUD

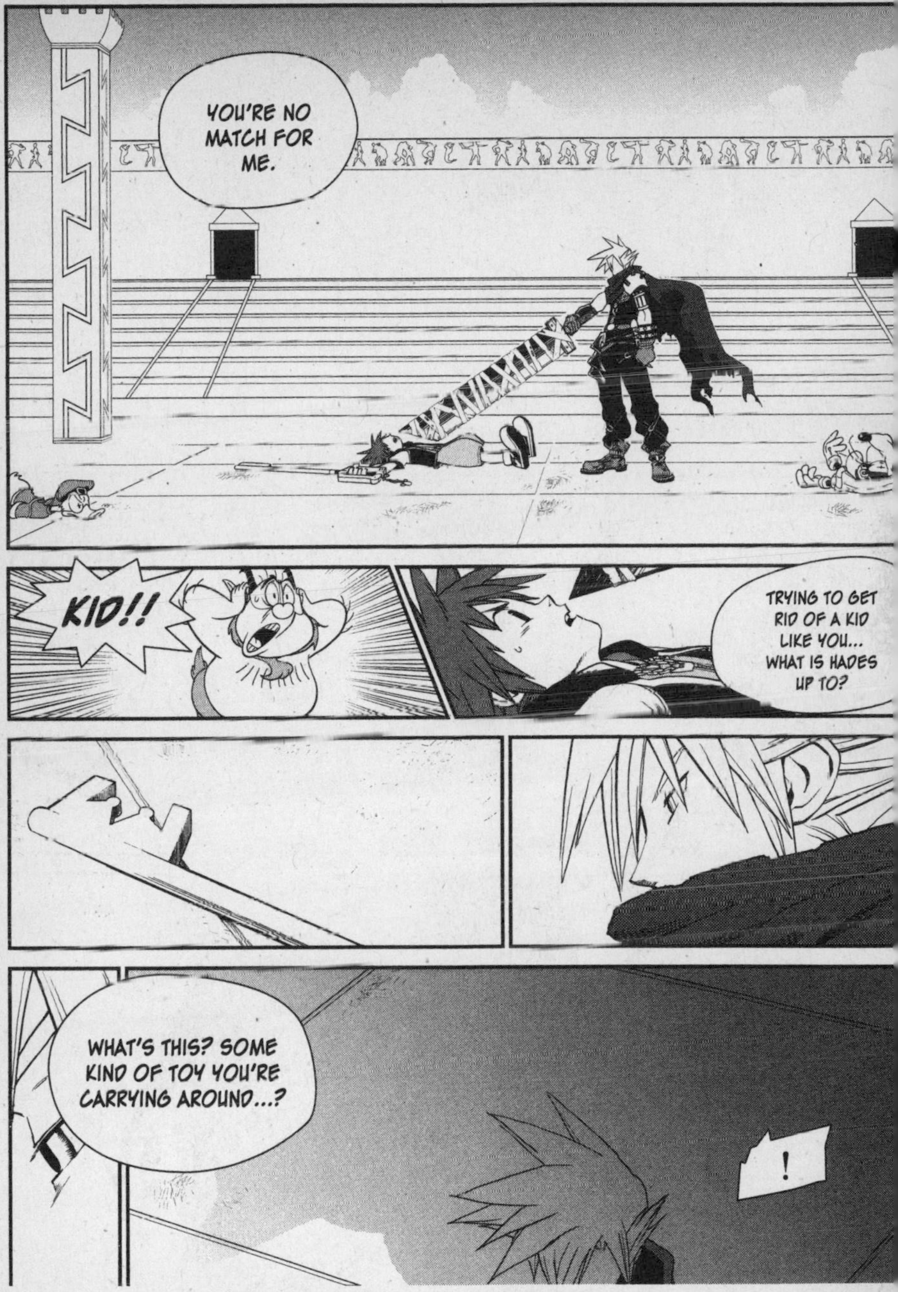
YOU'RE NO MATCH FOR ME.
KID!!
TRYING TO GET RID OF A KID LIKE YOU... WHAT IS HADES UP TO?
WHAT'S THIS? SOME KIND OF TOY YOU'RE CARRYING AROUND...?
!

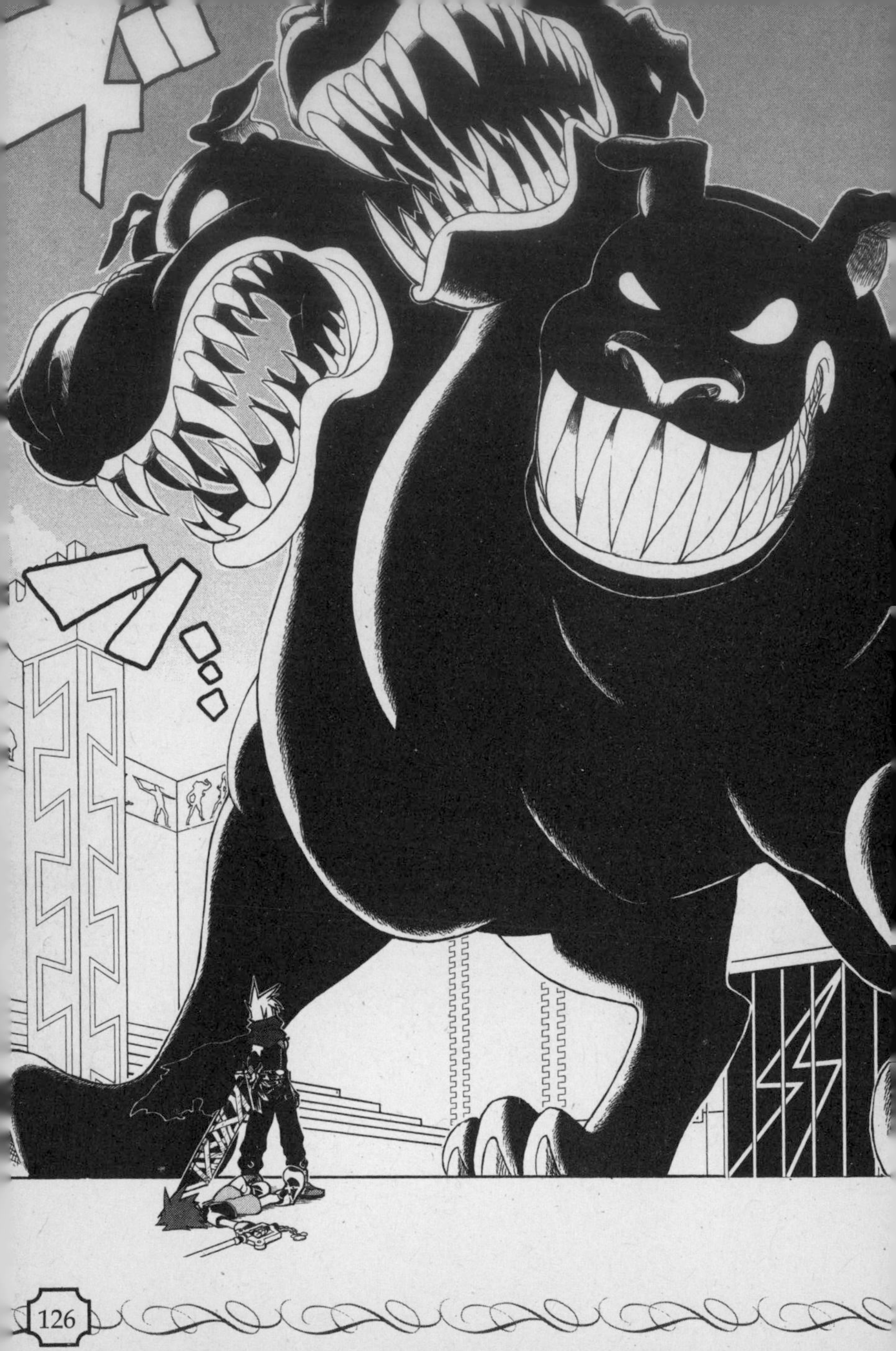

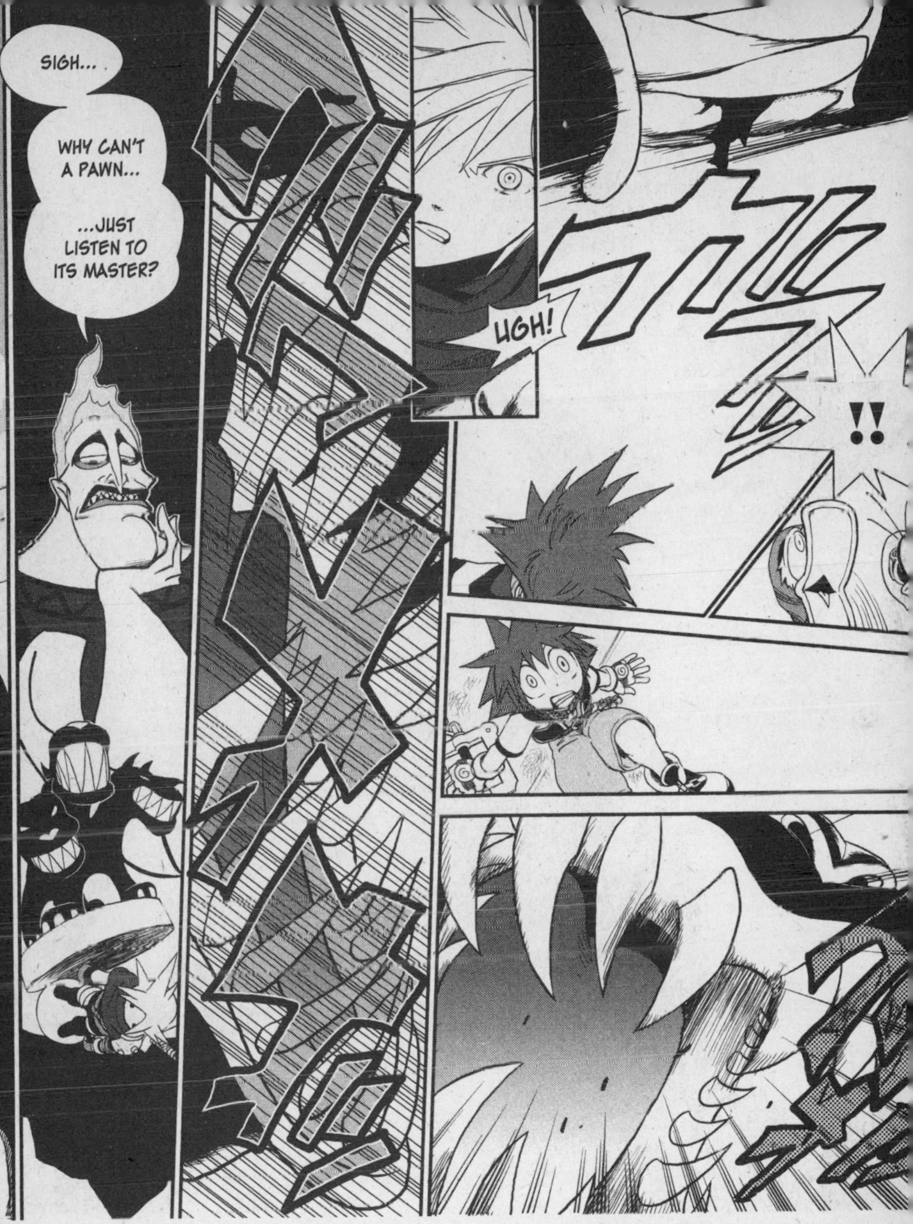
SIGH...
WHY CAN'T A PAWN...
...JUST LISTEN TO ITS MASTER?
UGH!
!!

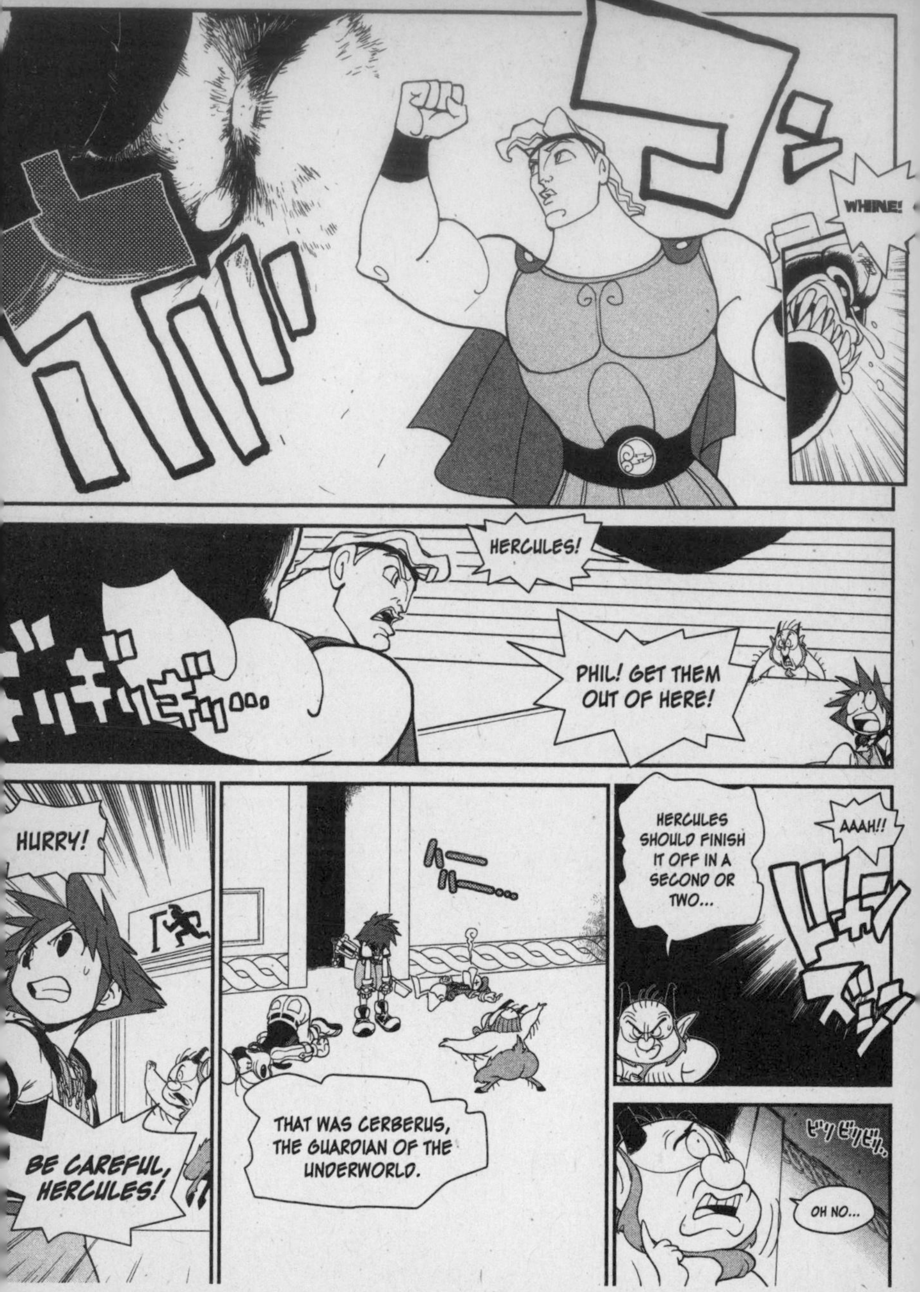
WHINE!
HERCULES!
PHIL! GET THEM OUT OF HERE!
HURRY!
BE CAREFUL, HERCULES!
THAT WAS CERBERUS, THE GUARDIAN OF THE UNDERWORLD.
HERCULES SHOULD FINISH IT OFF IN A SECOND OR TWO...
AAAH!!
OH NO...

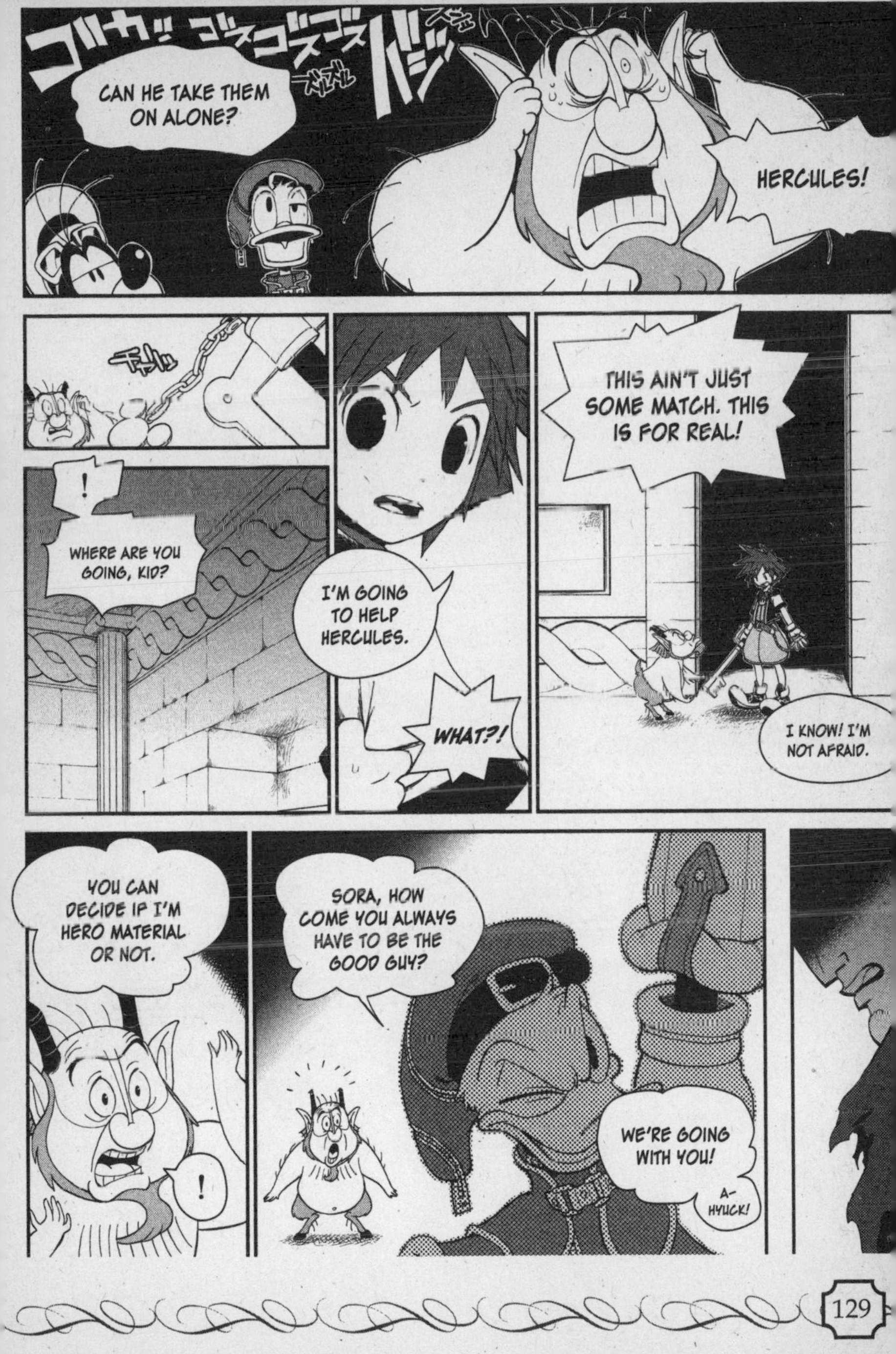
CAN HE TAKE THEM ON ALONE?
HERCULES!
!
WHERE ARE YOU GOING, KID?
I'M GOING TO HELP HERCULES.
WHAT?!
THIS AIN'T JUST SOME MATCH. THIS IS FOR REAL!
I KNOW! I'M NOT AFRAID.
YOU CAN DECIDE IF I'M HERO MATERIAL OR NOT.
!
SORA, HOW COME YOU ALWAYS HAVE TO BE THE GOOD GUY?
WE'RE GOING WITH YOU!
A-HYUCK!

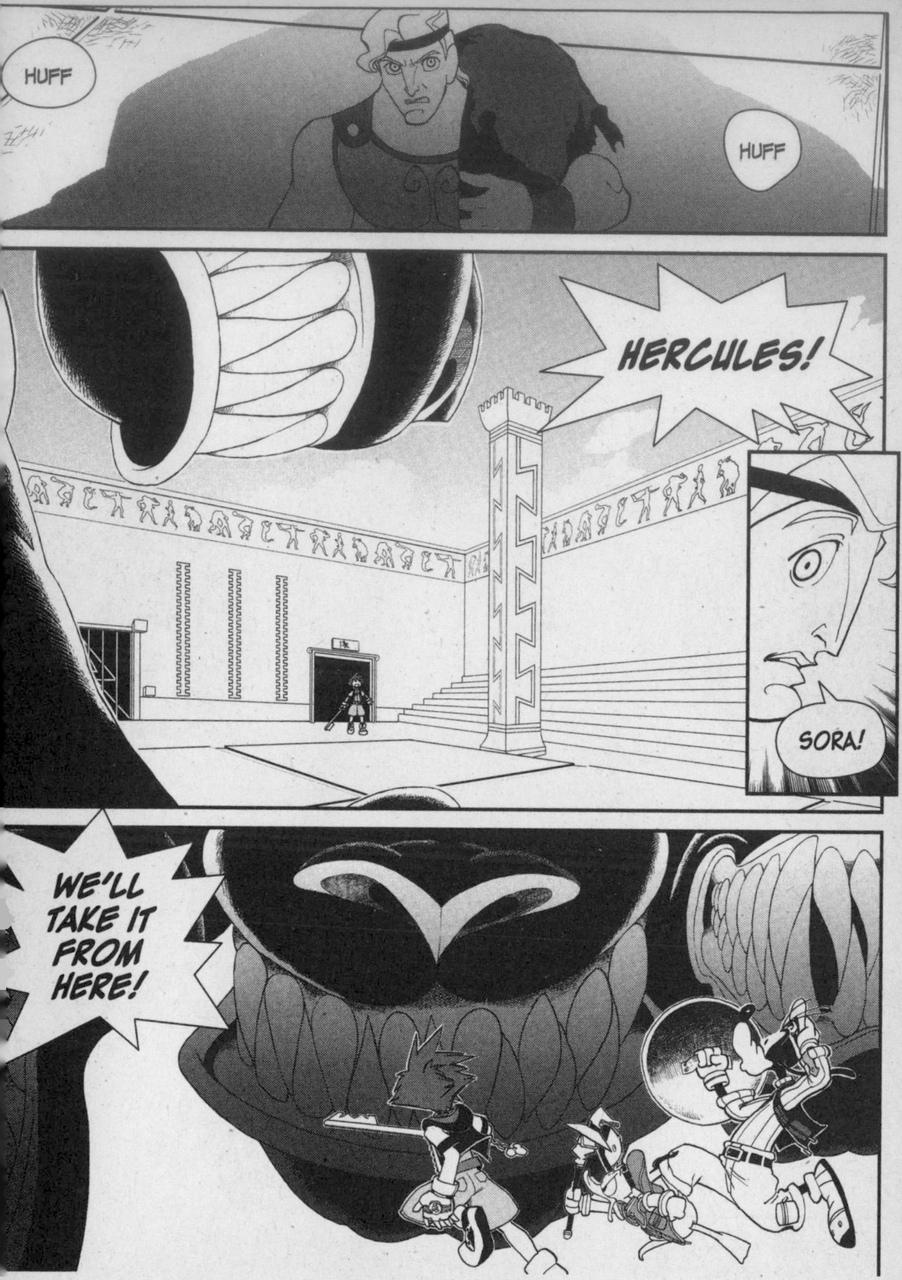

HUFF
HUFF
HERCULES!
SORA!
WE'LL TAKE IT FROM HERE!

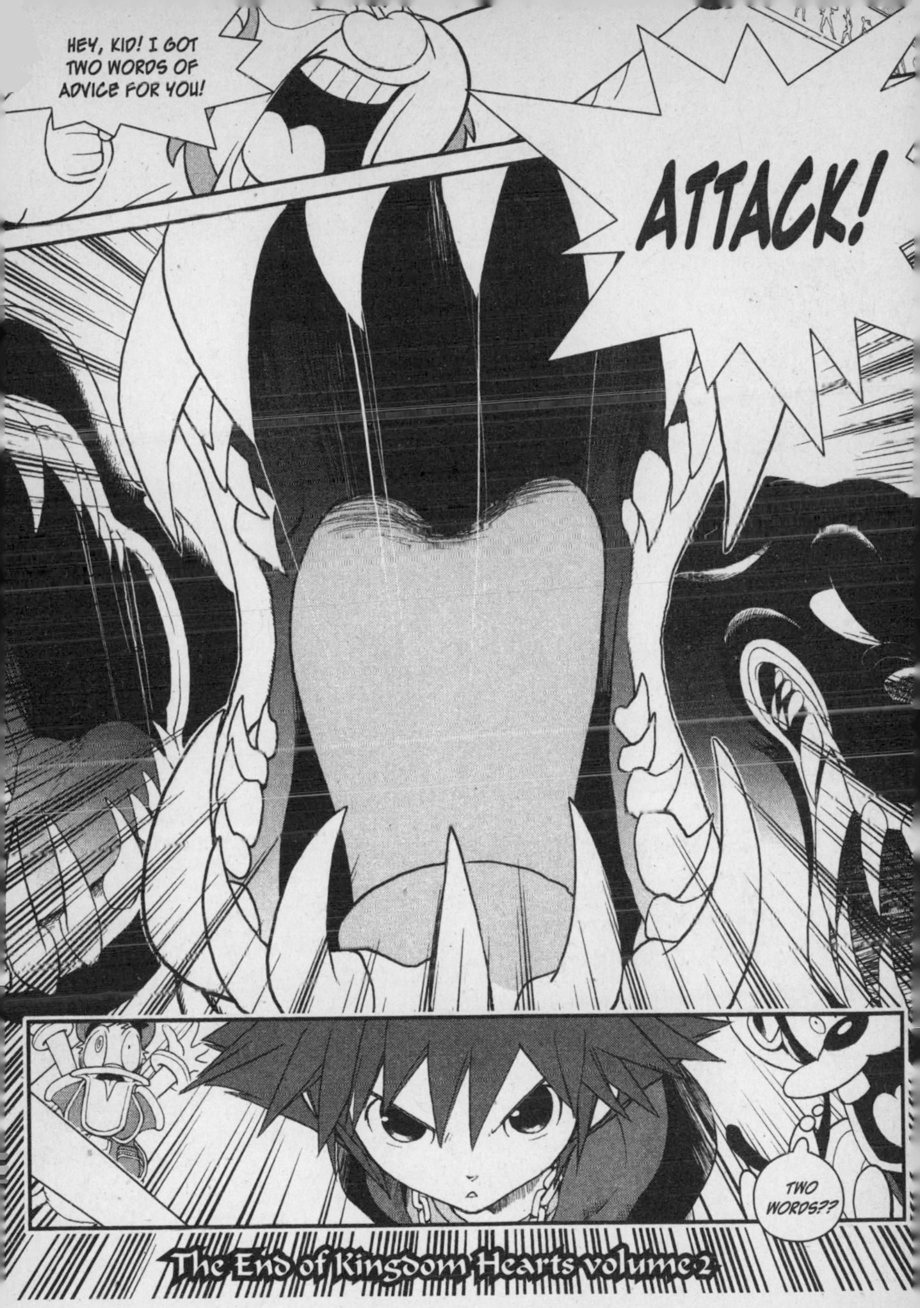
HEY, KID! I GOT TWO WORDS OF ADVICE FOR YOU!
ATTACK!
TWO WORDS??
The End of Kingdom Hearts volume 2

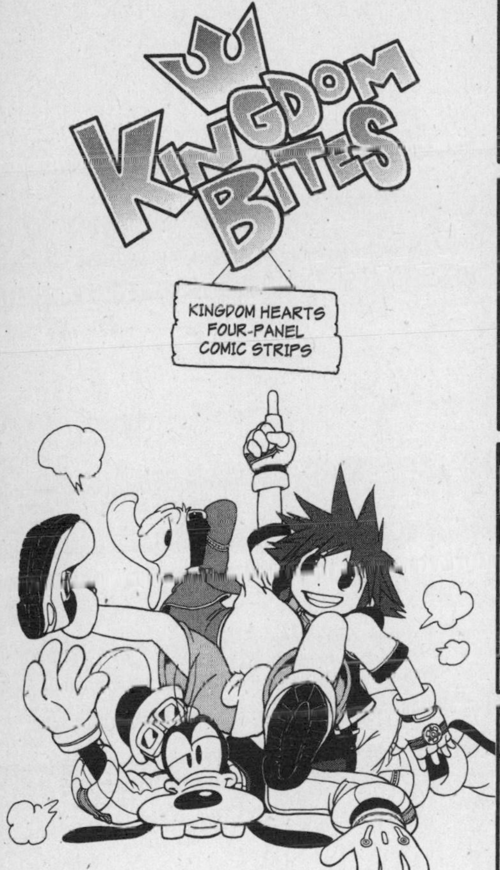
KINGDOM BITES
KINGDOM HEARTS FOUR-PANEL COMIC STRIPS

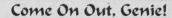

Come On Out, Genie!

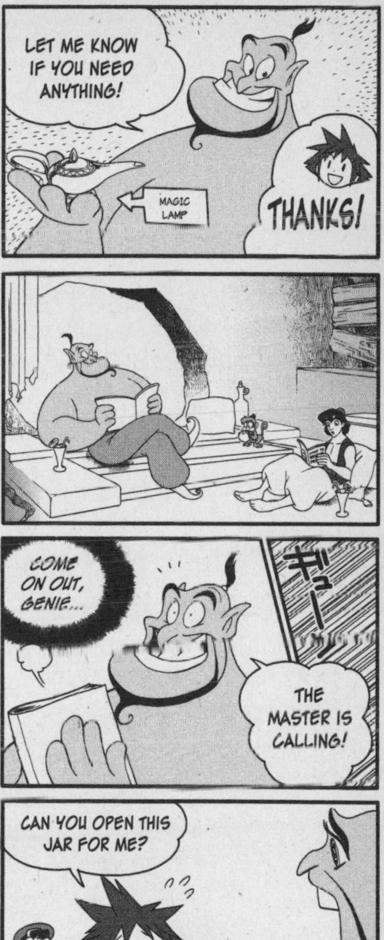
LET ME KNOW IF YOU NEED ANYTHING!
MAGIC LAMP
THANKS!
COME ON OUT, GENIE...
ギューン
THE MASTER IS CALLING!
CAN YOU OPEN THIS JAR FOR ME?

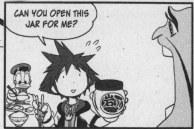

Café du Aerith

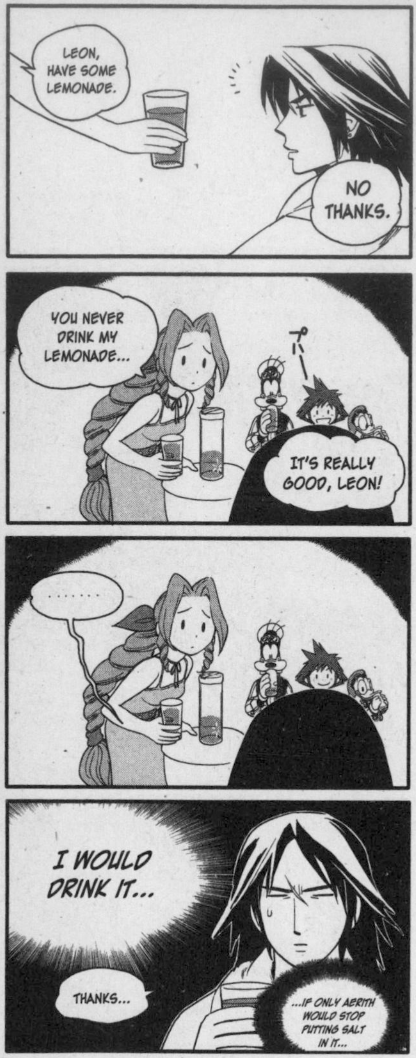
LEON, HAVE SOME LEMONADE.
NO THANKS.
YOU NEVER DRINK MY LEMONADE...
IT'S REALLY GOOD, LEON!
....
I WOULD DRINK IT...
THANKS...
...IF ONLY AERITH WOULD STOP PUTTING SALT IN IT...

A Day in the Life of Cid

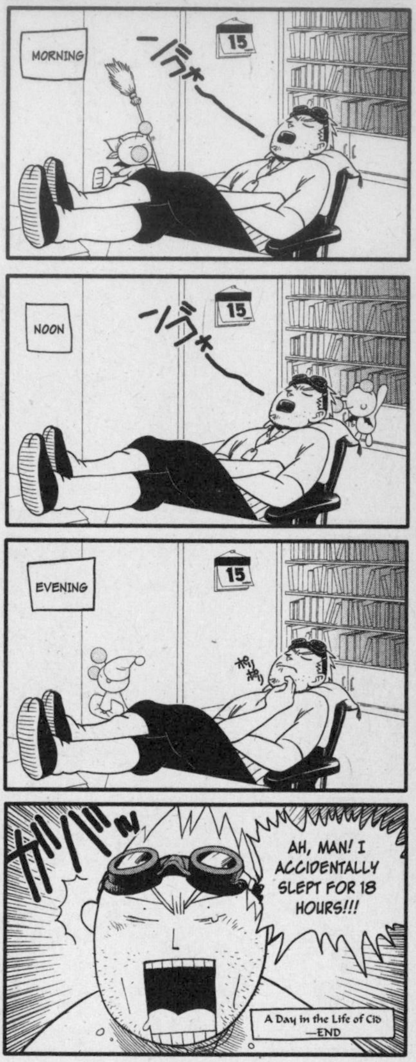
MORNING
15
NOON
15
EVENING
15
AH, MAN! I ACCIDENTALLY SLEPT FOR 18 HOURS!!!
A Day in the Life of Cid —END

Final Mix Juice

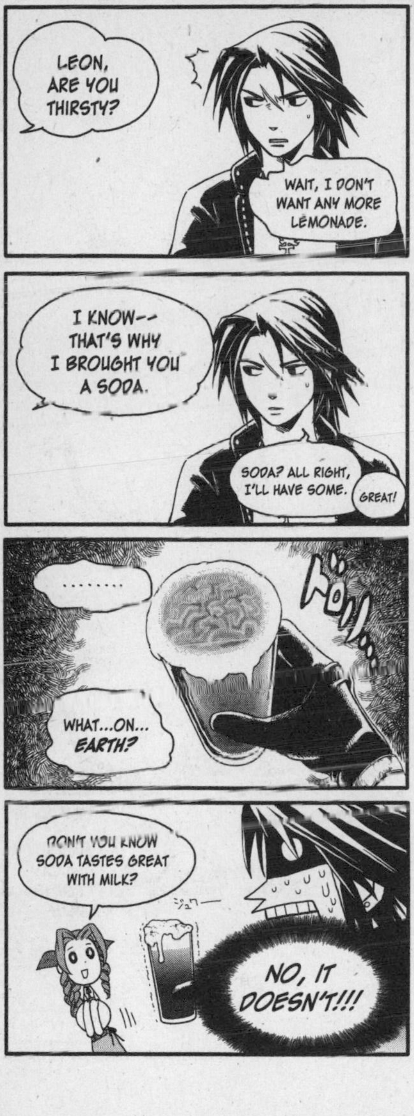
LEON, ARE YOU THIRSTY?
WAIT, I DON'T WANT ANY MORE LEMONADE.
I KNOW--THAT'S WHY I BROUGHT YOU A SODA.
SODA? ALL RIGHT, I'LL HAVE SOME.
GREAT!
....
WHAT...ON... EARTH?
DON'T YOU KNOW SODA TASTES GREAT WITH MILK?
NO, IT DOESN'T!!!

Mr. Fancy

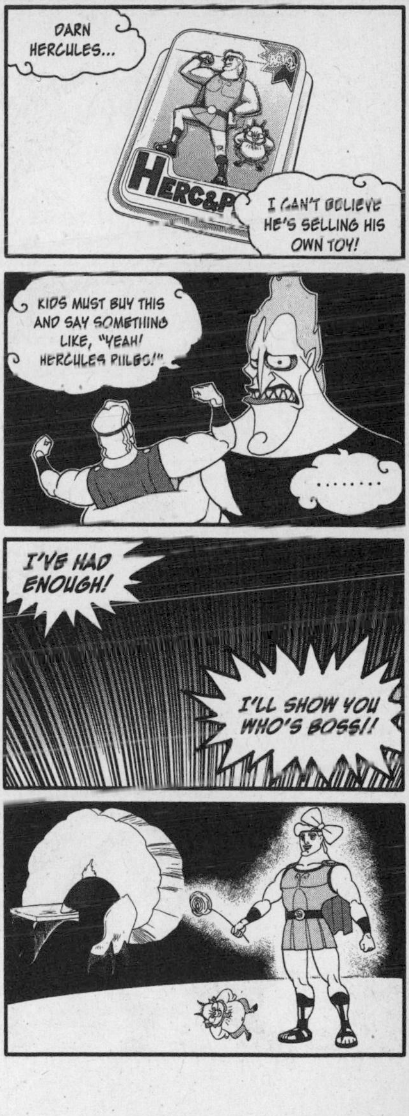
DARN HERCULES...
I CAN'T BELIEVE HE'S SELLING HIS OWN TOY!
KIDS MUST BUY THIS AND SAY SOMETHING LIKE, "YEAH! HERCULES RULES!"
....
I'VE HAD ENOUGH!
I'LL SHOW YOU WHO'S BOSS!!

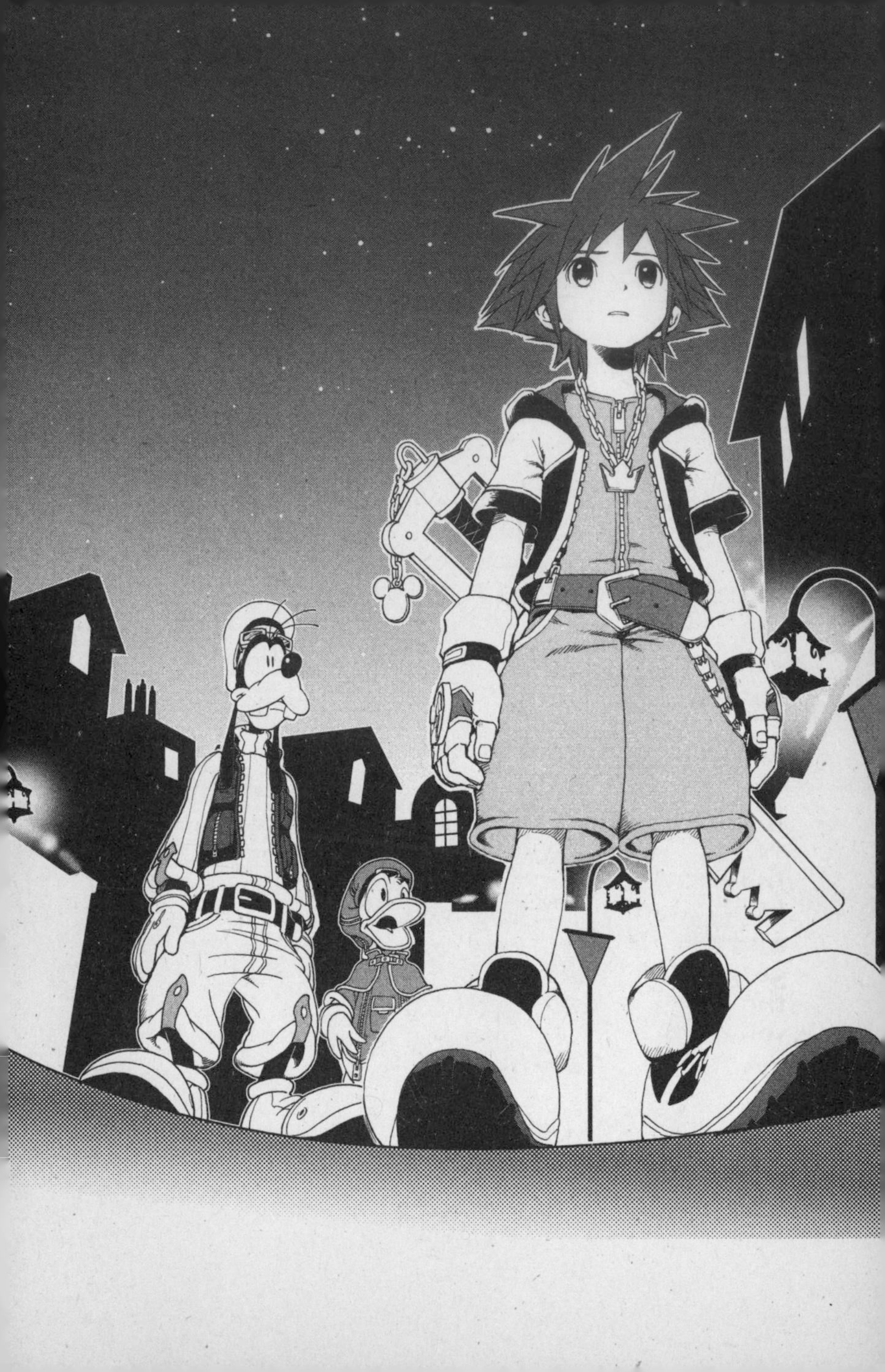

IN THE NEXT VOLUME OF

Disney SQUARESOFT

KINGDOM HEARTS

It's an ocean theme for Sora and the gang in volume 3 of *Kingdom Hearts,* featuring Monstro the whale, Ursula the Sea-Witch, and Captain Hook and his pirate ship! From inside the belly of a whale to great undersea kingdoms, the crew gets deeper into trouble the closer they get to the secret of stopping the Heartless. And all the while, Maleficent continues to plot and scheme against our heroes.

ALSO AVAILABLE FROM TOKYOPOP®

MANGA

.HACK//LEGEND OF THE TWILIGHT
ALICHINO
ANGELIC LAYER
BABY BIRTH
BRAIN POWERED
BRIGADOON
B'TX
CANDIDATE FOR GODDESS, THE
CARDCAPTOR SAKURA
CARDCAPTOR SAKURA - MASTER OF THE CLOW
CHRONICLES OF THE CURSED SWORD
CLAMP SCHOOL DETECTIVES
CLOVER
COMIC PARTY
CORRECTOR YUI
COWBOY BEBOP
COWBOY BEBOP: SHOOTING STAR
CRESCENT MOON
CROSS
CULDCEPT
CYBORG 009
D•N•ANGEL
DEARS
DEMON DIARY
DEMON ORORON, THE
DIGIMON
DIGIMON TAMERS
DIGIMON ZERO TWO
DRAGON HUNTER
DRAGON KNIGHTS
DRAGON VOICE
DREAM SAGA
DUKLYON: CLAMP SCHOOL DEFENDERS
ET CETERA
ETERNITY
FAERIES' LANDING
FLCL
FLOWER OF THE DEEP SLEEP
FORBIDDEN DANCE
FRUITS BASKET
G GUNDAM
GATEKEEPERS
GIRL GOT GAME
GUNDAM SEED ASTRAY
GUNDAM SEED ASTRAY R
GUNDAM WING
GUNDAM WING: BATTLEFIELD OF PACIFISTS
GUNDAM WING: ENDLESS WALTZ
GUNDAM WING: THE LAST OUTPOST (G-UNIT)
HANDS OFF!

HARLEM BEAT
HYPER RUNE
I.N.V.U.
INITIAL D
INSTANT TEEN: JUST ADD NUTS
JING: KING OF BANDITS
JING: KING OF BANDITS - TWILIGHT TALES
JULINE
KARE KANO
KILL ME, KISS ME
KINDAICHI CASE FILES, THE
KING OF HELL
KODOCHA: SANA'S STAGE
LAGOON ENGINE
LEGEND OF CHUN HYANG, THE
LILING-PO
LOVE OR MONEY
MAGIC KNIGHT RAYEARTH I
MAGIC KNIGHT RAYEARTH II
MAN OF MANY FACES
MARMALADE BOY
MARS
MARS: HORSE WITH NO NAME
MINK
MIRACLE GIRLS
MODEL
MOURYOU KIDEN: LEGEND OF THE NYMPH
NECK AND NECK
ONE
ONE I LOVE, THE
PEACH FUZZ
PEACH GIRL
PEACH GIRL: CHANGE OF HEART
PHD: PHANTASY DEGREE
PITA-TEN
PLANET BLOOD
PLANET LADDER
PLANETES
PRESIDENT DAD
PRINCESS AI
PSYCHIC ACADEMY
QUEEN'S KNIGHT, THE
RAGNAROK
RAVE MASTER
REALITY CHECK
REBIRTH
REBOUND
RISING STARS OF MANGA™,THE
SAILOR MOON
SAINT TAIL
SAMURAI GIRL™ REAL BOUT HIGH SCHOOL

10.19.04Y

ALSO AVAILABLE FROM TOKYOPOP®

**You want it? We got it!
A full range of TOKYOPOP
products are available now at:
www.TOKYOPOP.com/shop**

10.19.04Y

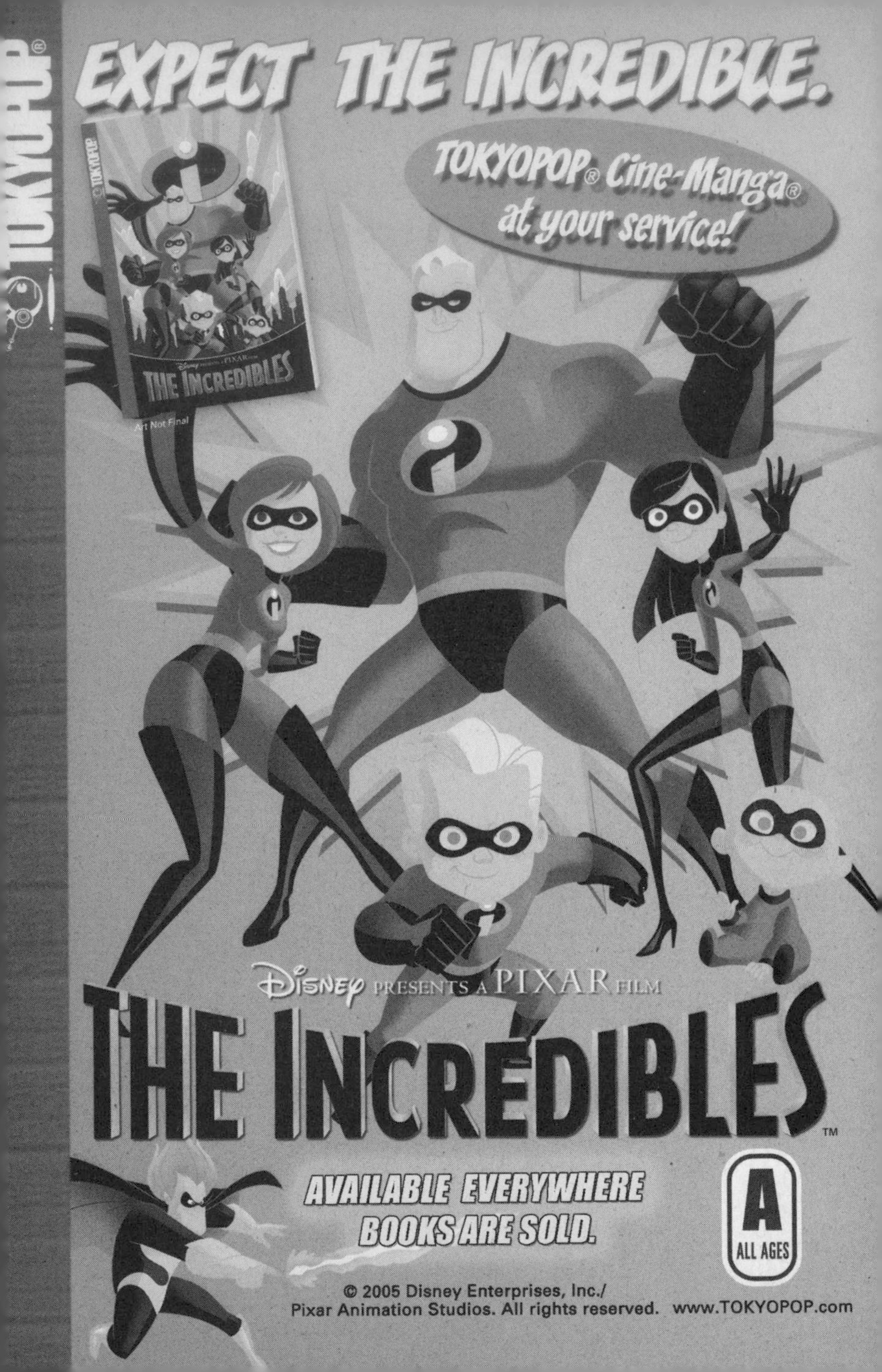
TOKYOPOP
EXPECT THE INCREDIBLE.
TOKYOPOP® Cine-Manga®
at your service!
Art Not Final
DISNEY PRESENTS A PIXAR FILM
THE INCREDIBLES™
AVAILABLE EVERYWHERE
BOOKS ARE SOLD.
A
ALL AGES
© 2005 Disney Enterprises, Inc./
Pixar Animation Studios. All rights reserved.
www.TOKYOPOP.com

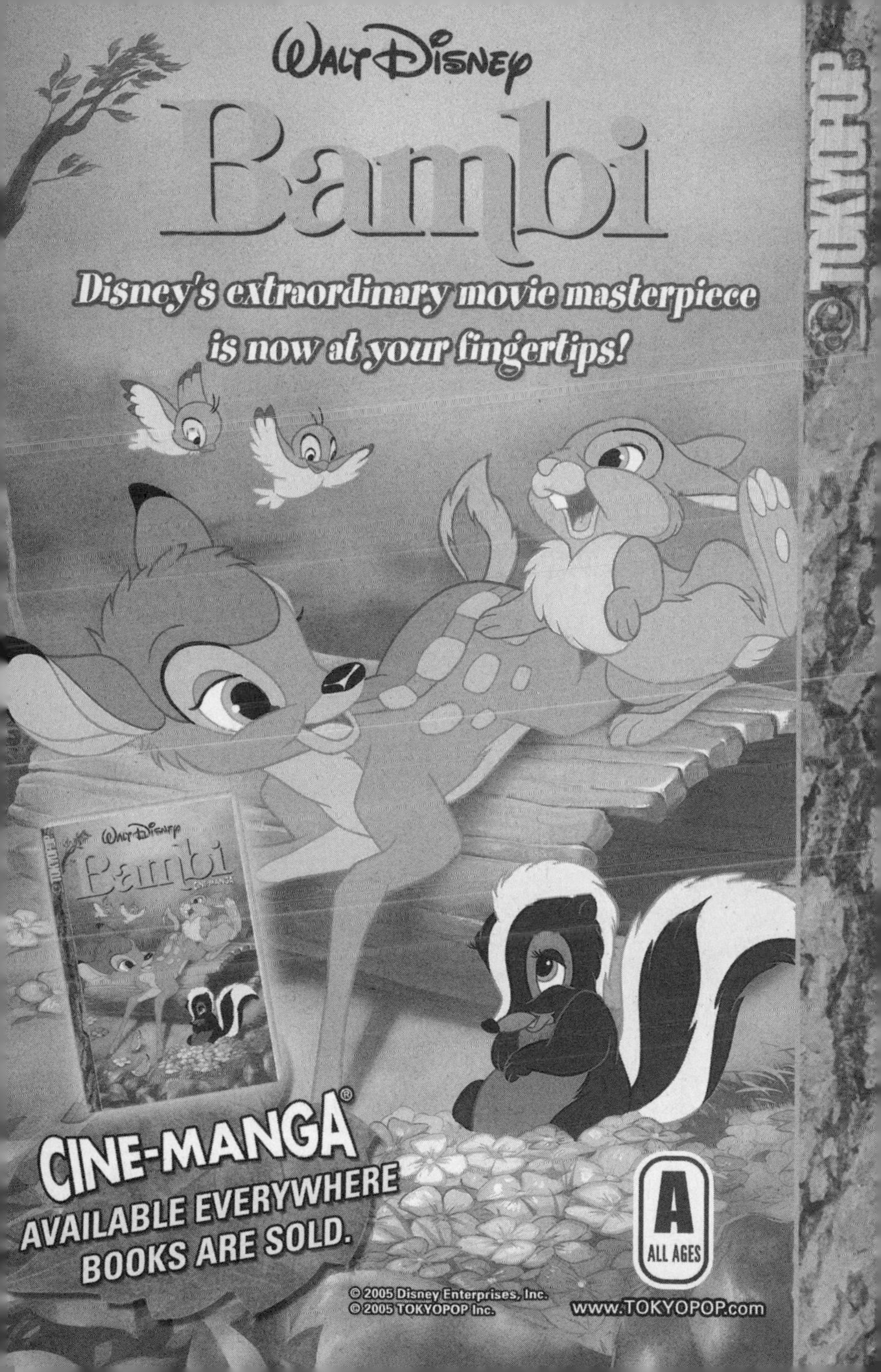

WALT DISNEY
Bambi
Disney's extraordinary movie masterpiece
is now at your fingertips!
TOKYOPOP
CINE-MANGA®
AVAILABLE EVERYWHERE
BOOKS ARE SOLD.
A
ALL AGES
© 2005 Disney Enterprises, Inc.
© 2005 TOKYOPOP Inc.
www.TOKYOPOP.com